BASTIONS AND BARBED WIRE

ALSO PUBLISHED AS VOLUME FOUR OF THE

JOURNAL OF CONFLICT ARCHAEOLOGY

Devoted to Battlefield and Military Archaeology and Other Spheres of Conflict Archaeology. Covering all Periods with a Worldwide Scope.

BASTIONS AND BARBED WIRE

EDITED BY

TONY POLLARD AND IAIN BANKS

BRILL

LEIDEN · BOSTON
2008

Cover Illustration: Buchenwald at Liberation (US National Archives), Auschwitz Fence (Photo by Adrian T. Myers). Cover Design: Alex Silberstein

This book is printed on acid-free paper.

Library of Congress Cataloging-in-Publication Data

A C.I.P. record for this book is available from the Library of Congress.

ISBN 978 90 04 17360 6

Printed and bound in Great Britain by
CPI Antony Rowe, Chippenham and Eastbourne

CONTENTS

 DOI: 10.1163/157407808X382719

Book Reviews

EDITORIAL

NAZIS, WE HATE THOSE GUYS!

Subjects under consideration in this volume range from Crimean war memorials, siege sites, through colonial architecture and experimental musket firings to Nazi concentration camps. It may at first be difficult to detect a unifying theme here, and indeed why should there be? One of the motivations behind this journal is to give expression to the broad scope of conflict archaeology, and at this we feel it continues to succeed. However, almost entirely by accident a core theme can be seen to run through the majority of papers within these covers.

That theme is confinement. It is most obviously present in Myers' paper, *An Archaeological Approach to Studying the Nazi Concentration Camps*, but more on this later. Other papers which touch on the same theme are presented by Passmore and Harrison, who set out the results of a field survey of earthworks created during the Battle of the Bulge in 1944. Both deliberately excavated entrenchments and shell craters were utilised by troops during combat, thus creating microenvironments within the wider geography of the battlefield which both confined and protected. In some respects, the occupant of a shell-hole may share some experiences with members of a besieged garrison, inability to move freely outside of the defences, difficulties of communication with comrades, shortages of supplies and ammunition, the uncertainty of relief etc. Some of these issues are apparent in the two papers by Pollard which deal with the archaeology of siege sites. The earliest of these took place in 1560 when a Protestant force of Scottish and English troops invested the Catholic French citadel of Leith, close to Edinburgh in Scotland. The second, smaller scale affair centred on Fort William on the north-west coast of Scotland, where Jacobite forces kept the government garrison bottled up for several weeks in early 1746. One of the aims of both of these projects was to address the wider social aspects of conflict, focusing not so much on the combat itself but exploring the civilian and non-combatant experiences of conflict. Thus far, perhaps, Fort William has achieved the greatest success here, with evidence recovered for the civilian settlement of Maryburgh which grew up outside the walls of the fort and was razed to the ground by the garrison prior to the commencement of the siege. In looking at the relationship between military and civilian settlements, coloniser and indigene, in the post medieval period, the Fort William project probably has more in common with the frontier studies taking place in North America and Canada than most of the research projects taking place in the UK at the moment.

 DOI: 10.1163/157407808X382728

In a paper co-authored by Pollard and Banks, the theme of confinement is clearly expressed through the investigation of defensive works on the island of Inchkeith in the Firth of Forth, not far away from the citadel of Leith on the shore to the south. The defences range in date from the 16th century up to the 20th, with hundreds of soldiers based on the island during the early part of WWII. It will not have escaped the reader's notice that no less than three papers in the current volume have Pollard's name attached to them. What this reflects is the amount of work being carried out in the field of conflict archaeology by the Centre for Battlefield Archaeology at Glasgow University, which over the past few months alone has completed the investigation of the deep dugout known as Vampir constructed by the British in 1918 just outside Ypres in Belgian Flanders and the evaluation of suspected mass grave pits related to the 1916 battle of Fromelles, in French Flanders. The pits were indeed found to contain the remains of Australian and British soldiers buried by the Germans after the battle and both governments have recently announced their intention to have these remains recovered and reburied in individual graves in a newly established cemetery.

Continuing the theme of confinement is Grguric's detailed study of colonial farmsteads in 19th century Australia, which the author convincingly argues are a reflection of the architecture of fear. Snead's study of conflict and destruction again looks at the relationship between settlement and conflict, this time among the Pueblo societies of the south western United States. Straying away from our theme but no less valued for that are a very useful study of musket ballistics by Roberts, Brown, Hammett and Kingston (which was carried out by military personnel as part of an ammunition technician's course) and a consideration of Crimean war memorials by Hughes and Trigg.

Before bringing this editorial to a close the editors feel it important to comment further on Myers' work on Nazi concentration camps, in which he explores the ways in which historical archaeologists can isolate the tensions between the past and the present and provide a nuanced means of exploring the processes which underpin memory and forgetting. There can be little doubt that the anthropological and archaeological study of incarceration and confinement, as expressed through prisons, asylums and prisoner of war camps is in the ascendant, with a session recently taking place at the World Archaeological Congress in Dublin and *Anthropology News* calling for papers on the subject. The editors are, however, particularly pleased to include a contribution dealing with concentration camps as we believe that archaeology has a vital role to play in our understanding of some of the key events of the 20th century, which included the atrocities perpetrated by the Nazi regime.

If ever there was time for archaeologists to engage with this material, then it is now. Any suggestion that Nazism was entirely snuffed out with the defeat of the Wehrmacht in 1945 is surely cast into doubt in the context of the thankfully limited resurgence of the neo-fascist British National Party (BNP) in the UK and disturbing news reports of racially motivated violence across Europe, some of which appears to be related to increased levels of economic migration. Nor is it just archaeologists who are becoming increasingly drawn to this difficult subject matter and the contested past embodied within it. The field of 'Dark Tourism' is a growing subject of study among geographers, and indeed may find some parallel with advances in the sub-discipline of conflict archaeology over recent years. The transformation of 'dark' sites such as concentration camps and battlefields into tourist attractions is a worthy subject of study and again one which archaeologists, who in some cases have been active participants in this process of transformation, should engage.

Returning to the themes picked up on by Myers; the dichotomy between memory and forgetting and indeed the relationship between the two is clearly an important one. Surely one of the primary functions of archaeology is to remember, but it has also, at least in a bastardised form, been called upon to promote forgetting, or even more insidiously to deny.

The culture-history paradigm which dominated archaeology in the 1930s was appropriated by the Nazis to underpin the myth of the Third Reich's Aryan origins and to legitimise the Nazi state's dominance of neighbouring peoples. In a similar fashion, today's scientific techniques are being put to equally chilling use by neo-Nazis in the quest to deny the Holocaust. *Dissecting the Holocaust*, edited by Germar Rudolf (2000), is a prime example of the Holocaust denier in action. Tellingly, the subtitle of the volume is *The Growing Critique of 'Truth' and 'Memory'*. These collected papers include historical approaches supplemented by a battery of forensic-type techniques; aerial photographs are analysed, samples removed from the walls of gas chambers are subject to chemical analysis (Rudolf trained as a chemist), architectural designs are examined and the practicalities of digging mass graves large enough to dispose of the many victims considered.

All of these investigations come to the same result: the claim that concentration camps were not used in the systematically-organised murder of 6 million Jews; in short, that the Holocaust did not happen. The book is banned in Germany and, after seeking asylum in the United States, Rudolf was extradited and in March 2005 sentenced by the Mannheim District Court to two and half years in prison for inciting hatred, disparaging the dead and libel. Contributors to the Rudolf volume regard their approach as 'revisionist' and refer to their opponents as 'exterminationists' (Faurisson 2000: 133); the French

Holocaust denier Robert Faurisson contributes the preface and also an article, the latter being just one that sets out to discredit eyewitness accounts of exterminations, which in his case include the writings of Primo Levi (ibid.). This is not the place for an in depth critique of the volume in question, but some examples of the arguments put forward will serve to give something of the flavour of the whole.

In a paper called *Do photographs prove the NS extermination of Jews?*, Udo Walendy argues among other things that the piles of shoes purporting to be removed from concentration camp victims prior to being gassed are actually nothing more sinister than items of apparel donated by the general population for recycling as part of the war effort (2000: 257). If anyone should need convincing of the fallacy of this statement then they only need look as far as the footnote which refers to a similar interpretation made by one E. Gauss, a name which just happens to be one of many pseudonyms used by Germar Rudolf in a sad effort to expand the academy of revisionist 'scholars' (Mazal 2005). There can be no doubting the central role played by Rudolf in the denier's project. In one of his contributions he uses chemical analyses to back up his thesis that the gas chambers at Auschwitz and Birkenau (Auschwitz II) were used for delousing operations and additionally that the crematoria were there for the disposal of the victims of epidemics in the camps (even he cannot stretch the evidence to suggest that large numbers of Jews were not present in the camps). In summing up his argument he states:

> . . . no mass gassings with Zyklon B can have occurred under the conditions attested to by alleged eyewitnesses, court witnesses, journalists, and academics or other popularisers (2000: 372).

It is all very unpleasant stuff, and there can be little doubt that these authors should be scorned rather than pitied, but whether the book should be banned is another matter, and it can be argued that such a sanction flatters with the implication of dangerous knowledge which needs to be suppressed. Is it not better to have such poor scholarship and twisted argument open to scrutiny and critique? Fortunately there are scientists willing to engage in this and Rudolf's gas chamber hypothesis was eloquently exposed as pseudo-science by Green (1997) who also rightly points out that the burden of proof lies with the deniers. When debate has taken place face to face it has been in courts of law, and it is the Holocaust deniers who have lost the fight, the burden of proof clearly being too heavy for them. It is leaving such ideas in the shadows rather than exposed to the harsh light of truth that allows them to grow and develop. Once these ideas are exposed as the perverse distortions that they are, they have less power to influence new generations further removed from the reality of the situation.

The best known legal case, at least in the UK, is perhaps that involving David Irving, who is name-checked in Myers' paper and is a writer of World War Two history with a particular interest in Adolf Hitler. Partially due to increasing criticism from one side and flattery from the other, Irving was lured from the world of respected historical research, albeit resulting in work which cast the Fuhrer in the best of lights, into the 'Revisionist' camp. In 1996, Irving filed a libel case against American academic Deborah Lipstadt and Penguin, which had published a British edition of her 1993 book *Denying the Holocaust: The Growing Assault on Truth and Memory* in the UK (again, notice the sub-title). Lipstadt was highly critical of Irving in her book, and among other things called him a 'Holocaust denier' (1993: 111, 179) and accused him of 'bending historical evidence' (*ibid*: 181). The court found against Irving, and on 11 April 2005, Justice Charles Gray passed down his judgment in which he stated that it was 'incontrovertible that Irving qualifies as a Holocaust denier' (Gray 2005). Irving escaped with payment of the extensive trial costs but was later to serve a short prison term in Austria, a country to which he had returned after delivering Holocaust denial lectures there in 1989. Irving's public humiliations may have inflicted a heavy blow against the deniers but the movement is still active, and is determined to turn the likes of Rudolf and Irving into martyrs for the cause.

It might seem that such issues are not of much importance. After all, the neo-Nazis exist on the fringes of society and political life, so how can their re-fashioning of the history of the Holocaust be of any great concern? Are we not just tilting at windmills? Certainly, both the Jewish communities that have found their property attacked and their synagogues defaced with swastikas and other graffiti, and Muslims who live in fear of attack by skinhead thugs, would see such groups as anything but straw men. However, while these people are a serious concern, they are not the only reason for making a stand. Undoubtedly of greater concern is the involvement of Middle Eastern politicians and activists in Holocaust denial. Iran's President Ahmadinejad stated publicly in December 2005 that he doubts the truth of the Holocaust (Al-Jazeera, 14 December 2005), calling it a fabrication and a myth. In 2006 Iran went further and hosted an 'International Conference to Review the Global Vision of the Holocaust' in Tehran, which attracted a number of notable deniers including Robert Faurisson and David Duke, former leader of the American racist organization, the Ku Klux Klan. Also present was Australian/German denier Dr. Fredrick Toben who caused controversy in the UK in October 2008 when he was arrested on arrival at Heathrow on the basis of a Holocaust denial related warrant issued in Manheim, Germany (British Liberal Democrat home affairs spokesman Chris Huhne became embroiled in the affair and risked criticism when, quoting Voltaire, he proposed that although he had no sympathy at all with Toben's views the issue was one of freedom of speech and because of this the European warrant should not be honoured. The fact that this argument was also put forward by David Irving with regard to the same case is a clear indication of the problems inherent in dealing with denial and deniers).

Pitched as an academic conference, the Tehran meeting was in reality nothing more than a forum for Holocaust deniers to express their opinions without the inconvenience of addressing dissent and facing up to hard evidence. It is one thing for deniers to rationalise their views by arguing that all historical truths should be open to scrutiny, it is entirely another to use lies and distortions as the tools of investigation. What is clear is that there is a growing movement of state sanctioned Holocaust denial in the Middle East, and that this is a new phenomenon. It is an expression of the conflict in the region, a way of reconfiguring one's enemy into a construct that better fits the role of villain in one's world view.

Conflict is, however, two sided and Israel also engages in the misrepresentation of its opponents, be they Arab, Palestinian or Iranian and while each side demonises the other and refuses to accept that there can be any truth or justice in the position of the other, there can be no hope of peace. Although there is little that archaeology can do to bring peace to the Middle East; it may at least be possible to use it to disarm one of the weapons used in that conflict.

If there is an intellectual battle against Holocaust denial and the neo-Nazism and anti-Semitism it serves, then it is one in which archaeologists have a role on the front line. This is not the archaeology of conflict but archaeology in conflict.

Tony Pollard & Iain Banks
October 2008

References

Faurisson, R 2000 'Witnesses to the Gas Chambers of Auschwitz', *in* Rudolf, G (ed) *Dissecting the Holocaust: The Growing Critique of 'Truth' and 'Memory'*. 2nd rev ed, first published in German 1994. Theses & Dissertations Press: Capshaw, Alabama. 133–145.

Gray, C 2005 *Holocaust Denial on Trial, Trial Judgement: Electronic Version*. www.hdot.org/trial/judgement (viewed on 7/9/08.)

Green, R J 1997 *Leuchter, Rudolf and the Iron Blues*. The Holocaust History website: http://www.holocaust-history.org/auschwitz/chemistry/blue/.

Lipstadt, D E 1993 *Denying the Holocaust: The Growing Assault on Truth and Memory*. The Free Press, New York (British edition published by Penguin Ltd 1994).

Mazal, H W 2005 *Whats in a Nym?* http://www.holocaust-history.org/denial/nym.shtml.

Rudolf, G 2000 'Some Considerations about the "Gas Chambers' of Auschwitz". *in* Rudolf, G (ed) *Dissecting the Holocaust: The Growing Critique of 'Truth' and 'Memory'.* 2nd rev ed, first published in German 1994. Theses & Dissertations Press: Capshaw, Alabama. 337–372.

—— (ed) 2000 *Dissecting the Holocaust: The Growing Critique of 'Truth' and 'Memory'.* 2nd rev ed, first published in German 1994. Theses & Dissertations Press: Capshaw, Alabama.

Waldeny, U 2000 'Do photographs prove the NS extermination of Jews?', *in* Rudolf, G (ed) *Dissecting the Holocaust: The Growing Critique of 'Truth' and 'Memory'.* 2nd rev ed, first published in German 1994. Theses & Dissertations Press: Capshaw, Alabama. 243–269.

A DETAILED STUDY OF THE EFFECTIVENESS AND CAPABILITIES OF 18TH CENTURY MUSKETRY ON THE BATTLEFIELD

N A ROBERTS, J W BROWN, B HAMMETT & P D F KINGSTON

Abstract

During the mid 18th century, the standard British Army issue weapon was the Brown Bess Musket. There are various accounts of the performance of this early form of firearm and its tactical deployment (e.g. Hanger 1816). Using a technical replica of the Brown Bess, range trials and computer modelling have been used to asses the weapon's capabilities and likely performance. The research found the Brown Bess musket to be a lethal weapon at the ranges at which enemy was commonly engaged, so long as it was accurate enough to hit the target. A single shot fired at 150 yards could penetrate at least two soldiers, even if bone were hit. The armour of the day (shields of wood, leather and sometimes steel, and the layers of woollen clothing) was easily pierced by the shot. The shot was found to readily deform on impact with metal targets. The maximum range could extend to around 1200m, with 202m reached when fired horizontally.

Introduction

Background

The nature of warfare is always dictated by the principle weapon systems available at the time. In the 18th century, the principle weapon system used by the British infantry was a smooth bore musket. The weapon was employed in platoon-sized groupings, which fired volleys of lead shot in the direction of the enemy (shots were not aimed). The musketeers would form a static location in front of an advancing enemy, or fire while advancing until close enough for hand-to-hand combat. It is clear that the performance of the musket would have a direct influence on the tactics and the outcome of the battle. However, historical sources provide many conflicting accounts of the capability, performance and reliability of this weapon system (Hughes 1974). Perhaps the most often quoted reference comes from the hand of Colonel George Hanger who saw service with the British Army during the American Revolution:

> 'A soldier's musket, if not exceedingly ill-bored, as many are, will strike a figure of a man at 80 yards; it may even at a hundred; but a soldier must be very unfortunate indeed who shall be wounded by a common musket at 150 yards, providing his antagonist aims at him; and, as to firing at a man at 200 yards with a common musket, you may as

 DOI: 10.1163/157407808X382737

well fire at the moon and have the same hope of hitting him. I do maintain and I will prove, whenever called on, that no man was ever killed at 200 yards, by a common musket, by the person who aimed at him (1816: 205).'

Aim

The aim of this research project was to conduct a thorough ballistic examination and provide a performance assessment of an 18th century musket. In recent years, there has been an increasing interest in the examination of the performance and capabilities of historic firearms, including artillery, through experimentation and replication (e.g. MacPherson 1994; Pollard & Oliver 2003; for a detailed study of cannon-fired case shot, see: Allsop & Foard 2007). This interest has also been reflected through the activities of hobbyist black powder shooters, most particularly in the USA (e.g. James n.d.). The project focused on the investigation of the Brown Bess Musket as used by the British Infantry at the Battle of Culloden on 5 April 1746. This battle is of particular interest as archaeological investigations have resulted in the recovery of numerous lead projectiles including musket balls and the present project received support and encouragement from Dr Tony Pollard, the archaeologist leading that work. This weapon was widely popular, and remained in use without major modifications until the 1800s, when rifles eventually made smooth bore muskets obsolete.

Approaching the problem

Due to the value, scarcity and deterioration of original Brown Bess Muskets, the firing of a technical replica Brown Bess was the most appropriate method of analysing the ballistic properties. Using a technical replica, with similar bore and barrel dimensions to the original, would ensure more consistent experiments could be carried out.

Range trials were conducted with the aim of replicating the known performance (particularly muzzle velocity) of the Brown Bess. Computer modelling was used concurrently to maximise the information obtained from each trial. The conditions derived from these trials enabled the setting up of accurate and realistic tests examining the wound effects the weapon could inflict in different tactical situations (such as closer ranges and differing amours). The effect of impact on the lead shot was also examined by using a soft capture box.

The Brown Bess

The historical context for this research project was the Battle of Culloden, where the British Infantry used the Brown Bess Musket. Existing documentary evidence of the performance of the Brown Bess from the majority of sources tends to provide a historical, rather than technical perspective. This project used technical methods to address the accuracy and veracity of these historical records. It is known that the weapon weighed around 10 lbs 8 oz (4.7 kg), had a 46-inch length barrel with a 0.75 inch (1.87 cm) bore diameter. The shot fired was 14 bore lead, contained in a cartridge made of hemp and cotton paper.

Description of the Brown Bess Musket

Capability

It should be borne in mind that the capability of the small arms system is not merely a function of the capability of the weapon. The human-weapon interface plays an important role, resulting in fluctuations in a soldier's performance depending on his size, physical state (tired, cold, wet), and mental state (scared if in battle). His weapon handling under these conditions will be improved by good training, which should go some way to minimise the effects of these conditions. The investigation of these variables falls out of the scope of this project, and a rigid mounting for the weapon was used to eliminate human variation. This allowed the investigation of purely the ballistic capabilities of the Brown Bess, operated at similar ranges to those fired during the Battle of Culloden (Pollard 2005).

Ammunition

The ammunition cartridges were made of paper containing one lead shot and a quantity of gunpowder, and tied off with twine. The concept of using cartridges was introduced to make firing the weapon easier whilst ensuring a more consistent amount of gunpowder. It also assisted in keeping the powder dry and reduced windage (the small gap between the lead shot and the calibre of the barrel) as the paper also served as wadding (see below).

Propellant

Little evidence exists as to the exact scientific details of the gunpowder used, but it is believed to be a mixture of saltpetre, charcoal and sulphur in the ratio of 75:15:10, and of mixed grain size. The amount in each cartridge was between 5 and 6 drams (8.89 to 10.66 g), of which 10 grains (0.65 g) was used for priming (Harding 1999: 105).

Cartridges

The lead shots used in the cartridges were cast in moulds and quenched in water. A small burr was left from where the lead was poured into the mould. Paper used to make cartridges in the 18th century differs from today's paper, as it was made from a linen or cotton texture, like fine rags. The lead shot was placed at the bottom corner of the paper, which was then folded over it. The cartridge was rolled by using a wooden rolling rod (0.65 in diameter) to form a cavity for gunpowder. The end with the shot was tied off with twine, and the gunpowder poured in through the open end.

Operation

Musketeers would bite off the end of the cartridge, pour a small amount of gunpowder into the flintlock pan, with the remainder being poured down the barrel. The shot was then rammed down the barrel with a rod and the cartridge paper became wadding. This protected the shot during ramming, held it in place between loading and firing, and provided forward obturation during shot travel down the barrel. On pulling the trigger, a flintlock produced a flash that ignited the powder in the pan, burning through a tiny hole into the chamber. This would then ignite the gunpowder confined inside, producing rapidly expanding hot gases that forced the lead shot and the wadding out of the barrel. In this simple explanation of the firing procedure, it is already obvious how much room for variation there would be, potentially affecting the ballistic performance.

Muzzle Velocity

When examining the performance of a small arms weapon, muzzle velocity is the conventional measurement taken. Unfortunately, there are no records of the muzzle velocities of the Brown Bess from the mid 18th century, and not many experiments appear to have been conducted in that era. However, Mordecai (1845) conducted a series of experiments in the mid-19th century which can be extrapolated to estimate the likely muzzle velocity of the Brown Bess. The gunpowders he used were mainly from the US, but the figures obtained generally corroborate the data for the few British powders that he tested. Robins also conducted research on ballistics, published in 1742, which along with Mordecai's work, show that muzzle velocities of 1500 feet per second (fps) or 457.2 metres per second (m/s) were being obtained from muskets (Harding 1999: 371). The velocity of sound in air is 1100 fps, showing that the projectile travelled at supersonic speeds.

Until manufacturing processes were improved in the late 18th century, gunpowder was extremely variable in quality (Nonte 1969: 191). There were numerous reasons for this, including: inconsistencies in the charcoal produced by charring timber in stacks; the type and age of wood used; impurities in the saltpetre and sulphur; and method of formulation and mixing. When in use, this resulted in unpredictable muzzle velocities on firing the weapon. The tactical manner of using soldiers in long lines firing in the general direction of the enemy, however, meant that variations in muzzle velocity did not matter greatly for battlefield effectiveness.

The Battle of Culloden

Background

The Battle of Culloden took place on the afternoon of 6 April 1746. On one side were 5,000 Jacobite troops (including Highlanders, Lowlanders, some French and a few Irish), equipped with muskets, pikes, axes and other hand-held weapons, commanded by clan chiefs loyal to Bonnie Prince Charlie. Their enemy numbered around 9,000 Government troops, well equipped with the Brown Bess musket. The Jacobites were tired after an unsuccessful attempt at a surprise attack the previous night, which had failed due to navigational errors. At the start of the battle, the government lines stood around 500 m away, separated by ground entirely unsuitable for the traditional Highland charge (victory at Killiecrankie in 1689 resulted from Jacobites charging down hill—the ground at Culloden was variably wet and despite various topographic variations was far more level in character).

As a precursor, both sides engaged with artillery, first in counter-battery fire, with the Government guns then switching to the Jacobite infantry once the artillery had been knocked out. When the order to charge was given the message was not passed properly, and the Jacobite advance became dislocated. While charging to engage in hand to hand fighting, the Jacobites suffered further attrition from heavy volley fire from the Brown Bess Muskets of the Government troops. They did break through the Government lines in some places, but were defeated by depth in the Government lines. A disorderly retreat followed, and combined with successful flanking manoeuvres by the government cavalry, the Jacobites were routed in less than an hour. Government losses were just 350 men dead and injured compared with at least 1,200 Jacobites dead.

Tactics

The Government troops employed volley fire from their muskets. This broke down charges, and reduced numbers of enemy able to engage in hand to hand fighting. Ranges varied from around 150 yds down to point blank range. The soldiers were told not to aim, but simply hold the weapon horizontally and fire. Although firing by platoon was normal by the time of the battle this was dispensed with in favour of volley fire by battalions deployed in triple lines—thought by General Hawley as the only way to break a Jacobite charge. The front rank, probably kneeling, kept their bayonets charged and did not reload after the first volley, thus providing a protective hedge of bayonets in front of the two firing ranks (Reid, in press).

Historical Sources

Some sources would suggest that the Brown Bess did not perform well ballistically, proposing that shot penetration of the body was rare, and could be prevented by wet clothing or shields. Contradicting this, there was also circumstantial evidence that a single shot could penetrate two men standing one behind the other. There are also doubts about accuracy over engagement ranges, and the wounding characteristics that were produced:

> *Accuracy of the Brown Bess was, as with other muskets, low. The effective range is often quoted as 100 yards (91.4 m). The combination of large calibre of the projectile, the heavy weight of its lead construction, and its unstable aerodynamic shape (a round ball marred by hand casting) contributed to its low effective range* (historical plaque at battle site).

> *It is my conclusion that effective musket fire was not possible at ranges above 150 yards. This echoes the sentiment of some contemporary writers. Furthermore given the poor field conditions and the little or no target practice that the conscripts had, really effective fire could probably not be delivered at ranges above 100 to 150 yards* (Willegal, 1999: 9).

There has also been a modern fascination with the supposed high recoil resulting from firing a Brown Bess. It is believed by some that government soldiers lessened the painful effects of this by reducing the amount of powder rammed down the barrel. This would reduce the muzzle velocity of the shot, and so affect the range, accuracy and penetration of the shot. Finally, further to a recent find of interestingly deformed shots from the site of Culloden (Pollard 2005), trials were conducted to simulate the lead shot colliding with metal edges, such as sword blades or belt buckles.

Replicating the Brown Bess

Weapon Selection

The aim of this project was to, as realistically as possible, analyse the ballistic properties of the 18th century Brown Bess musket. An ideal way to have done this would have been to acquire, test fire, and measure the performance of an actual Brown Bess musket. However, while considering the use of an original or replica musket, a number of practical issues became immediately apparent.

Firstly, original 18th century Brown Bess muskets are now historical artefacts, and could be considered more works of art than functioning weapons. Even though an original musket could be obtained, preserving the condition of the weapon could not be guaranteed with the range of conditions under which it would have been fired. Furthermore, the material integrity of a 250 year old weapon would have posed a potential safety hazard to personnel and property at the experimental range.

Secondly, consideration was given to using a replica Brown Bess, which would at least solve the question of material integrity. However, given the range setup, properly mounting the weapon for repeatable firings proved to be unworkable without causing damage to the weapon. Limited finance was also a limiting factor for this option. It was therefore decided that a technical replica musket, which matched the pertinent specifications of the Brown Bess, would be designed, fabricated, and used during the project's experimental firings.

Design and Operation of the Technical Replica Brown Bess

The design of the technical replica Brown Bess was kept very simple. A 42 in (1066.8 mm) long EN 24 steel tube was used to replicate the barrel. The inner diameter of the tube was 19 mm, which closely matched the Brown Bess's 0.75 calibre. The tube's wall thickness was 3 mm thicker than the original Brown Bess's barrel. This was chosen to ensure safety on the range, whilst having a negligible effect on the ballistics of the weapon. It allowed varying amounts of gunpowder to be used knowing that the barrel would not fail under the high pressures.

The chamber end of the barrel was threaded to accept an adapter used to fit the barrel in the firing mount found at the Small Arms Experimental Range (SAER). An off-axis cavity was drilled into the side of the adapter to replicate the musket's flashpan. A 2 mm touch-hole was drilled through this cavity into the chamber of the barrel. In this way, gunpowder initiated in the cavity would ignite gunpowder in the chamber via the touch-hole causing the replica to function in the same manner as the flintlock Brown Bess. The gunpowder in the flashpan was initiated remotely using a Vulcan Fusehead (an electric matchhead), 20 ft of copper wire and a 9 V battery.

The replica Brown Bess was therefore a series of screw thread applications put together to measure safely the performance of the weapon in a controlled environment. Table 1 shows a summary of specifications for the Brown Bess technical replica.

Property	*Details*
Calibre	19.05 mm
Barrel Length	1066.8 mm
Shot Diameter	17.53 mm
Touch-Hole Diameter	2 mm
Loading Method	Muzzle Loaded
Firing Method	Electrically
Bore Type	Smooth

Table 1. Brown Bess Technical Replica Specifications

The Replica Cartridge

Paper

The paper used for the replica cartridge was obtained from Falkiner Fine Papers of London via their manufacturer, Griffen Mills in the Republic of Ireland, and mirrored as closely as possible that used in the 18th century. The paper type used was called 'Wove', made from a blend of cotton and hemp fibres, cream in colour and weighing 80 g/m^2 (about 0.004 in in thickness). The cartridge paper was cut to size and rolled as described earlier to incorporate the lead shot, before pouring in the gunpowder. Thin strands of parcel string were used to replicate the twine.

Shot

There was much debate about the purity and density of lead used in the 18th century for the shot. The shot used in this research was cast from pure lead, identical to that used for roofing houses. Using modern day moulds, the shot was cast in the traditional method by the 'Muzzle Loaders Casting Shack' in Clacton on Sea. Research suggests that during the Battle of Culloden in 1746, the Brown Bess fired 14 bore lead shot. The closest obtainable match to this was 0.691 inches in diameter, which was used during the research.

Gunpowder

Gunpowder is not now made to the same standards or using the same process as in the 18th century (Buchanan 1996). The old method involved using a pestle and mortar to incorporate the saltpetre, sulphur and charcoal; a process which would last up to eight hours. This would now contravene modern safety regulations, so it is not possible to replicate this important step.

Even if it could be attempted, it would be virtually impossible to match all the characteristics of the powder exactly due to the complex nature of gunpowder. Additionally, as mentioned previously, the gunpowder was extremely variable in quality. Therefore, replicating true 18th century gunpowder would involve incorporating a degree of inconsistency.

A partial aim of this project was to assess the ballistic properties of a Brown Bess, it was decided to use modern gunpowder in order to ensure reliability when examining the ballistic effects. Due to lack of records, the specifications of the powder used in the Brown Bess are unknown, although there is circumstantial evidence to suggest that it was of mixed grain sizes. Three modern day gunpowders were obtained: Black powder Type 3A (fine); G12; and blasting powder, with the aim of testing them individually and mixed, in order to find the closest match to 18th century gunpowder. Measuring the muzzle velocity would give an indication of how similar in terms of power each gunpowder was to that used in the 18th century.

Computer Modelling

Internal Ballistics Modelling

The program used to model the internal ballistics of the Brown Bess technical replica was HMSOV, which was created with the Matlab computing language. By inputting the weapon's specifications (and making realistic assumptions where necessary), the program calculated muzzle velocity, peak pressure, and defined a pressure/travel history curve. Three input files were created; one to represent each of the charges used: 7.5 g, 10 g, and 15 g.

Defining the Parameters

An input file was used to define the parameters of the projectile. These parameters included muzzle velocity, projectile mass, shot calibre, angle of elevation, initial height, and coefficient of drag (C_D). Based on the input parameters, the external ballistics modelling program calculated the trajectory. For every metre of range, the program output listed values for total velocity, horizontal and vertical components of velocity, vertical displacement, C_D, Mach number, and elapsed time.

Calculating Muzzle Velocity

Once the likely muzzle velocity of 1500 fps (457.2 m/s) was identified through the use of data from historical sources, it was a simple matter of

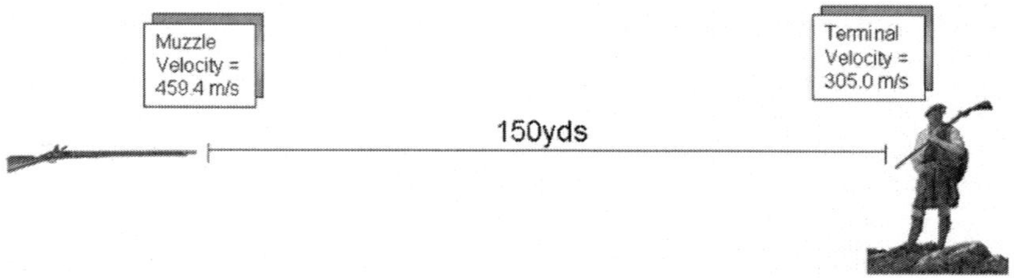

Fig. 1. Terminal Velocity measurement for an historical engagement

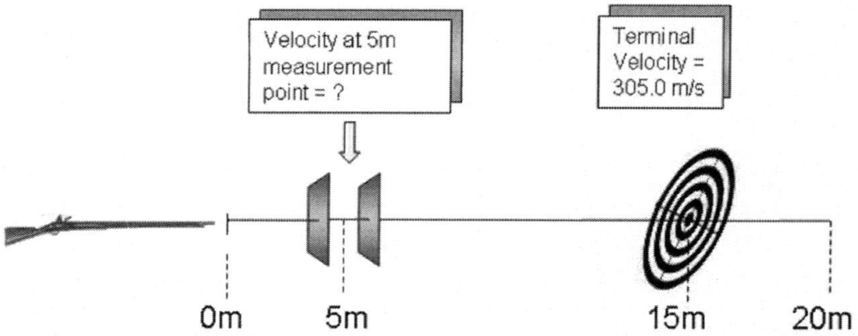

Fig. 2. Range scaling for target at 15 m on a 20 m range

defining parameters for the input file to determine what the terminal velocity would be at a given target range. Normal engagement ranges during the 18th century have been quoted as being 150 yards (137 m). The output data found the terminal velocity at a 137 m target would be approximately 304 m/s. It should also be noted that when fired from a height of 1.5 m (roughly shoulder height), at 137 m the shot would have dropped to approximately 0.9 m above the ground. Also, if no target were hit, the shot would travel until it hit the ground at approximately 201 m.

The external ballistics modelling program also aided in the design of the terminal ballistics experiments. For simulating a 150 yd engagement, and with a muzzle velocity of 459.4 m/s from range data, the computer model predicted a terminal velocity of 305 m/s, as depicted in Fig 1.

To simulate this engagement on the 20 m firing range (with the target located at 15 m), it was required to know what velocity needed to be registered at the measuring point 5 m from the barrel, as shown in Fig 2. The 127 m entry in the output file (137 m–10 m) indicated that the velocity at that point will be 313 m/s. Thus, by measuring a velocity close to 313 m/s on the range, it could be confidently estimated that the terminal velocity would be near the expected value of 305 m/s.

Maximum Range

As the replica musket could only be fired using the clamp at the 20 m range, maximum range could not be measured practically. Ballistic modelling was therefore also employed to predict the maximum range achievable, and at what angle of elevation this would occur. By inputting the relevant parameters, it was found that around 1,200 m could be reached when firing at 35° of elevation, compared to 202 m when firing horizontally.

Ballistic Experiments

Experimental set up

All of the trials were conducted at the Cranfield University SAER; an indoor range with a remote firing capability and ability to fire replica barrels. The replica musket was mounted in a clamp which eliminated human based firing variations. Equipment was available for measuring projectile velocity as well as weighing facilities for gunpowder. The cartridges to be fired were pre-made using the method described previously. The replica musket was positioned in a clamp at the end of the 20 m range. Aluminium laminates mounted in stands were used to measure shot velocity.

Preparing the Cartridge

The gunpowder was weighed out at the range and then placed inside the cartridge, with 0.65 g of the total amount weighed separately to be used for priming. The quantity and type of gunpowder used varied depending on which experiment was being conducted. Exact details are described in the methods later in the Chapter. After fixing the replica musket in the stand, the cartridge was loaded into the barrel in the same manner as used in the 18th century: the top of the cartridge paper was bitten or ripped off, and the powder it contained placed into the barrel.

Loading the Cartridge

As the barrel was fixed in the stand, it was not possible to tilt the weapon and pour the powder down the barrel. Instead, a small scoop mounted on a wooden pole was used. The powder was poured onto the scoop, inserted in the barrel and emptied at the chamber end of the barrel. The remainder of the cartridge was then inserted down the barrel using a ramrod. The paper end went in first in order to act as wadding, with the shot (still wrapped in paper) separated from the gunpowder by this wadding.

Firing the Weapon

The remaining powder (the 0.65 g kept aside for priming) was then poured into the recess created to represent the pan found on a musket. An electric match head was positioned in the pan, ensuring it made contact with the powder. With the weapon prepared, all personnel retreated to another room. The weapon was fired by connecting the wire from the match head to a 9V battery. This caused the match head to burn, igniting the powder in the pan. The flames went through the touchhole to the powder in the chamber, which in turn ignited. The expanding gases provided the force to accelerate the shot down the barrel and towards the target.

Experiment to find Gunpowder equivalent to 18th Century Gunpowder

The aim of this experiment was to trial several modern gunpowders in order to find a composition and amount that achieved the closest match to that used in the 18th century. The intention was to obtain a muzzle velocity of 1500 fps (457.20 m/s), whilst using a quantity of gunpowder as close as possible to that used with the Brown Bess.

Results

A total of 21 firings were conducted using 3 different gunpowders. It was found that the type 3A and G12 both produced similar muzzle velocities, which were higher than that of the coarse Blasting Powder. When 3A and G12 were combined whilst keeping the same total mass, an even higher muzzle velocity was obtained. It was found that using 15 g 3A and G12 in a ratio of 1:3 achieved an average muzzle velocity of 459.4 m/s (1507.2 fps).

The results, shown in table 2, demonstrate the unpredictable and inconsistent performance of a gunpowder fired weapon, particularly noticeable with G12.

Conclusion

During the 18th century, about 10 g of gunpowder was used, achieving a muzzle velocity of around 1500 fps (457.2 m/s). As the modern powder used was not as powerful as that of the 18th century, 457.2 m/s could not be obtained using the same quantity of powder. This was expected as the modern powder was created for a different intended use. However, the most powerful effect was found by mixing 3A and G12, rather than using them

Firing No.	*Amount of Powder (g)*				*Velocity (m/s)*
	3A	*G12*	*Blasting Powder*	*Total*	
1	10			10	314.7
2	10			10	282.2
3	10			10	204.9
4		10		10	130.2
5		10		10	329.3
6		10		10	210.7
7			10	10	138.4
8			10	10	110.7
9			10	10	186.6
10	5	5		10	305.3
11	5	5		10	271.6
12	5	5		10	295.0
13	2.25	7.75		10	336.5
14	2.25	7.75		10	310.0
15	2.25	7.75		10	291.6
16	4.5	13.5		18	448.7
17	4.5	13.5		18	476.7
18	5	15		20	513.9
19	3.75	11.25		15	447.1
20	3.75	11.25		15	473.8
21	3.75	11.25		15	457.2

Table 2. Varying Gunpowder Type and Quantity

individually. 15 g of 3A and G12 mixture in a ratio of 1:3 gave the closest match to the desired effects, producing an average muzzle velocity 459.4 m/s (marginally above 1500 fps). This increased velocity from mixing the powders could be due to the powders having individual pressure/travel curves, which peak at different distances down the barrel. When mixed, the pressure/travel curves are combined, leading to a longer peak pressure (larger area under the graph) and therefore higher muzzle velocity.

Experiment to Synthesise hitting Targets at 75 and 150 yds

Having achieved the muzzle velocity of the 18th century, the amount of gunpowder used then was scaled down to achieve the desired terminal velocities for the future experiments. Given that the SAER range was 20 m long and the targets positioned at the 15 m point, the ballistic modelling found that to achieve the effect of hitting a target at 150 and 75 yds, muzzle velocities of 313.0 and 379.0 m/s respectively were required. This experiment aimed to find how much powder was needed to obtain these values. Different quantities of the 1:3 mix of 3A/G12 gunpowder were fired using the replica musket, and the quantity varied until the desired muzzle velocities were achieved.

Results

Using the results from the previous experiment, the average muzzle velocity of 312.7 m/s obtained with 10 g of gunpowder was deemed close enough to the required 313.0 m/s to replicate firing at 150 yds. 14 g was found to give an average muzzle velocity of 383.9 m/s, with the results shown in Table 3. This was regarded sufficiently near to the required 379.0 m/s to replicate firing at 75 yds.

Amount of powder (g)	*Achieved muzzle velocity (m/s)*
14	388.0
14	365.1
14	398.7

Table 3. Replicating Firing at 75yds

Conclusion

Due to the variable nature of gunpowder in the replica musket, it was decided that obtaining the calculated muzzle velocities exactly was not necessary, and small differences were tolerable. 10 g of the 3A/G12 mixture provides a close enough muzzle velocity to that desired for the 150 yds, whilst 14 g would be used for 75 yds.

Wound Effects

Target Analysis

At the battle of Culloden, the target was a Jacobite warrior wearing a woollen garment known as a plaid, which in various forms could constitute a kilt, a shirt and or a waistcoat. The armour consisted of large shields known as targes. The targe was constructed from an irregular number of thin planks of pine glued edge to edge, which was then laid crossways over another series of similar planks, so the grain of one is set across the other. This cross ply construction made the shield stronger and much improved sword or bullet-stopping capabilities. The front of the targe was then covered in cowhide and nailed at the back. Targes were between 18 and 24 inches in diameter, with the wood around half an inch thick. Based upon this data, and ignoring some of the decorative features, a replica was produced from pine cross ply, and covered in cow leather.

The targets used to mimic the human torso were produced from a mix of water (85% by weight) and ballistic gelatine (15% by weight). This mix has a similar density (1.06 g/cm^3) and elastic modulus to human tissue, while accounting for variances in density within a real human torso. A thick woollen blanket was cut to cover the face of each target block. This represented the likely clothing worn by Jacobite forces during the battle. In some trials, it was wetted to assess any differing effects, as claimed by some historians.

Wound Effects Experiments

Eight experimental firings were used to examine the wounding effects of the technical replica and deformation of the lead shot. The same range set up described earlier was used, with a high speed camera focused on the target end in order to capture temporary cavitation effects. The technical replica Brown Bess was mounted on the stand at the SAER, and fired using an appropriate amount of modern gunpowder to achieve the terminal velocity expected at the likely distance of engagement with the enemy.

Experiment investigating Effect on Gelatine Block at 150 yds

The first experiment was designed to simulate the effect of the musket shot hitting a man in the torso at 150 yds—the likely distance of engagement. A blanket was placed around the gelatine block to replicate clothing. An entry wound 38 mm across was inflicted, and an exit wound of 65 mm. The maximum permanent cavitation was around 40 mm. It is assessed that this level of damage to the ballistic gelatine block represents a catastrophic effect on a human torso at the likely maximum distance of engagement, assuming a strike to the torso.

Experiment investigating Close Distance Engagement (75 yds)

Next, the effects of the musket shot hitting the chest of a man at 75 yds were measured. 14 g of gunpowder was used to achieve the 379.0 m/s muzzle velocity to simulate this engagement range. The high-speed camera captured evidence of some extremely large temporary cavitation, stretching the gelatine block to twice its original height and volume. The entry wound was 48 mm across, and exit was around 55 mm. The maximum permanent cavitation was 80 mm across, and the wound track had forced off a chunk of ballistic jelly. The temporary cavitation is much greater at 75 yds compared to 150 yds, meaning that considerably more damage would have occurred, that would almost definitely have been fatal.

Experiment to measure the Penetration of Replica 18th Century Armour (150 yds)

The third experiment was designed to measure the effectiveness of battlefield protection available at the time of the battle of Culloden. A smaller mould of ballistic gelatine was used, replicating the thickness of a human arm, which would be supporting a targe in battle. Both the targe and the ballistic gelatine were penetrated, with a clear wound track visible through the depth of the gelatine block. Small pieces of wood and woollen material were dragged into the wound track. The entry wound was 20 mm in diameter and the exit wound 25 mm. Considerable translation occurs, with both the targe and the gelatine block knocked off the target frame. Permanent cavitation in the form of small bubbles in the gelatine block could be seen, 38–40 mm in diameter.

The presence of an exit wound in the gelatine block shows that not all of the kinetic energy was transferred to the gelatine block. However, the translation of the apparatus implies that the force may be great enough to knock over a soldier holding a targe. A considerable amount of the displaced wood from the targe could be seen in the ballistic gelatine block. This would drag any dirt and pathogens into the wound, likely to cause death by secondary infection if the soldier survived the impact.

Experiment investigating Effect on Replica Armour with Steel (150 yds)

The fourth experiment was a repeat of the previous, but with a 1 mm steel plate placed in front of the targe to replicate the reinforced shield sometimes utilised. The steel plate was easily penetrated, as was the targe. This proved that the steel plate provided little additionally resistance to the shot. However, the steel may have improved the targe's performance against other hand-held weapons such as axes or maces.

Experiment investigating hitting two Ballistic Gelatine Blocks with Clothing and a Pork Ribcage (150 yds)

The fifth experiment was designed to evaluate three effects. Firstly, the shot hitting bone, achieved by placing a pork ribcage between the clothing and the gelatine block; secondly, another gelatine block was placed 20 cm behind the first to see whether two Jacobite soldiers may be incapacitated by the same shot; thirdly, the second block was placed behind six layers of fabric that were saturated with water. This would investigate the theory that wet blanket may prevent penetration by the lead shot.

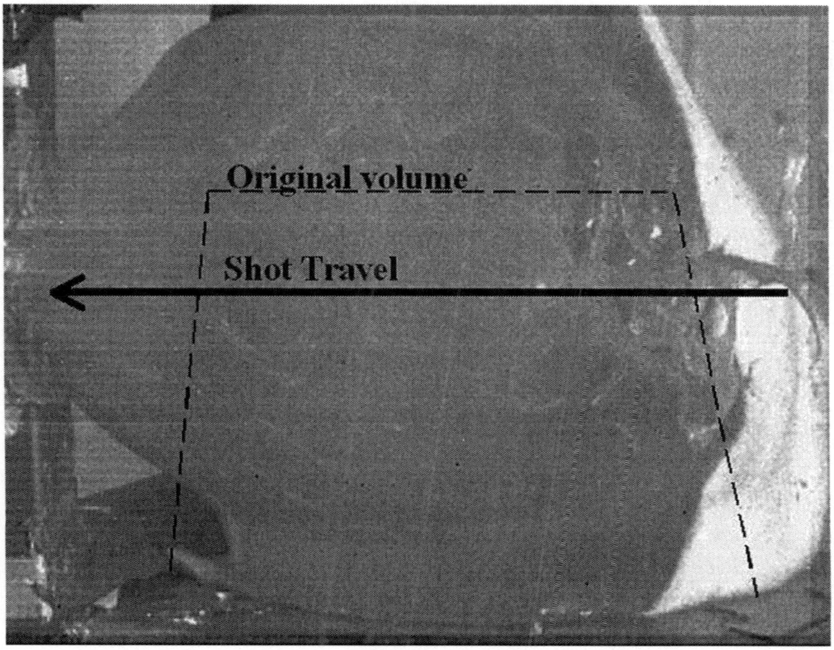

Fig. 3. High Speed Camera Footage Showing Temporary Cavitation

Both gelatine blocks were penetrated, and large temporary cavitation was captured on high speed camera, shown in fig 3. Significant debris from clothing and pork ribcage is visible in the wound track of the first gelatine block. There is fabric debris in the second. This proved that the same round could well incapacitate two or more (closely spaced) Jacobite soldiers. It also disproves any idea that wet clothing may protect against penetration from lead shot. It was evident that a large amount of debris gets dragged into any cavity formed by the shot, likely to lead to infection if the wound is survived.

Experiments examining the Effects on Modern ceramic body armour (CBA) (150 yds)

The next two experiments were designed to compare the Brown Bess effects on modern day battlefield protection; CBA with and without a ceramic plate. Without the ceramic plate, the shot hit the fabric lining of the CBA, perforating it. The shot was caught inside the fabric and bulged the inside lining. The shot itself became deformed, with the appearance of it having been squashed. The inside of the fabric protruded sharply around 2–3 inches into the body behind the armour. With the ceramic plate inserted, the plate was

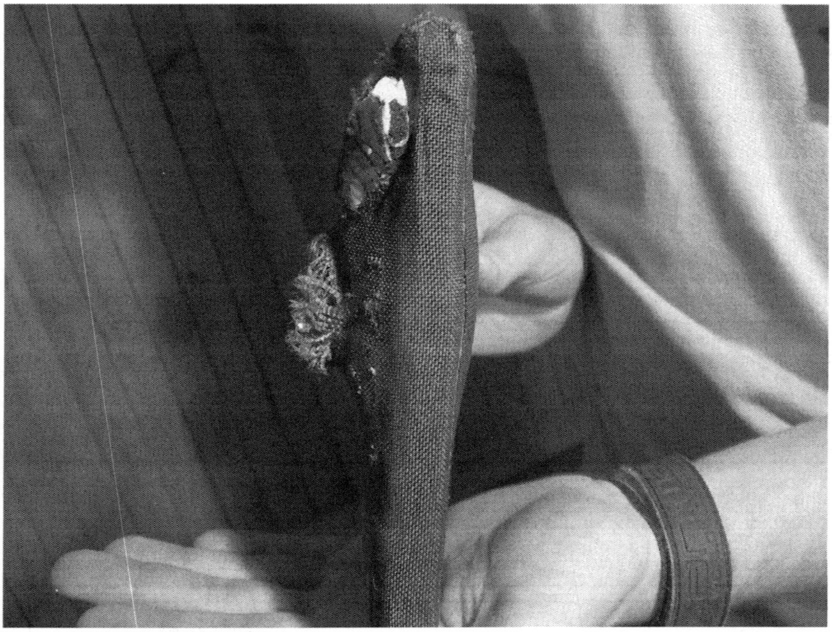

Fig. 4. Damage to Ceramic Plate

shattered and only a slight bulge occurred to the fabric. The damage to the ceramic plate is shown in fig 4. The high speed footage appeared to show the lead shot shattering.

While the CBA stopped the shot, the behind armour effects were considerable. It is assessed that the lead shot would incapacitate a man wearing CBA without ceramic insert plate. With the plate, incapacitation was unlikely to have occurred, but the wearer would probably have been knocked over.

The Effects of Musket Balls striking Sharp Metal, such as Sword Blades (150 yds)

Previous archaeological investigations at Culloden have uncovered musket balls which appear to have been deformed, perhaps by striking a sword blade or other metallic item such as a belt buckle. The former hypothesis was drawn from musket balls which had been almost cleaved in two, leaving the two halves hinged like a scallop shell (Pollard 2005). An attempt was mad to replicate this circumstance by positioning mesh wire garden fencing at the end of the range, with a 'soft capture' box containing rubber chunks behind it. The fencing used was steel with plastic coating. The horizontal and vertical strands of the fence formed 45 mm by 45 mm squares. The soft capture box was intended to decelerate and contain the lead shot.

Unfortunately, the soft capture box failed to adequately decelerate the shots, resulting in deformation occurring on hitting the back wall of the box. It was not therefore possible to examine whether the shot had cleaved. All shots caused dislocation and bending of the strands in the fencing, or the removal of one side of a square in the fencing. This implies that metal, such as a belt buckle, would be unlikely to stop a lead shot.

Terminal effects summary

The effects demonstrated using ballistic gelatine at realistic engagement ranges have shown that if struck by a lead shot, the human body will at the very least be incapacitated, and most probably fatally injured. In this respect, the ballistic performance of this weapon system can be said to be excellent, with its effect on modern CBA showing it to be comparable to modern weapons (except enhanced penetrating ammunition). It would certainly cause attrition to advancing enemy who entered the zone where the shots were fired.

Accuracy

The experiments have not investigated the issue of accuracy of the weapon, which has obvious ramifications for the overall effectiveness. However, the technical replica used during the project did display a consistent level of performance, with entry holes on a witness screen behind the targets often overlapping, and all occurring within an area of an A4 piece of paper at a range of 20 m. Given the reports of extreme inaccuracy, this result was surprising. However, many variables that are known sources of inaccuracy were eliminated during the range sessions. The recoil of the weapon is known to be huge, and likely to be the largest cause of variability, as it would be impossible to hold the weapon still when firing. The more consistent modern gunpowder used would also have reduced the muzzle velocity variation, which in turn affects the trajectory.

Conclusion

The aim of the project was to conduct a detailed study of the effectiveness and capabilities of the 18th century Brown Bess musket. Experiments were designed and conducted which investigated the ballistic effects of the Brown Bess, and answered the questions posed at the start of the project. A replica musket was created, which was able to fire replica cartridges with accurate recordings made. Having researched the historical accounts, key claims of the Brown Bess's capabilities were chosen for investigation. Experiments were then designed to assess their legitimacy. In all cases, meaningful results were obtained, which could be related back to the historical evidence.

Gunpowder

Gunpowder in the 18th century was made using a lengthy procedure which contravenes modern health and safety regulations. The modern gunpowders that were sourced to fire the weapon were not as powerful per unit mass to the 18th century gunpowder in terms of muzzle velocity achieved. 15 g of modern powder was required to achieve the same velocity as 10 g of the old powder. This could be attributed to the modern powder not being designed to fire a musket, and so having different specifications.

Cartridges

Replica cartridges were successfully constructed following the 18th century method, using paper and lead shot that were a close match to the original.

Modelling

The computer modelling proved invaluable when calculating how to scale down the powder to achieve the correct muzzle velocities for the terminal effects. The models also provided information about the range of the weapon, which could not be performed experimentally. The maximum calculated range was around 1,200 m when firing at 35° of elevation, and 202 m when firing horizontally.

Wound Effects

All but one of the experiments examining terminal effects used a muzzle velocity equating to being hit at 150 yds (137 m). The damage caused to the target indicates that immediate death would be almost certain due to the large temporary and permanent cavitation. This confirms the effectiveness of the weapon at relatively long range, contradicting the historical accounts of it being ineffective at 100 yds (91 m). At 75 yds (69 m), the effects were even more damaging, causing much greater cavitation. It was also proved that a single shot could penetrate more than two soldiers, and would shatter bone, dragging fragments throughout the wound. The outer clothing layer was also dragged through the wound, along with any dirt and pathogens. If the soldier survived the impact, death would still be likely through secondary infection. The damage caused to the modern CBA again shows the harm that the shot could cause against today's armour.

Bibliography

Buchanan, B 1996 *Gunpowder: The History of an International Technology*. Bath University Press: Bath

Crocker, G 1986 *The Gunpowder Industry*. Shire Publications: Oxford

Hanger, G 1816 *Colonel George Hanger's Advice to all Sportsmen, Farmers and Gamekeepers*. Printed for JJ Stockdale: London

Harding, D 1999 *Small arms of the East India Company 1600–1856, Volume III: ammunition and performance*. Forsight Books: London

Hughes, BP 1974 *Firepower: Weapons Effectiveness on the Battlefield, 1030–1650*. Charles Scribner's and Sons: New York

James, G (no date) *Britain's Brown Bess*. http://www.rifleshootermag.com/featured_rifles/bess_092407/

MacPherson, D 1994 *Bullet Penetration: Modeling the Dynamics and the Incapacitation Resulting from Wound Trauma*. Ballistic Publications, El Segundo, CA

Mordecai, A 1845 *Report of Experiments on Gunpowder*. Washington

Moss, G M, Leeming, D W & Farrar C L 1995 *Military Ballistics*. Brassey's: London

Nonte, G 1969 *Black Powder Guide*. Stoeger Publishing Company: New Jersey

Pollard, T 2005 *Culloden Battlefield: Report on the Archaeological Investigation*. GUARD report no. 1981, University of Glasgow

Pollard, T and Oliver, N 2003 *Two Men in a Trench II: Uncovering the secrets of British Battlefields*. Michael Joseph: London

Reid, S (in press) 'The British Army' *in* Pollard, T (ed) *Culloden 1746—The History and Archaeology of the Last Clan Battle*. Pen and Sword: Barnsley

Richardson, T 1999 'Ballistic testing of historical weapons', *Royal Armouries Yearbook 1998*. Royal Armouries. 50–52.

Robins, B 1742 *New Principles of Gunnery*: London

Sellier K G & Kneubuehl B P 1994 *Wound Ballistics and the Scientific Background*. Elsevier: Amsterdam

Textbook of Ballistics and Gunnery 1984, Vols I and II. Her Majesty's Stationery Office

Thompson, A L 1969 'The Brown Bess Musket', *Guns Review*

Willegal, M, 1999 *The Accuracy of Black Powder Muskets*. www.willegal.net/iron_brigade/musket.pdf

AN ARCHAEOLOGICAL STUDY OF TALAMANCA BATTLEFIELD

XAVIER RUBIO CAMPILLO

Abstract

The Peace of Utrecht (1713) ended the War of the Spanish Succession as a global European conflict. However, the treaty abandoned to their fate the Spanish territories that had supported Archduke Charles. Resistance to the House of Bourbon was focused in the city of Barcelona, which was immediately put under siege. However, the Catalan government managed to create a powerful army outside the siege belt of the capital. This force, comprising almost 5,000 soldiers, attacked a similar Bourbon army in the small town of Talamanca on 13 August, 1714. The Catalan commander, the Marquis of Poal, successfully launched three simultaneous attacks against the Bourbon force. This study is an approach to this battle, using the results of archaeological fieldwork undertaken in the area. The study of material evidence is combined with GIS and statistical analysis in order to better understand the armies of the 18th century.

Introduction: Local Epilogue of a Global Conflict

The War of the Spanish Succession (1700–1714) was one of the major engagements of the 18th century. The origin of the war was the struggle for hegemony between the different royal European houses, particularly involving the Austrian Hapsburgs and the French Bourbons. The death of Charles II, the king of Spain, without heirs left this kingdom open to the claims of both houses, which presented their candidates to the crown: Philip, Duke of Anjou and grandson of Louis XIV of France, and the Archduke Charles, son of the Holy Roman Emperor Leopold of Austria.

Initially, Philip was accepted as king; this succession had been specified in the will of Charles II. However, the prospect of France and Spain united under a common Bourbon crown was a potential threat to the European balance of power. This was the main reason why England, the Dutch Republic and Austria created a Grand Alliance to declare war against Louis and Philip. Portugal and Savoy soon joined the coalition, and a major part of Europe began the preparations for war, which now seemed imminent.[1]

[1] Other smaller states joined the war: Prussia and Denmark sent troops to help the Grand Alliance, and the elector of Bavaria signed a treaty with Louis XIV, opening the gates of South Germany and Austria to the French army.

 DOI: 10.1163/157407808X382746

The armies were sent to the usual European conflict zones: northern Italy, the zone of the High Rhine which led to the heartland of Austria, and particularly the Low Countries. In 1705, another theatre of war was opened as Catalan representatives in Genoa signed the union of Aragon, Catalonia and Valencia to the Grand Alliance.[2] A substantial fleet disembarked in the city of Barcelona, and Valencia fell under their control within a few weeks. From this point, the War of the Spanish Succession gained an additional dimension as a political and military struggle between the territories of the Spanish crown, as well as a wider European conflict. Castile supported the centralist policies of the Bourbon house, while the territories of the Aragonese crown desired to gain political control through the Hapsburgs.

Barcelona became the heart of the Alliance in the Iberian Peninsula, operating as a logistical and military base for the allied forces. Charles was crowned king, and held his court in the city throughout the war. In 1706, a powerful Bourbon force tried to conquer Barcelona, but the Alliance managed to break the siege and defeat the army of Philip, initiating a pursuit that finished in Madrid. The arrival of French reinforcements, commanded by the Duke of Berwick, reversed the situation. The Allied army was forced to retire towards Valencia, where they were soundly defeated in Almansa on 25 April 1707. This battle had important consequences, as the Allied army was virtually destroyed, and Philip was able to regain control of Valencia, most part of Aragon and the Catalan city of Lleida.

Elsewhere, however, events were more favourable to the Grand Alliance. Their most important army, commanded by the Duke of Marlborough, defeated the French armies in Blenheim (1704), Ramillies (1706), Oudenaarde (1708) and Malplaquet (1709). Moreover, the victories of Prince Eugene of Savoy in northern Italy left Philip with insufficient resources to conquer the rest of Catalonia, and in 1710 the Allies managed to create another powerful army based in Barcelona.

After the victories of Almenar (1710) and Saragossa (1710), the allied Commander-in-Chief, Guido von Starhemberg, marched again on Madrid under the influence of James Stanhope, leader of the English troops in the Catalan theatre of war. Taking Madrid was a high water mark for the Allies, however, as massive French intervention again altered the course of the campaign: the army of the Duc de Noailles invaded northern Catalonia, and the Spanish army was rebuilt near Valladolid. In November 1710, Starhemberg

---

[2] These territories comprised the Crown of Aragon, which still had their own constitutions and laws under the Spanish monarchy. This was the main reason of their treaty with the Grand Alliance, as the coronation of a Bourbon king like Philip would be an important step towards centralism.

had to retire from Madrid, and then from Central Spain entirely, to defend his own logistical base in Barcelona. The English contingent, which was isolated in Brihuega, had to surrender; Stanhope spent the next year as a prisoner. Ironically, on the day following the fall of Brihuega, Starhemberg defeated the Bourbon army in Villaviciosa, winning his army some time to retreat towards Catalonia.

In 1711, Holy Roman Emperor Joseph I, brother of Charles, died and the Archduke was crowned the new Emperor. An important part of the English government wanted to end the war and started peace negotiations with France, culminating in the Peace of Utrecht (1713), where Philip was recognized as King of Spain, at the cost of renouncing his rights to the French crown. England, Portugal and the other states signed their own treaties with Louis XIV of France and Philip V of Spain. Only Austria, guided by Archduke Charles (now the Holy Roman Emperor Charles V) continued the war.

The signing of the treaties left Catalonia in a difficult position, as the full force of France and Spain could be directed against it with no fear of external interference. The Emperor and his court, as well as the entire Allied army, retired from the zone and handed over most of the fortresses to the Spanish army. Despite this, the Catalan government decided to continue the war alone. On 6 July, 1713, a new Catalonian army was founded to organise the defence against the Bourbons. Winning the war was impossible in the long term, but the possibility of aid remained, given the complexities of European politics.

As Barcelona had plenty of military and economic resources, the raising of the new Catalan army took only a few weeks. Antonio de Villaroel, a brilliant officer of the old Allied army, was named Commander-in-Chief, and the recruitment of soldiers commenced; most of the recruits were from the old Allied army, but there were also local troops. Within 12 days, the Catalan army had almost 4,000 soldiers, forming 3 cavalry and 5 infantry regiments (Hernàndez & Riart 2007: 27) with plenty of veterans and officers.

On 25 July, 1713, the commander of the army of the Two Crowns,[3] the Duke of Popoli, started the siege of Barcelona with an army of almost 20,000 soldiers. Popoli knew that this was the main stronghold of Catalan resistance, and the fall of this city could probably finish the war. The Catalans raised new forces in the surrounding countryside which, located in the almost impregnable fortress of Cardona, tried to distract the Spanish forces from the siege of the capital. In the summer of 1714, the siege was proving to be a complete failure for the besiegers. Popoli and the Spanish army were incapable

---

[3] This is the common name of the Bourbon forces in Spain, given by most of the primary sources.

of conquering Barcelona, so Louis XIV sent one of his finest generals, the Duke of Berwick,[4] with numerous reinforcements. The Bourbon force amounted to 39,000 soldiers in the siege of Barcelona, with an additional 37,000 Spanish and 10,000 French soldiers deployed across the Catalan countryside.[5]

Berwick started a formal siege, battering the walls of the city with cannon fire. During the night of 13 August, 1713, he launched a massive assault against the city. However, the attack was a failure and was beaten off by the defenders. Casualties were heavy, both sides suffering more than 1500 casualties in the engagement.

At the same time, the Catalan army that had been raised in the surrounding area marched from Cardona in an attempt to break the siege and bring reinforcements into the capital. This force, shadowed by strong detachments of the Bourbon army, kept to the mountains to avoid being attacked by Bourbon cavalry on the plains. The Catalan army had a high percentage of mountain infantrymen (known as *miquelets*), and their knowledge of the landscape was one of the major benefits of using these routes instead of better tracks. On 13 August, the day of the major assault against Barcelona, the Catalan army was located in the small town of Talamanca, facing a large Spanish force on the other side of a stream. The Catalan commander, the Marquis of Poal, decided to cross the stream and surprise the enemy with a three-pronged attack against the hills where they were deployed. This engagement, known as the Battle of Talamanca, was the last important engagement of the war apart from the siege of Barcelona, as more than 5,000 soldiers fought in the area for an entire day.

Sources about the Battle

The most important source of information about the battle is an encrypted letter that the Marquis of Poal sent from Olesa to the Catalan government inside Barcelona, dated on 20 August, 1714 (AHCB: *Consell de Cent, Lletres Originals*, 1B-X-127, doc 337). In the text, the Catalan commander describes the dispositions of the troops before the engagement, as well as the detailed order of battle of his own army (3 mountain infantry regiments, 2 cavalry regiments, plus some grenadier companies and 2,000 militiamen known as

---

[4] James Fitz-James (1670–1734), duke of Berwick, was an illegitimate son of James II of England and nephew of Marlborough. He had shown his military skills in victories like Nice (1706) and Almansa (1707). Given the importance of his role in the Bourbon armies, his memories are a valuable source for the war.

[5] Ostwald gives an interesting comparison of the sieges of this war (2007, 341–43). As can be seen, the siege directed against Barcelona in 1714 is one of the longest of the entire conflict.

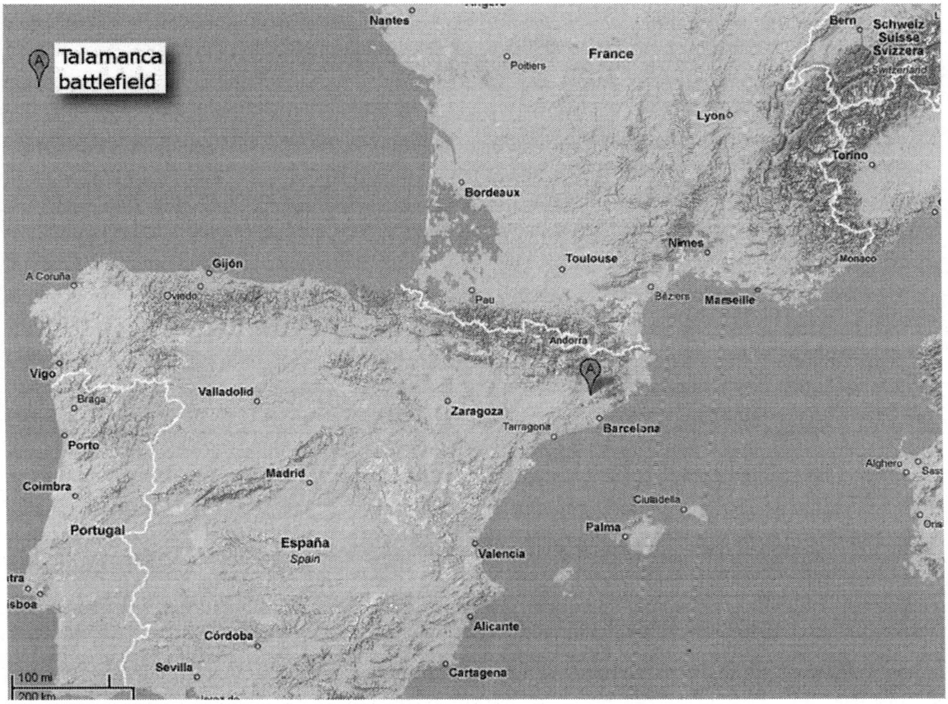

Fig. 1. Map of Iberian peninsular showing location of Talamanca battlefield

sometents). In contrast, the disposition of the enemy is only known in general terms (the columns of Montemar, Vallejo and Gonzalez, adding up 1,500 horsemen and a larger number of infantrymen). The Poal letter describes the battlefield, and his plan of attack against the Bourbon forces, composed by three different assaults across the stream. A first assault was conducted by his left wing, headed by 2 mountain infantry regiments (commanded by Colonels Segimon Torres and Martirià Massegur). Their target was the hill where the Bourbon infantry was deployed; the assault was a success. A second assault, starting from the Catalan centre, launched a regular infantry regiment (led by Francesco Busquets Mitjans) and a high number of *sometents* against the other hill in the area, which was held by dragoons; this assault was also successful. The final assault was a diversionary attack, launched with part of the Catalan reserve (two cavalry companies and *sometents*). They followed an alternate route towards the Bourbon command post, attempting to distract the Bourbon reserve from the main attack and destroy the powder magazine, which was located in a farm. This attack was a complete failure, but the Catalan army had succeeded in its main objectives and had managed to defeat the Bourbon troops on both hills. The arrival of Bourbon reserves stopped the advance of Poal's troops, but the counter-attack was repulsed by two companies of Grenadiers deployed in the Catalan centre. On the following day, the Bourbon commanders ordered the retreat. They were harassed by the Catalans all the way to the safety of Terrassa.

In his letter, Poal specifies the casualties on both sides (650 Bourbon soldiers against 35 Catalans).[6] He ends the document expressing his desire to take advantage of the victory by trying to break through the blockade to send reinforcements to Barcelona.

There are some other sources about the engagement, such as a reference in the work of Lord Mahon (Mahon 1832: 385), and another in Berwick's memories (Berwick 2007: 408), but none of them provides better information than Poal's letter, as most of the sources about the war were focused on the assault of Barcelona that was launched the same day.

The Research and the Battlefield

The main objective of the battlefield study was to confirm the historical information about the engagement. As there are only a few references for the battle, the archaeological analysis of the findings could help understand the size and importance of the clash, as well as the reliability of Marquis of Poal as a primary source. This is an important point, as there are several other encrypted letters from this commander, particularly about the war outside Barcelona's siege. By assessing the accuracy of the information in Poal's letter through the physical evidence provided by the archaeological survey, we can either accept or deny this important figure as a reliable source in understanding this period of the war (1713–1714).

The second point of the research is related to Spanish Bourbon and Catalan armies. There has been almost no research about the weapons of these two forces, or about their composition and size. The recovery of lead bullets and other military artefacts can be valuable in defining the type of firearms, as well as their calibres. Barcelona had a strong military industry, as the existence of contracts regarding weapon and ammunition production testifies. In these contracts there are references to three different calibres (pistol, carbine and musket), but the diameter is not specified in any of the sources currently

[6] Numbers seem exaggerated, especially about Bourbon casualties. However, in 1970 a mass grave was found near Talamanca's church, with up to 70 human remains buried at the same time. Unfortunately, no forensic studies were undertaken, but it seems quite probable that this mass grave was the place where the dead of the battle were buried.

known. The intention of the archaeological survey was to get some additional information, if this were possible.

Furthermore, the research was designed to improve and refine some important aspects of methodology. The battlefield of Talamanca is extraordinary rough, with noticeable slopes and a dense wood. This is a typical landscape for the North-West Iberian Peninsula, so all the experience coming from this survey will be useful for other projects developed under the same type of terrain.

The area of the engagement seemed to be big for the numbers involved (more than 300 ha; fig 2). Poal describes the Catalan force as being deployed under Talamanca's castle. Three infantry regiments (those commanded by Segimon Torres and Massegur were composed of *miquelets*, while the other, lead by Colonel Mitjans, was made up of regular infantrymen) and a detachment of grenadiers were to be the main assault force. Supporting these forces were a significant number of militiamen, known as *sometents*, numbering up to 1,500 men. Finally, the Marquis of Poal left all of his cavalry and 1,500 infantrymen as a tactical reserve, near the town of Talamanca. Opposing these regiments, the Bourbon army was divided in three corps. The left side, probably composed of dragoon regiments (up to 1,500 soldiers), was deployed on a hill, probably dismounted given the roughness of terrain. The right side, with more than 1,500 infantrymen, was located on another hill, just in front of Talamanca's castle. Finally, a large reserve corps held the Bourbon headquarters, the farm of Mussarra, in an area that dominated the battlefield in terms of height.

In terms of the landscape, the area of the battlefield today is covered by a dense wood. At the time of the battle, the vegetation was different; traces of human activity survive in the form of the remains of vineyards, while historical sources confirm that the general landscape of the area in 18th century was one of viticulture.[7]

A first analysis of the terrain slopes, developed under GRASS (Geographic Resources Analysis Support System), gives some clues about the attack zones, given that most of the area is inaccessible, and the stream was deep enough to stop any co-ordinated movement by hundreds of soldiers bar a couple of crossing points (fig 3). Following the historical references, as well as Poal's indications, it was possible to define the main focus of the engagement, and thus to start the archaeological surveys in the correct location.

[7] For references about the landscape of the zone see Ferrer 1998.

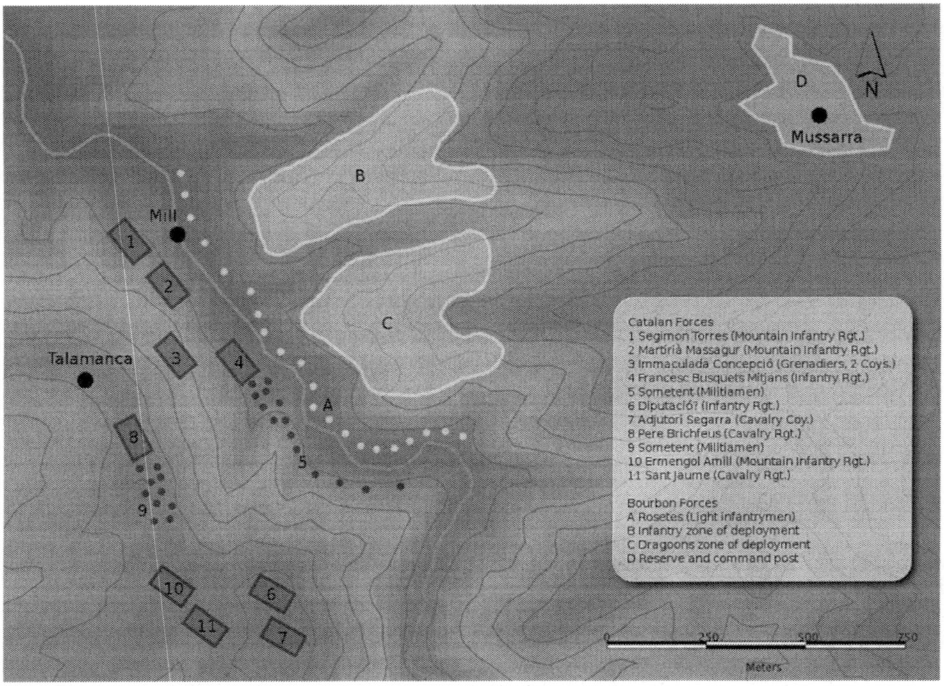

Fig. 2. Deployment of forces, as described by Poal's letter

Methodology and Works

The archaeological team explored the battlefield using metal detectors to collect lead bullets and other types of metallic items related to the battle. In order to classify and record information, each survey team was provided with a GPS, with instructions on how to geo-reference all the findings, tracking the different routes inside the battlefield.

Given the roughness of the terrain and the difficulty of walking through vegetation, the archaeologists were unable to delimit transects to explore the terrain on a regular grid. Some of the areas were completely inaccessible, given the slopes of the terrain and the presence of deep ravines. As these geographical features were present in 1714, the potential attack routes are limited, and the exact location of the battlefield can be easily found, given the information provided by the Poal letter.

The methodology followed was to divide the area of the battlefield into different zones delimited by the terrain itself, working systematically using four different teams. These archaeologists explored the zones in parallel courses, and the track information was recorded every 15 seconds using GPS. When the team detected metal artefacts, they were extracted and stored in indi-

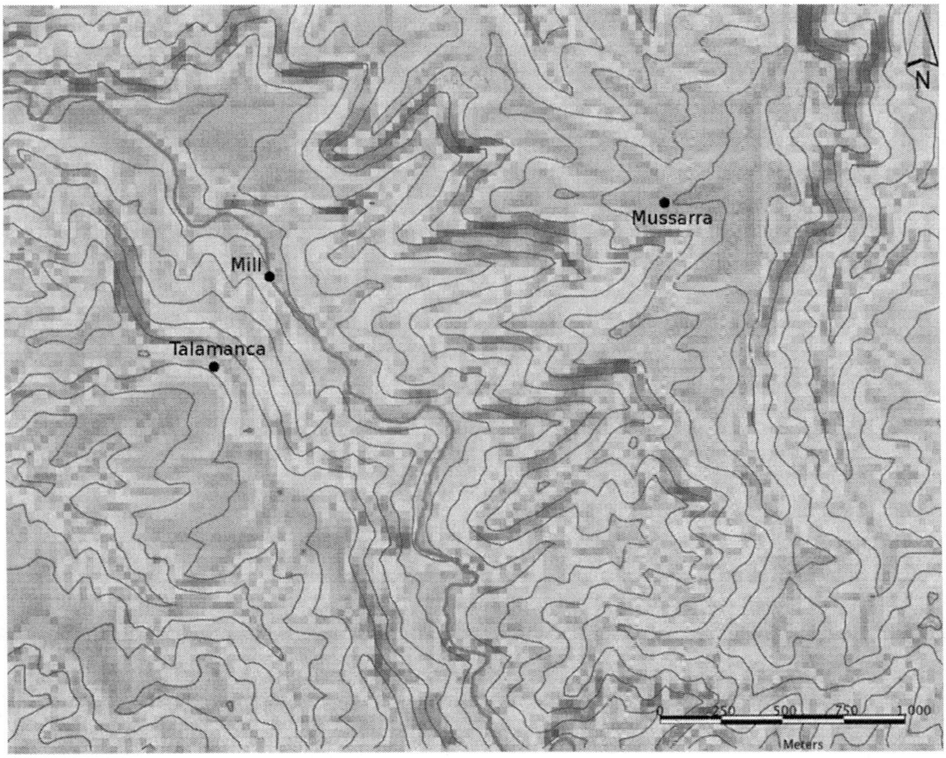

Fig. 3. Slope analysis of the battlefield

vidual bags; the bags were marked with GPS waypoint, team identifier, time and type of metal.

The survey was conducted in March 2008 over 5 days. The number of artefacts recovered is sufficient to confirm the scale of the engagement, while the amount of terrain explored is significant (almost 45 ha). Zones were chosen to cover the maximum terrain in order to fix the exact location of the battle.

Gis Analysis of the Findings

After the survey, a GIS database was created gathering all the data collected from the battlefield. The system, designed with QGIS, was filled with all GPS tracks and artefacts possibly related to the battle (up to 210 artefacts), as well as terrain analysis information. Figure 4 shows the collection over a DEM model of the terrain. Every item was photographed, weighed and measured to record its dimensions. Given the information that lead bullets can provide, they were additionally recorded by calibre when possible,

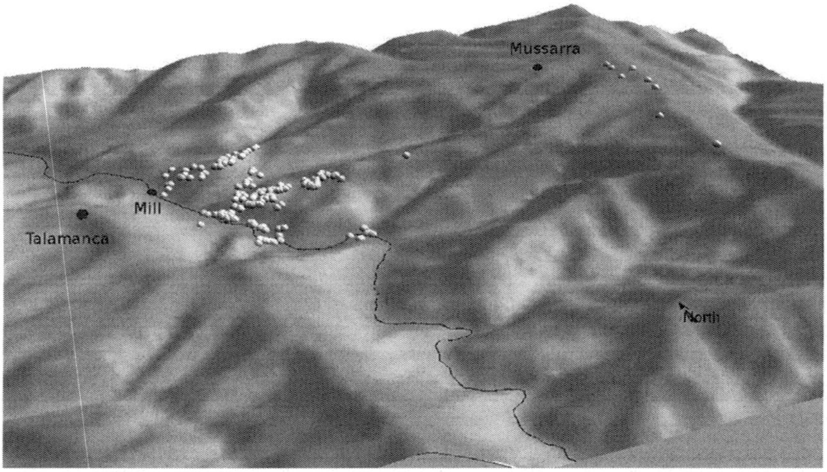

Fig. 4. Virtual reconstruction of the battlefield, with findings marked in white

given the state of the lead. The survey collected 73 bullets, and a high percentage of them seemed to be fired. The ones found over rocky soil were completely flattened, given the effect that an impact against harder surfaces can produce on a lead bullet.

The bullets were dispersed over the two hills where theoretically the Bourbon forces were deployed. Artefacts were recovered over a considerable area, far away from the initial line of attack (up to 500 m). This fact seems to indicate the success of the Catalan effort, consistent with the primary textual source. The exploration of the area where the diversionary attack against Mussarra took place produced some additional bullets. The distribution of the artefacts is related to the alternate route from Talamanca towards this Bourbon command post. The artefact distribution here was not as dense as the main zone of combat, but their location relative to Mussarra's farm gives a clue about the failure of this attack (300 m). The Catalan force was defeated by the Bourbon reserves and was unable to destroy the command post where the powder magazine was located. This is probably the reason why no bullets were found near the farm.

Coming back to the main area of action, the presence of a high number of horseshoes and related nails in the eastern hill proves that it was a suitable zone for cavalry. These artefacts could derive from agricultural activity and be unrelated to the battle but their presence, combined with the lack of horseshoes on the other hill, strongly suggests that this was the only location where a dragoon deployment may have taken place.

The locations of military artefacts (bullets, uniform items, etc.) on the battlefield are concentrated around two narrow tracks, as the terrain roughness mentioned before delimits the attack routes. One of the areas, corresponding to the attack of the left Catalan wing (composed of two mountain infantry regiments), starts near the watermill, where there is still an easy crossing of the stream. It continues towards the western hill of the battlefield up to the summit, with bullets distributed on a regular pattern.

The second track is aligned with the other currently possible crossing of the stream, where the centre of the Catalan deployment was located (Mitjans' regular infantry regiment, and up to 2,000 militiamen). From this location onwards, the artefacts were found up to the eastern summit. The hilltop consists of a small plain of rocky soil, where most of the deformed bullets were found.

Nine lead bullets were located near the stream, in areas where climbing the hill was practically impossible. Poal stated that a firefight developed for almost two hours before the crossing of the stream, so these bullet may be the result of this combat, when both armies were separated by a short distance, and a line of Bourbon light infantrymen (known as "Rosetas") held the northern side of the stream.

A number of special bullets were found distributed across the battlefield. In contrast to the standard, spherical bullets, these projectiles seemed to have been created from old lead objects. The survey teams gathered nine of these improvised bullets. They vary substantially in terms of weight, and the shape in most of the objects is cylindrical.

Even though it is quite difficult to specify the origin of these bullets, it is feasible that these projectiles were created and used by *sometents* (militiamen consisting of inhabitants of Catalan towns and villages). The other forces, both Catalan regulars as well as the entire Bourbon army, had their own logistical sources and cartridge supplies. Upcoming archaeological surveys on other battlefields could determine whether this unusual type of bullet was made by irregular troops or whether regular soldiers also used improvised bullets depending on the situation.

Statistical Analysis of the Bullets

Given the number of lead bullets found on the battlefield, it is possible to get an idea about the nature of the projectiles from a statistical point of view. The most valuable data are weight and calibre of bullets. In the first case (see Graph 1), improvised bullets somewhat distort the histogram given that, not being spherical, their weight is higher than it should be. Nevertheless, the information provided by this analysis is highly valuable, as will be seen below. In the second case, the count had to be done with just 60% of recovered bullets, because some of the projectiles were so deformed that measurement was impossible (see Graph 2). Graph 3 shows the relationship between weight and calibre. Apart from improvised bullets (with high weights that modify their positions in the graph), most of bullets show the correct pattern between both variables as they are spherical lead objects.

With this information, there is enough data to make a calculation of densities, using bullets that still retain a perfect spherical shape. The analysis shows that, although the theoretical density of lead is fixed at 11.34 g/cm^3, the bullets found have values distributed on a range between 10 and 11 g/cm^3. This is the consequence of imperfect manufacture, as air bubbles and impurities are located inside the bullet, thus lowering the final weight of the projectile. These defects have an important impact on accuracy of muskets, because the gravity centre of the bullet is displaced from the centre of the sphere, modifying the path of a fired bullet.

With regard to the possible identification of calibres, both histograms shows three different peaks. In the histogram of weights, these peaks are 4 g, 12 g and 21 g. These values strongly correlate to the three peaks in the histogram of calibres: 8 mm, 11 mm and 15 mm. The lighter values are probably not related to the battle, as they may be hunting lead shot. The bigger peak corresponds to musket bullets, as it can be converted to 21 bullets to the pound, a measure that matches contemporary musket calibres. Finally, the survey found a high number of medium calibres. They can be associated with carbine and pistol shots; the presence of mountain infantry and dragoons indicates that firearms of these types would have been a major element of the weaponry used during the fighting.

Linking all this information with geographical location, it is apparent that improvised bullets are distributed on an apparently random fashion between both hills. As the Catalan left wing theoretically did not have *sometents*, it seems to suggest that these projectiles were not only used by militiamen; *miquelet* forces that comprised the mountain infantry regiments also used them, as is shown by the archaeological records.

Musket bullets are concentrated on the eastern hill, following the path of Mitjan's regular infantry regiment. Mixed with these bigger projectiles are high quantities of medium calibres, probably corresponding to the fire of Bourbon dismounted dragoons against the Catalan assaulting troops, as well as *sometent* non-standard firearms.

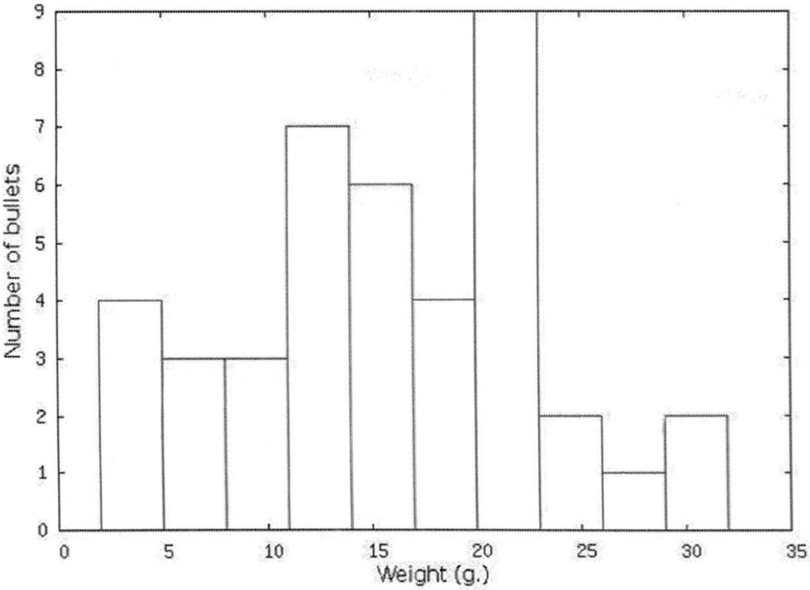

Graph 1. Histogram of the weights of found bullets

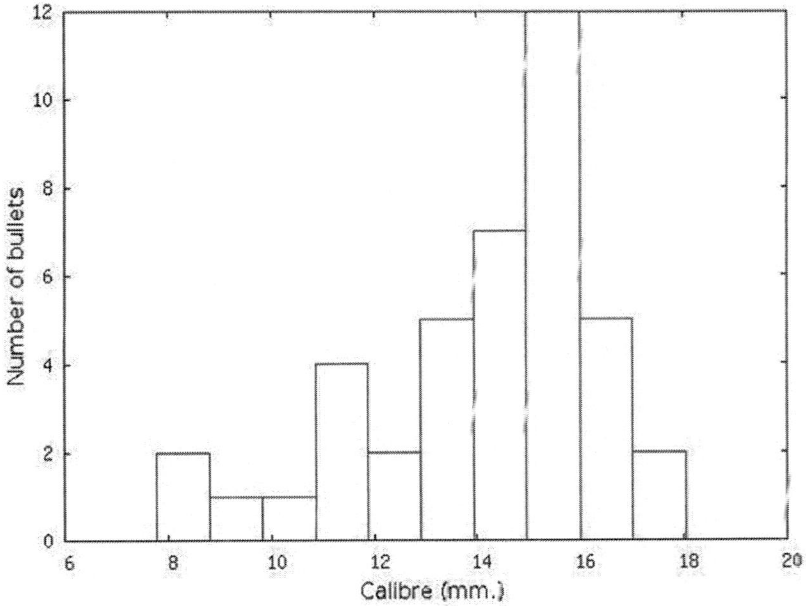

Graph 2. Histogram of calibres of found bullets

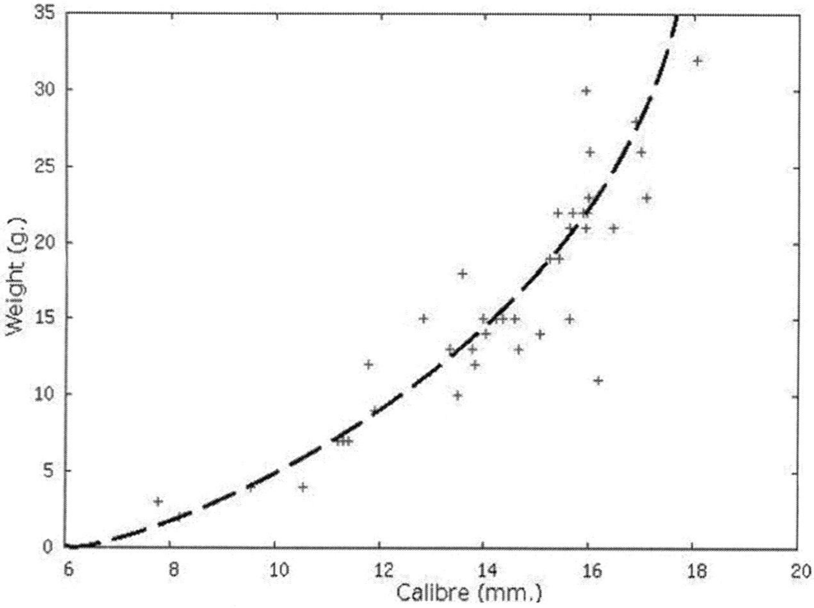

Graph 3. Relation between weight and calibre of found bullets

Conclusion

As an initial conclusion, the archaeological record extracted from Talamanca battlefield matches the information provided by the Marquis of Poal. The survey confirms that three attacks were launched across the stream, and it also confirms the success of the left wing and centre of Poal's army. Although additional surveys should be undertaken to gather more data, this first work has managed to depict a clear picture of the battle, marking the main engagement points as well as the path followed by soldiers.

In addition, all the information regarding calibres, uniforms and miscellaneous equipment collected in the battlefield is extremely valuable, as the number of historical sources about these topics is scarce. Other contemporary battlefields need to be examined to cross-reference the data of different armies and engagements in the zone, but these results seem a good starting point of the research.

The definition of a well-established methodology approach to this battlefield was difficult, given its particular topographic features. The selection of the explored areas was carefully considered to avoid holes in the data, as well as the concentration on theoretically richer zones.

To conclude, we can affirm that this survey has contributed important information to the study of the later years of the War of the Spanish Succession. This is the second excavated battlefield of this conflict in the Iberian Peninsula, and its records are quite different from the first one, Almenar (Rubio 2008). The nature of the engagement is truly different to bigger, famous battles like Blenheim (1704), Almansa (1707) or Oudenaarde (1708). The archaeological records remark the nature of the battle: uneven terrain covered by vineyards or wood, where cavalry charges and linear tactics were completely impossible. In these circumstances, the tactics of the *miquelets*, skilled mountain infantrymen at the service of Archduke Charles, were highly valued. These types of forces were also used by the Bourbon armies, combined with dragoons to gain mobility (first references of *miquelet* mountain regiments in French army are dated back to 1640, see Sales 1984). The importance of the Battle of Talamanca is summed up in hundreds of references to clashes in mountainous terrain, where constant fighting for supply paths and key fortresses is shown (see Castellví 1999). All this information throws some light onto the importance of uneven terrain in the Spanish theatre of war throughout all the War of the Spanish Succession.

Finally, this work shows that the war between the Catalan army and the Bourbon forces was not limited to the siege of Barcelona. The army commanded by the Marquis of Poal was capable of defeating large detachments, like the one concentrated in Talamanca. Even though in the end he was not capable of breaking the siege, he was a real threat to Berwick's effort, distracting thousands of soldiers from the capital and, with his presence, prolonging the war for almost two years.

Bibliography

AHCB (Arxiu Històric de la Ciutat de Barcelona). *Consell de Cent, Lletres Originals*, 1B-X-127, doc 337.

Bacallar, V 1957 *Comentarios de la Guerra de España e Historia de su rey Felipe V, el Animoso*. BAE: Madrid.

Berwick, Duke of 2007 *Memorias del duque de Berwick*. Pere Molas Ribalta (ed.), Universidad de Alicante: Spain.

Castellví, F 1999 *Narraciones Históricas*. 4 vols. Fundación Elías de Tejada: Madrid.

Chandler, D 1990 *The Art of Warfare in the Age of Marlborough*. Sarpedon Publishers: USA.

Coxe, W 1815 *Memoirs of the Kings of Spain of the House of Bourbon: from the accession of Philip V to the death of Charles III, 1700–1788*. Longman, Hurst Rees, Orme & Brown: London.

—— 1820 *Memoirs of John Churchill, Duke of Marlborough, with his original correspondence: collected from the family records at Blenheim and other authentic sources*. Longman, Hurst, Rees, Orme & Brown: London.

Duffy, C 1998 *The Military Experience in the Age of Reason*. Wordsworth Editions: London.

Ferrer i Alòs, L L 1998 *La Vinya al Bages*. Centre d'Estudis del Bages: Manresa.

Hernàndez, X & Riart, F 2007 *Els Exèrcits de Catalunya 1713–1714.* Rafael Dalmau: Editor: Barcelona.
Mahon, L 1832 *History of the War of Succession in Spain.* John Murray: London.
Ostwald, J 2007 *Vauban under Siege: engineering efficiency and martial vigor in the War of the Spanish Succession.* Brill Academic Publisher: Netherlands.
Parner, A 1905 *The War of the Succession in Spain: during the reign of Queen Anne, 1702–1711.* G Bell & Sons: London.
Rubio, X 2008 *Almenar 1710. Una victòria anglesa a Catalunya.* Llibres de Matrícula: Barcelona.
Sales, N 1984 *Senyors Bandolers, Miquelets i Botiflers.* Editorial Empúries: Barcelona.

REMEMBERING THE CHARGE OF THE LIGHT BRIGADE: ITS COMMEMORATION, WAR MEMORIALS AND MEMORY

GAVIN HUGHES & JONATHAN TRIGG

Abstract

This paper takes a broad approach to the British and Irish commemoration of the Charge of the Light Brigade (CLB), by assessing the contemporary documentary and memorial evidence and providing useful case-studies for further research. It builds upon the 1858 study by Captains Colbourne and Brine on Balaklava memorials and cemeteries by including an appreciation of those memorials and graves in the United Kingdom and the Republic of Ireland. In contrast to Colbourne and Brine's purpose, which was to provide a catalogue of graves and memorials, this paper seeks to interpret their impact, imagery or importance as required.

Introduction

Since the commencement of hostilities in the Crimea, the campaign's imagery and powerful influence has grown. Yet it remains an extremely maligned campaign with associated myths which are hard to expel. Despite recent and current military historical research, which has re-evaluated it within wider European, Imperial, Colonial and warfare contexts, from a British perspective, the Crimean War remains a period which is often popularly characterised by the efforts of Florence Nightingale and the Charge of the Light Brigade (CLB). Whilst the Crimean campaign was so much more than this, it is the Charge which still holds fascination for us today, almost as much as it did to Victorian society. Consequently, this paper explores some aspects of its commemoration and offers some observations on the same. Our intention has been to assess the historical and monumental sources, through active fieldwork and archive research, in an attempt to compose a useful record of such monuments. Whilst it cannot claim to be comprehensive, this paper hopes to tie together certain important themes in the CLB and examine them in view of current archaeological thinking. In particular, the attitudes to death and the dead of the CLB will be examined, as will any consequential historical implications, where appropriate. The commemoration of the Crimean War as a whole has been a much neglected subject for research and it is interesting to note that the only major published work on this area remains that of Captains Colbourne and Brine in 1858. It is also of interest to note that recently there has been an upsurge in commemorative activity, but these issues are beyond the scope

 DOI: 10.1163/157407808X382755

of this paper, and will be investigated in a future publication. In the meantime, we wish to consider aspects of commemoration that were contemporary with the veterans of the Crimean War, until the last surviving veteran, Rookes Evelyn Bell Crompton, died in February 1940 (Cliff, pers comm.).

For the Crimea, it is the battles of the winter of 1854 that perhaps have the greatest resonance in British memory and national consciousness. On 25 October 1854, the events of the so-called Battle of Balaklava were played out with its various phases, now forever linked with the Charge of the Light Brigade. Given the importance of sustained communal memory within the military mind and the need to commemorate fallen comrades and honour past campaigns, it is perhaps unsurprising that Britain's 'Army of the East' was commanded by a man who was fixated by both. Any commander of his generation would have had understood—to greater or lesser degrees—the need to have a unified military identity and the importance of remembering its war dead (Keegan 1991; 1994). Raglan despised giving orders to his subordinates and frequently 'suggested' rather than overtly ordered and this trait, admirable in other walks of life, dogged the campaign and eventually doomed the Light Brigade (Dixon 1994: 37–44), especially as his leading subordinates were mostly incompetent and inexperienced—combined with that most poisonous mix, an unbelievable arrogance (Brackenbury 1856; fFrench-Blake 1974; Barbary 1975; Adkin 2000; Small 2007). Indeed, within a military context, this becomes a pivotal point in the narrative of events regarding causes of the loss of the Light Brigade and, because of the shock such a loss caused, perhaps explains why it has been remembered and commemorated ever since.

Just as the perceived popular memory of the Great War revolves around the stagnant trenches of the Western Front, the power of memory regarding the Crimean War focuses upon the CLB and the stagnant trenches around Sevastopol. As will be discussed further, the events of the War and, most particularly, those at Balaklava on 25 October 1854 similarly captured the Victorian imagination for many years following. Just as the 'Old Contemptibles' have a near-legendary status amongst military veterans in Britain for much of the Twentieth century post-1918, the survivors of 'the Six Hundred' held similar sway until the late 1920s.

Attitudes to Death, the Body and the Disposal of the Dead after the CLB, October 1854

When George Dallas of the 46th Regiment of Foot entered the Battle, 'all we could see was the ground strewed with dead horses and men' (Mawson 2001: 41). This section seeks to deal with the attitudes of the soldiers at Balaklava to the dead and the manner of disposal of the bodies. It appears that not all the dead were treated with respect. This treatment began contemporaneously with the Charge itself. At the same time as the survivors were trying to get back to British lines, the Cossacks had moved in to finish off the wounded and pillage the dead.

Donald Thomas (1974: 251) recounts the following conversation between the Earl of Cardigan and Sir James Scarlett regarding Captain Louis Nolan:

> 'Imagine the fellow screaming like a woman when he was hit, said Cardigan to Scarlett. 'Say no more, my lord,' answered Scarlett, 'I have just ridden over Captain Nolan's dead body'.

An alternative version of this exchange (Woodham Smith 1953) has it that it was Cardigan who rode over the body of Nolan. The discrepancy can be explained by the fact that the former was written in reply to the latter, more adverse, portrayal of Cardigan. Unfortunately, the two accounts cannot be investigated critically, as neither provides their evidence of the encounter. It may well lie in the, now missing, Blunt Papers, a fascinating series of 'lost' recollections written by John Blunt, civilian Turkish interpreter on Lucan's staff and, incidentally, one of the few men to hear the exchange between Lucan and Nolan before the CLB. The other witness, Captain Walker, was Lucan's ADC (Adkin 2000: 269, n9). The treatment of, and attitudes to, Nolan's corpse is pivotal to assessing the attitude and treatment of other British casualties, as will be discussed below.

After the CLB, according to Hibbert (1961: 153) the dead were brought back under flags of truce. In this, Hibbert appears to be half right. He may have been confused in his reporting of the dead being carried back; rather it seems that shortly after the battle, a Russian officer came in under a flag of truce to arrange the burial of the dead (Barrett 1911). If this is so, then he could be fusing certain accounts of the Russians seeking permission to bury the bodies with the British intention to do so. In fact, Captain Fellowes and Trumpet-Major Joy were indeed sent under a flag of truce by Raglan to discuss terms of removing the dead for burial on 26 October but, interestingly, this was refused by the Russians, on the grounds that, being Christians, they were perfectly able to bury the bodies themselves. On 27 October, however, another British party attempted again and this time secured the names of those taken prisoner on the day of the battle, but nothing more (Adkin 2000: 226). This jousting of protocol could all simply revolve around the military principle of possession of ground. If the British sought permission to bury their dead, it tends to suggest that the ground was seen by them as 'un-owned', but the Russians may have felt otherwise. Colonel Whinyates (1884: 142) commented that the ground surrounding the redoubts was 'abandoned that night, and for a certain period of time considered neutral.' The fact that the Russians were left, in effect, to bury the dead tends to suggest that the ground was in their possession.

Despite such issues of military etiquette, clearly a number of individuals were not recovered from the battlefield. In a letter dated 2 June 1855, Roger Fenton describes the macabre scene he came across in the Balaklava Valley. He writes that he

> "came upon many skeletons half buried, one was lying as if he had raised himself upon his elbow, the bare skull sticking up with still enough flesh in the muscles to prevent it falling from the shoulders; another man's feet and hands were out of the ground, the shoes on his feet and the flesh gone" (quoted in Gernsheim & Gernsheim 1954: 87).

For this reason, he did not photograph Balaklava Valley. However, by writing of the scene in such a vivid manner, he reveals a fascination with the ghoulish and gruesome details of war not represented in the photography of the time (Groth 2002).

From contemporary accounts, it would appear that only Captain Nolan's body was individually recovered and certainly no mention can be found of other single casualties being buried at this time. Indeed, the exact opposite seems to be the case (Russell 1855; Whinyates 1884; Hamley 1891). That this was the case may be down to a few pertinent factors. Firstly, Nolan was laid in the ditch of No. 5 Redoubt, close to where he was killed. As Hamley wrote, it was near here that they saw '. . . the body of Nolan on its back, the jacket open, the breast pierced by the fatal splinter' (Hamley 1891: 121). As such, it appears to have been the nearest and most appropriate place to bury the officer. Captain Branding of C Troop, Royal Horse Artillery, was in charge of the burial, with Bombardier Ormes and four gunners. The incident was well documented by Whinyates (1884: 142), as Ormes

> ". . . on his return, said that the poor fellow's [Nolan's] chest had been quite broken away, and that the gold lace and cloth of his jacket very much burnt by the shell which killed him, and must have burst very close by; also that there was only one officer present [Morris], who appeared to be a friend and was much affected".

The badly wounded Captain Morris removed Nolan's watch and sword; according to Whinyates (1884: 142) '. . . the body was lain in the earth as it was, there was no time to dig a deep grave, as occasional shots were fired at the Troop'. Attempts have been made to locate the grave of Nolan, although these have failed to produce any positive results (Gilchrist, pers comm.).

However, there has been some debate as to whether Nolan's corpse has already been found at the battlefield. Some years ago, a skeleton was rumoured to have been discovered close to the British Balaklava Obelisk. This monument is thought to be sited over the area where Redoubt No. 5 was once situated. The human remains, however, disappeared sometime after their discovery and were apparently not related to any associated finds (see below; Horton, 7/8/99, CWRS Disc. Grp). It is not known whether or not the location surrounding the Obelisk has since been archaeologically investigated to indicate signs of disturbance or artefacts. Whilst the identity or antiquity of the skeleton was not proven and, indeed, has since been hotly contested, the issue over the exact location of Nolan's possible interment is becoming increasingly pertinent.

Many theories exist regarding the correlation between the place where Nolan was killed (largely believed to be near Redoubt No 4.) and where he was buried (Redoubt No. 5). The debate has been succinctly and expertly put in the correspondence of Horton and Austin (for Redoubt No. 5) and Robinson and Hargreaves Mawson (for a site elsewhere in the North Valley, possibly Redoubt No. 4); both sides weigh up the likelihood, or otherwise, of suitable locations. Horton, as shown above, was convinced that the body was deposited in Redoubt No. 5 as stated in many sources. Yet, Robinson places considerable—and perhaps understandable—emphasis upon Captain Brandling's own recollection on the siting of the grave '. . . on the outer plain, and there is a slight bend inwards in the ridge near that place' (Whinyates 1884: 142). Whilst Horton maintained that this referred to Redoubt No. 5, Robinson interpreted this as relating to a ditch (possibly dug by Brandling's troop) in the North Valley, as yet undiscovered. One point worth noting is that Nolan may have been killed near Redoubt No. 4, but many witnesses saw his horse carrying him back for a while before he toppled to the ground (Hargeaves Mawson 1/11/04, CWRS Disc. Grp). The over-riding impression from the burial party, however, is that they took Nolan to the most easily accessible spot and placed him quickly into his final resting place.

Another puzzling issue is the lack of a marker, temporary or otherwise, for Nolan's burial site. Again, if one considers the surrounding events and context of the burial, then one explanation may lie in the fact that the area was simply considered too dangerous. Brandling's troop came under fire whilst hastily burying Nolan and, under such circumstances, they may be forgiven for not remaining long enough to erect a marker of some description. That one was not erected later may also be explained by Colonel Whinyate's comment that the site '. . . would not be visited by the English for some months' (Whinyates, 1884: 142).

Most of the other deceased were less fortunate, as the family of Captain George Lockwood, of the 8th Hussars and ADC to Cardigan, were to discover. Like Nolan, Lockwood was killed during the early part of the Charge but, unlike him, his body was never found (Adkin 2000: 176). Indeed, it may well have been pulverised by either shell blast or horses hooves, as it simply disappeared as the recognisable corpse of an officer. There is a memorial to Lockwood on the south wall of St Mary and All Saint's Church, Lambourne, (Essex), with the inscription

> TO THE MEMORY OF GEORGE LOCKWOOD CAPTAIN 8TH HUSSARS, SECOND SON OF WILLIAM JOSEPH LOCKWOOD OF DEWS HALL. BORN 16TH JUNE 1818. HE FELL OCTOBER 25TH 1854 IN THE MEMORABLE CAVALRY CHARGE OF BALACLAVA WHILE ACTING AS A.D.C. TO MAJOR GENERAL THE EARL OF CARDIGAN. EVERY EFFORT TO RECOVER HIS REMAINS HAVING BEEN PROVED INEFFECTUAL THIS MONUMENT IS ERECTED BY HIS MOTHER AS A TRIBUTE OF LOVE TO AN AFFECTIONATE AND DUTIFUL SON

Indeed, for the remainder of the Light Brigade, the dead were unceremoniously removed of valuables, boots, socks, bits of useful kit etc. and then left on the battlefield for those left in possession of the ground to bury, as was the custom (Adkin 2000; Howard 2002: 61; Keegan, 1994; Osgood 2005: 167 *et alia*). As William Russell noted on 28 October, with the British casualties still lying on the field the '. . . Russians stripped our dead' (Russell 1855: 236).

At Balaklava, it later transpired that the Russian burial of the mass dead of the Light Brigade was not very effective and was possibly hastily done. In this, it may be somewhat reminiscent of the way Custer's troopers were buried after the battle of the Little Big Horn in 1879 (see below). In May 1855, when C Troop were again on manoeuvres over the terrain in the North Valley, they were greeted with the gruesome sight of remains of men and horses in roughly covered slit-graves. Bones could clearly be seen emerging from the pits and uniforms could still be clearly made out adhering to the human remains; so much so that the regiments were easily distinguished (Adkin, 2000: 226).

Landscapes of Balaklava as Places of Pilgrimage

Despite the fact that the Crimean theatre was effectively closed to non-Soviet, non-military persons for much of the post-Crimean War era and (more significantly) distance and expense were an issue some veterans did return to the battlefields after the cessation of hostilities (Freeman, forthcoming). One such returner was Evelyn Wood, who toured the battlefields accompanied by Viscount Wolsey, a fellow veteran. He describes viewing 'the now smiling scene, where many of our comrades froze, starved, or bled to death . . . perhaps the saddest recollections were connected with the harbour of Balaklava'

(Wood 1895: vii–viii). He also states that, despite the change in nature of the Balaklava terrain from grassland to cultivation,

> "its shape cannot alter, and to the end of Time anyone interested in the deeds of our cavalry, when standing on the edge of the Upland, will have no difficulty in tracing the course of those who, it may truly be said, in devoted obedience to orders rushed 'to glory or grave'" (Wood 1895: 123).

The significance of making such pilgrimages was emphasised by the fact that the British, with the exception of high-status figures such as Lord Raglan, buried their dead at the site of their death (*cf* Freeman 2001).

Contemporary CLB Monuments, Memorials and Burial Grounds at Balaklava

A monument to the CLB stands in Balaklava at the point where the Charge began. It was placed on the 'ridge between Light and Heavy Cavalry Charges' and took the form of an obelisk on which was inscribed 'IN MEMORY OF THOSE WHO FELL IN THE BATTLE OF BALAKLAVA 25TH OCTOBER 1854' on the front. On the right panel there was a carved cross and, on the left, were the words 'ERECTED BY THE BRITISH ARMY A.D.1856'. Indeed, Winston Churchill visited the site of the CLB in 1945, whilst in the Crimea for the Yalta Conference; during this pilgrimage, Churchill visited the white obelisk (Strauss 2004).

In October 1854, the Light was comprised of five cavalry regiments; the 4th (Queen's Own) Light Dragoons, the 13th (Light) Dragoons, the 11th (Prince of Wales' Own) Hussars, the 8th (King's Royal Irish) Hussars and the 17th Lancers. A troop of Royal Horse Artillery was also present (A Troop) but this did not commit itself to the Charge. As it is memorials pertinent to the above regiments which concern this work, it is interesting that individual memorials to members of the Light Brigade, especially those wounded and taken to Scutari following the CLB, do not seem to feature in the region. Why this should be the case requires further examination (see below) and from this, some pertinent observations may be made. Whilst cavalry burials are recorded in Colbourne & Brine's 1858 catalogue of memorials, only six regiments are noted and, of these, exactly three are of the Light Brigade (4th (The Queen's Own Light) Dragoons, 11th (Prince Albert's Own) Hussars and the 13th (Light) Dragoons). From Colbourne & Brine's inventory, it can be noted that individual Light Brigade interments or memorials are rare but do occur. When they do, they are mainly in small regimental cemeteries near to where their camps had been set up, or by areas close to the hospitals. Of these, the burial grounds at Kadakoi may seem the most likely resting places for many of the Light Brigade wounded following the CLB. On the road going toward Karani was a burial ground with 38 graves, relevant to the 13th Light Dragoons, with four wooden grave markers (Colbourne & Brine, 1858: 32) all of which date to 1855. Of these, two are from mid-summer of this year and one is to the baby daughter of one of the 13th's troopers.

There was an uncommemorated plot (or at least not marked with a lasting memorial) to the 4th Light Dragoons, which contained 23 graves, between Kadikoi and Karand (Colbourne & Brine, 1858). There are, however, three memorials to individual 4th Light Dragoons on the spot, none of whom rode in the Charge. The others are equally intriguing and could possibly relate to troopers wounded in the CLB or fatalities due to illness.

Another small burial ground lay next to the 4th Light Dragoons, between Kadikoi and Karani, holding 24 graves belonging to the 11th Hussars. Above the gate entrance to the cemetery—at both the front and rear—was a plaque inscribed 'ELEVENTH (Prince Albert's Own) HUSSARS'. Inside was a wooden memorial tablet which declared that it was 'SACRED TO THE MEMORY OF THE MEN OF THE 11th HUSSARS WHO DIED IN THE YEARS 1855 & 1856' and twenty-five names are listed. Of interest is that seven individuals are capitalised, marking them out, it would appear, for special notice. Of these seven, Ptes W. Taylor and E. Wilcox rode in the charge. Quite why these seven individuals should be capitalised is unclear.

The only memorial to a 17th Lancer (whether they were present at the Charge or otherwise) appears to be at Scutari. Here, there was a grave marker slab to Captain A.F.C. Webb, also commemorated at home (see below) which bore the words

> "S.M. Aug. Aug. F.C. Captain XVII Lancers wounded at Balaklava Octr. 25th Died at Scutari Nov. 6th 1854. Aged XXII." (Colborne and Brine 1858: 54).

This is intriguing; as it tends to suggest that only one wounded 17th Lancer was recovered from the battlefield, or at least only one who was commemorated; a figure which seems surprisingly low.

During the war, the Army had enclosed cemeteries such as these in the region with small low walls, including those in and around Balaklava, to a fairly regular pattern. When the Army was withdrawn, the British, quite literally, locked the gates of many of these behind them before returning home. Those burial grounds which had no gates or doors to close had their entrances blocked up as best as possible. For example, the Guards' Cemetery had special gates hastily made from the iron hoops of Commissariat barrels to barricade it from unwanted attentions (Colbourne & Brine 1858: A). As such, by 1872, burial grounds around Balaklava and in Crimea in general were falling into disuse. The historian Kinglake wrote to the Secretary of State for

War, Edward Cardwell, asking who had responsibility for the care of these memorials. Cardwell replied to his friend that:

> "Officially the graves in the Crimea belong to the Foreign Office, and I have asked Enfield to put that mighty body in motion. My province is to grovel to the Treasury every now and then, which I have done to perfection." (Kinglake to Cardwell 24th April 1872, Smyth/Kinglake Archive, Cambridge University Library, CUL Add.9554/5/26, courtesy of Tom Muir/David Kelsey)

However, by 1891, many of these smaller cemeteries and graves had become completely 'ruinous' and visitors to them were horrified to find bits of bones amidst the memorial stones. The state of disrepair that these cemeteries were in caused much national outrage (Hamley 1891) and soon the human remains were gathered where they could be found and removed to Cathcart Hill, along with their associated memorial stones (Hamley, 1891:306). The graves of the dead, where they were yet undisturbed, were left *in situ*. Presumably, the mass grave sites are still in and around Kadikoi, Karani, Balaklava and other locations. Consequently, the emphasis on the Light Brigade memorials in the region takes on a slightly different slant; there being a possibility that the remains of the war dead are still present in the area, undisturbed since the removal of the markers and, possibly, since the actually end of the conflict itself.

In this aspect, a possible close parallel can be shown between the grave sites on and around the battlefield at Balaklava and those at Custer's Last Stand at the Little Big Horn (LBH). There, the issue of the 'headstones' or 'marble markers' on the present battlefield had the added importance to military historians who traditionally took them to be the actual—and unequivocal—sites of death. Whilst at Balaklava such issues may not be as pertinent (with the possible exception being the location of Nolan's grave site), the removal of markers and visible remains to Cathcart's Hill provided a more concentrated locus for commemoration. Of interest is that both sites seem to follow as specific phases of burial; the first is bodies left on the battlefield: the second is either heaps of earth hastily placed on top of the those bodies found (LBH) or dragged off to shallow hastily dug pits (CLB). Later, when the area is no longer a site of danger and has been consolidated by the side who own the war-dead, memorials are placed in the location—or nearby—to remember them. Interestingly, there is a major divergence here between the sites and one which is of direct importance to aspects of Balaklava remembrance. When it comes to active commemoration within the living memory of the participants, in the CLB's case, we find evidence of memorial to the *event* rather than individuals on the battlefield. A point which may be significant is that individual commemoration appears to be both widespread and primarily done at home rather than 'in the field' The comparatively simple markers to where the Charge began, just as other similarly modest Victorian markers of battlefields or events elsewhere in the Empire, may indeed demonstrate that the more impressive or personal memorials to the CLB were to be restricted to within the shores of Britain and Ireland itself. Whilst Cathcart's Hill was notably impressive, with its obelisks, crosses and pillars, its purpose was to act as the concentrated focus of commemoration for the entire war. This would seem to be in contrast to some of the rather more transient memorials erected in, for example, the small burial ground of the 11th Hussars at Kadikoi.

Memorials at Home

The UK National Inventory of War Memorials (UKNIWM) lists 331 memorials to the Crimean War in the United Kingdom, although the original number is bound to be larger owing to the fact that a significant number are listed as lost, many due to enemy action in the Second World War. Presumably, a significant number of lost memorials will not have been recorded. Furthermore, some of the listed memorials are questionable in their status as war memorials, at least for the purposes of this study. This category includes a number of the Russian cannon which were purchased by towns and cities after the war, and the recording of such monuments is inconsistent in this database. Of the overall total of 331 memorials, 60 make reference to Balaklava, although there are several examples of what could be considered war memorials that are not listed in the UKNIWM. The nature of what is considered a war memorial, the nature of the collection of the material and the consistency of recording methods are problems inherent in this project. These issues are, however, pertinent to discussion elsewhere and are not within the remit of this paper. The dead of overseas campaigns such as the Crimean were, until relatively recently, buried near to where they died. This fact deprives the grieving relatives of a place to mourn their loss, and the memorials at home provided a locus for grief, either as separate monuments or as additions to existing family headstones. In Drumbeg Parish Church, on the outskirts of modern Belfast, is a stained glass window to the memory of Hugh Montgomery, 13th Light Dragoons, who was a 'charger' on the 25th October, whilst his name is also inscribed on the memorial stones of the family vault outside. Beneath the inscription to his mother, Cornet Montgomery is further commemorated as having been

> KILLED IN THE MEMORABLE CHARGE OF THE LIGHT CAVALRY AT THE BATTLE OF BALAKLAVA, 25TH OCTOBER 1854, AGED 24 YEARS.

Memorials also have a political perspective. On Sarsfield Bridge, Limerick, there used to be a monument to Lt J.C. (Viscount) Fitzgibbon, 8th Hussars, who was reported as 'killed (doubtful)' after the CLB (Estcourt 1854: 3459). The monument was originally intended to be sited elsewhere, but placed on Sarsfield Bridge due to the political, religious and historical sentiments of the time. This monument, which had Fitzgibbon in uniform on a plinth with the names of those who fell in the Crimean War, was erected in 1857, but was blown up by the Irish Republican Army on 9 June 1930 (information from the Republic of Ireland *National Inventory of Architectural Heritage*).

As Natalie Houston (2001; 354ff) has demonstrated, the CLB became a spectacle for the British public, one which was originally a matter of pride in the sacrifice of the Charge in the early days of public enthusiasm for the war. This mood is reflected in a number of the memorials of the period. That to A.[F.]C. Webb at Raskelf, (North Yorkshire), for example, refers to his death

> AT THE HOSPITAL, SCUTARI, FROM WOUNDS RECEIVED IN THE BRILLIANT CHARGE OF THE LIGHT CAVALRY DIVISION ON THE 25TH OCTOBER 1854 AT THE MEMORABLE BATTLE OF BALACLAVA

Of particular interest here is that Captain Webb is commemorated on at least three memorials; one at Scutari (see above), one at Raskelf and one at Newstead Abbey (Nottinghamshire). The last of these is inscribed

> IN MEMORY OF AUGUSTUS FREDERICK CAVENDISH WEBB, CAPTAIN 17th LANCERS WHO DIED AT SCUTARI 6 NOVEMBER 1854 OF WOUNDS RECEIVED AT THE CHARGE OF BALACLAVA 25 OCTOBER AGED 22 YEARS. ERECTED BY HIS BROTHER WILLIAM FREDERICK WEBB

Also, there is a memorial to Cornet Archibald Cleveland, 17th Lancers, at St John's Church, Instow (Devon) which well epitomises Houston's observations. Cleveland had survived the CLB only to be fatally wounded at the Battle of Inkerman on 5 November, but the memorial inscription is very long and detailed, giving his brief military career whilst on active service in the Crimea. Of extreme relevance here is that two sentences refer to Inkerman and his death from a shell fragment; three refer to his part in the CLB:

> HE WAS ONE OF THE RENOWNED FIVE HUNDRED [sic] IN THE/ BATTLE OF BALAKLAVA, WHERE HE IMMORTALISED HIMSELF BY HIS COOL AND DAUNTLESS BRAVERY, WHICH WILL EVER BE REMEMBERED WITH HONOUR. AFTER FIGHTING THROUGH A LARGE BODY OF THE ENEMY AND WHEN/ ESCAPING TO THE CAMP, THREE COSSACKS PURSUED HIM. HE MORTALLY WOUNDED THE THREE AND ARRIVED AT THE CAMP LEADING HIS WOUNDED CHARGER, FAINT FROM LOSS OF BLOOD.

In addition to this, he is commemorated by way of a Bible which is held in the Pickwell Chapel of St George's Church, Georgeham, also in Devon. This is inscribed

> "This bible was presented by Caroline Dene to Georgeham Church in remembrance of her father The Reverend Francis Hole (Rector 1831–1866) and her brothers Rev Thomas Hole and Rev Francis Hole Rectors (1869–1871) This bible was originally given to her husband Henry Dene by Mrs Clevland [sic] of Tapley Park North Devon as a memento of her son and his great friend Archibald Clevland [sic] a colonel (or cornet?) in the 17th Lancers who after taking part in the Charge of the Light Brigade at Balaclava was killed at Inkerman on the 5th day of November 1854." (Harris 2001).

Remembering the Survivors

It is not only the directly deceased who are commemorated on the memorials covered in this paper. For example, a memorial stone in All Saints' Churchyard, North Collingham, (Nottinghamshire) not only marks the death of two related individuals who died in the CLB (William Bacon and George Broome), but also records the safe return of a third family member (John Bacon) who had taken part in this battle. Interestingly, at the base of the stone is a poem which is clearly based on Tennyson's *The Charge of the Light Brigade* but with significant divergences.

It is clear that participation in the action at Balaklava was something which was considered of great acclaim until long after the event, and many memorials reveal the desire of former soldiers and their families to record their glory in battle. This is evidenced by the regular inclusion of references to the event on the later graves of survivors. The family gravestone of Lt Frederick Henry Cheshire in Whipton records that he was "LATE 8TH HUSSARS ONE OF THE SIX HUNDRED" (emphasis in the original). This is intriguing on a number of levels. Cheshire is not one of the officers listed as being with the 8th Hussars on 25 October; they were famously under-strength at the time and he may have been sick, but here he is actively listed as a 'charger'. At the CLB, there were four Lieutenants (Clutterbuck, Fitzgibbon (see above), Heneage and Philips) and two Cornets (Clowes and Mussenden) involved. In checking Hart's Army List for the years 1853, 1855 and 1861, no record of such an officer could be found. Neither could any mention of this officer be recovered from Rev. Robert Murray's (2004: 724) official *Regimental History of the 8th Hussars and List of its Officers for the Crimean War.* However, using the extremely thorough *EJ Boys Archive* (aka 'Lives of the Light Brigade') conserved by Roy Mills & Philip Boys for the CWRS, one Private Henry Cheshire [No. 1201] 8th Hussars is discovered. This highlights a classic issue with memorialisation of the CLB; identifying men and officers from the purely physical monumental evidence, which can be misleading, and then reconciling this with known historical records. Men on memorials can be 'aggrandised' in death, with their participation in events—or organisations—built up for the sake of their family or their memory. Sometimes, the memorials can be misleading to give the impression to the viewer that the subject had a higher status; in this case, being an officer involved in the CLB when he was historically recorded as no such thing during this period. This leads us to another interesting case study.

At Leamington Churchyard, the gravestone of Pvt. Job Allwood, recorded him as

> ". . . 13th Light Dragoons and 17th Lancers. A native of Leamington who rode in the Light Cavalry charge at Balaclava and served in the Indian Mutiny campaign. He died at Leamington on the 18th December 1903 and was buried with military honours. Erected by his friends and admirers."

Although Allwood charged with the 13th Light Dragoons, he later transferred to the 17th Lancers in 1857 where, presumably, he saw service in India. However, his name could not be found on the Indian Mutiny Medal Roll, although this is sometimes not unusual (E J Boys Archive). Quite simply put, this would rather tend to suggest that Pvt. Allwood was not entitled to the Mutiny medal and, ergo, was not actually present during the fighting parts of the campaign, when his memorial clearly implies that this was the case. Whether family history, personal aggrandisement or simple bureaucratic error has occurred, it highlights the problematic nature of some memorial evidence during the period.

Frederick Short, whose name was added to his son's gravestone at Beckett Road Cemetery, Leeds, had a similar epitaph to Cheshire's and Allwood's (Barnard 1990); one emphasising his role in the CLB. At the same cemetery, the gravestone of Sgt William Notley of the 13th Hussars contains, picked out in black paint with the initials in red, lettering reading

> ERECTED BY HIS COMRADES, AS A TOKEN OF RESPECT TO ONE WHO HAD SERVED 20 YEARS, AND WAS IN THE ENGAGEMENTS OF ALMA, BAL-ACLAVA, INKERMANN, AND SEBASTOPOL" (Barnard 1990: 129).

In County Louth, in the churchyard of St. Peter's Church of Ireland, Drogheda is a very fine gravestone to John Duggan, 17th Lancers, with the inscription 'DEATH OR GLORY' upon it. Duggan was a Drogheda man before enlisting and is stated as a survivor of the CLB, Alma, Sevastopol and Inkerman, although it appears that he was actually in hospital at Scutari at the time of this latter battle, presumably from wounds received at the CLB. Upon discharge from the Army, he returned to Drogheda where he became Sexton of St. Peter's in 1871, until his death in 1881 (Rev. Graham, pers. comm.). A similar design can be found in the churchyard of St Michael, Lichfield, where there is a memorial stone to Trumpeter John Brown who sounded the trumpet at the CLB. It is a flat stone surmounted by a skull and crossbones with the motto "OR GLORY" and indicating (unusually) that he is buried near the location of the memorial. Confusingly, it transpires that there were two Trumpeter John Browns with the 17th Lancers (indeed, there were four with the same name in total, but all have different Army Numbers, the two trumpeters being Nos 476 and 926; E.J. Boys Archive). Either of these two may have 'officially' sounded the charge—or 'Drill Calls'—passed on from the Call of the Brigade Orderly Trumpeter (see below). As such, this may be the cause of any confusion and, if it is, it is certainly not an isolated claim. Another 'Balaklava Trumpet' is on display at the Royal Hussars' Museum, Winchester, belonging to Trumpeter Keats, 11th Hussars, who is claimed as 'Lord Cardigan's Orderly' (Cliff 1986) with the very clear implication that Keats sounded the Charge. Another Balaklava bugle now on display at the National Army Museum belonged to Trumpet Major Joy, 17th Lancers, who was Lucan's Orderly Trumpeter and, as such, would have sounded the initial Drill Call to 'Mount the Division' in the desperate moments before the CLB (Cliff nd; Adkin 2000: 130). Joy is buried at St. Nicholas' Church, Chiswick. The inscription on his gravestone reads

> AS STAFF TRUMPETER TO GENERAL THE EARL OF LUCAN SOUNDED THE MEMORABLE CHARGE OF THE LIGHT BRIGADE AT BALACLAVA

Yet, the actual dubious honour to initiate the Charge fell to Trumpeter William 'Billy' Britten of the 17th Lancers, who was Orderly (Brigade) Trumpeter to Cardigan. It was Britten who sounded the order to 'Walk' and then 'Trot' and his bugle (the 'Balaclava Bugle') is on display at Belvoir Castle (Lincolnshire), the Regimental Museum of the 17th/21st Lancers (Cliff nd). Britten was seriously wounded at the CLB and was later transferred to hospital at Scutari, where he died of wounds on 14 February 1855 (Adkin 2000: 226). No mention of his grave or memorial in this region can be found in the relevant works.

In York Cemetery, there are two interesting Balaklava memorials; the first names William Pearson 'Hero of Balaklava' who died in 1909, aged 84. The other in York Cemetery records a memorial to Troop Sergeant-Major William Bentley, 11th Hussars, who is described as '. . . one of the Six Hundred at Balaklava 1854'. Sgt-Major Bentley died in 1891, aged 74. Another memorial to an 11th Hussar—Luke Oakley—can be found at Wirksworth Church (Derbyshire) and records that he too saw service at Balaklava and throughout the war. He died at the age of 88, in 1906. The memorials reflect the social conditions of the period, and it is noticeable that the vast majority of monuments to individuals are of officers, many of whom would have bought their rank and therefore came from families of substantial means and class, and all of the key players in the CLB were memorialized in one form or another. The social exclusivity in life continued into death. For example, Troop Sergeant-Major John Berryman, of the 17th Lancers, became a national hero and is commemorated by a very fine 'Celtic Cross' memorial in St. Agatha's Churchyard, Woldingham (Surrey) (Arthur 2005: 632). However, James Thomas Brudenell (the Earl of Cardigan) was memorialized to an even greater extent with, arguably, lesser reason. On his death, the uniform he wore at Balaklava was a major part of the centrepiece at his lying-in-state (Thomas 1974). There is a memorial window to him in the church at Deene St. Peter. Not only is Cardigan's memory preserved, but also that of his charger at the CLB, Ronald, who died in 1872. His head, tail and a hoof are preserved at Deene Park (Cavendish 1997). Ronald is not the only horse to be commemorated. Sir Briggs, the charger of Godfrey Morgan (Vaughan 1990), is commemorated in the cedar garden of Tredegar House, Newport (Gwent). A memorial to him reads

> A FAVOURITE CHARGER HE CARRIED HIS MASTER THE HONOURABLE GODFREY MORGAN CAPTAIN 17TH LANCERS BOLDLY AND WELL AT THE BATTLE OF ALMA IN THE FIRST LINE IN THE LIGHT CAVALRY CHARGE OF BALACLAVA AND AT THE BATTLE OF INKERMAN 1854

Lord Tredegar (as Morgan became), and by extension Sir Briggs, is also commemorated in the form of an equestrian statue in Cardiff by William Goscombe John. This monument, which depicts Tredegar as he was in 1854 and carries a frieze depicting the charge of the 17th Lancers at the CLB, was unveiled in 1909 on the 55th anniversary of the Charge (Massie 2003).

Until recently, a very fine stone memorial plaque was in existence for Captain Louis Edward Nolan, paid for by Generals Berkeley, Airey and other friends who had it erected at Holy Trinity Church, Maidstone. The plaque was dedicated to 'Lewis Edward Nolan' and inscribed

> CAPTAIN OF THE 15TH OR KING'S HUSSARS, AND ADC TO MAJOR-GENERAL AIREY, QUARTER MASTER GENERAL TO THE FORCES IN THE CRIMEA HE FELL AT THE HEAD OF THE LIGHT CAVALRY BRIGADE IN THE CHARGE AT BALAKLAVA, ON THE 25TH OCTOBER 1854, AGED 36. GENERAL SIR GEORGE BERKELEY, K.C.B., ON WHOSE STAFF HE SERVED IN INDIA, GENERAL AIREY, HIS BROTHER OFFICERS AND OTHER FRIENDS HAVE ERECTED THIS TABLET AS A SLIGHT TRIBUTE OF THEIR ESTEEM AND AFFECTIONATE REGARD FOR THE MEMORY OF ONE OF THE MOST GALLANT, INTELLIGENT AND ENERGERTIC OFFICERS IN HER MAJESTY'S SERVICE.

From the wording on the plaque it is clear that Captain Nolan's loss was deeply felt and that he was, genuinely, highly regarded by many of his peers and brother officers. Unfortunately, the memorial has since been lost as in 1997, Holy Trinity Church was converted into apartments and the memorial now seems likely to have been destroyed.

Furthermore, of a number of Crimean War participants to be buried in the Liverpool area, the only individual with a noteworthy memorial is that of Lt-Gen. Edward Seager (see plate 1), in stark contrast to those who have no marked grave such as James Glanister (see below) and Robert Martin (buried in Bebington Cemetery), or that of William Sewell, buried in St. Peter's Church, Woolton on a family grave, with no indication of his career (see plate 2). This, in itself, is most interesting. Private William Sewell [no. 1452] 13th Light Dragoons, was born in 1830 and received such a serious head wound as a result of the CLB that he had a metal plate fitted over the wound thereafter. He died at his home in Liverpool (18 Rose Lane, Mossley Hill) on 6 January 1910 and was buried at the above churchyard on 13 January. Sadly, the achievements of many of those who survived the action at Balaklava were less well represented in the manner of their treatment post-service. Many left the army life in humble circumstances and received no commemoration after their death. Private Samuel Parkes, who survived the Charge of the Light Brigade, and who was also one of the first servicemen to receive the Victoria Cross (VC), was buried in an unmarked pauper's grave in London (Harvey 1999). Likewise, James Glanister was buried at West Derby Cemetery, Liverpool in an unmarked grave.

Plate 1. Memorial to Edward Seager (1812–83) [*Photo*: Jonathan Trigg]

Plate 2. Family grave of William Sewell (1830–1910) [*Photo*: Jonathan Trigg]

A final note of caution is relevant here. In some cases, the presence of an inscription is directly suggestive of a presence at the CLB, when no such connection can be authenticated. For instance, there is a memorial to William Rhys Llewellyn in Cathays Cemetery, Cardiff. The inscription on this memorial quotes from Tennyson's poem, implying that Rhys might have been involved in the Charge, but research to date has failed to confirm presence. It is possible, in this case, that Mr. Llewellyn simply liked the poem and considered the CLB a glorious thing to be associated with. As we have seen through the use of memorialisation at Balaklava and at home, it would appear that many Britons of his generation would have whole-heartedly agreed.

The CLB—Legacy and Conclusion

The Crimean campaign was a shadowy herald of modern warfare for, although it seems to have echoed the battles of Napoleon or Wellington, within three weeks it had evolved into a trench war with possibly more in common with First Ypres than Fontenoy. Principal in this change was, perhaps, the technical developments in longer-range rifled muskets and especially artillery—and, of course, it was singularly around this very objective that Balaklava will forever be remembered, either rightly or wrongly. The solid defence of the 93rd Highlanders at the start of the day's engagements, followed by the success of the Heavy Brigade and 'C' Troop, R.H.A., were unfortunately bound to be eclipsed by the terrible events later on in the North Valley. The Light Brigade's Charge was certainly one of the turning points of the war. Had its aim been to pursue the fleeing Russians immediately after Scarlett's attack, then it may have made subsequent events surrounding Sevastopol redundant. As it stood, it became something perhaps even more powerful in popular memory. It acted as a focus and symbol for so many aspects of the Victorian military ideal, both impressively admirable and desperately unappealing. As Mark Adkin (2000: 253) has commented, the Charge of the Light Brigade '. . . came to represent the embodiment of the cavalry spirit . . . that anything was possible with enough dash and daring.' These sentiments were taken up by the Victorian public, and can be seen to be reflected in the breadth and diversity of the memorials to those who charged.

Acknowledgements

We owe a great debt to Phil Freeman for his tireless assistance in research and for the many useful suggestions his considerable knowledge enabled him to make. We would also like to thank Professor Fergus D'Arcy, UCD, Dennis Pillenger, MHS, OMRS, Sarah Kirkham, Glass & Ceramics Specialist (Sothebys) and members of the CWRS for their generous sharing of scholarship, namely: David Cliff, David Williams, Stephen Lewis, Tom Muir, Philip Boys and Roy Mills (E.J. Boys Archive). We also wish to thank the Revd. Michael Graham, St. Peters Church, Drogheda.

Bibliography

Adkin, M 2000 *The Charge: the Real Reason Why the Light Brigade was Lost.* Pimlico: London.

Arthur, M 2005 *Symbol of Courage: the men behind the medal.* Pan: London.

Barnard, S M 1990 *To Prove I'm Not Forgot: living and dying in a Victorian City.* Manchester University Press: Manchester & New York.

Barbary, J 1975 *The Crimean War.* Puffin Books: London.

Barrett, C R B 1911 *History of the XIII Hussars.* William Blackwood & Sons: Edinburgh and London.

Brackenbury, G 1856 *The Campaign in the Crimea: an historical sketch.* Longman, Brown, Green & Longman: London.

Cavendish, R 1997 'Deene Park, Northamptonshire', *History Today,* 47 (1997), 62–63.

Cliff, D nd *Items of Crimean Interest in the Regimental Museum of the 17/21st Lancers, Belvoir Castle, Near Grantham, Lincolnshire.* Crimean War Research Society Information Sheet, No. 44.

Cliff, D 1986 *Items of Crimean Interest in the Regimental Museum of the Royal Hussars (formerly 10th and 11th Hussars), Lower Barracks, Winchester, Hants.* Crimean War Research Society Information Sheet, No. 57.

Colborne, J & Brine, F 1858 *Memorials of the Brave, or Resting Places of our Fallen Heroes in the Crimea and at Scutari.* Ackermann & Co: London.

Dippie, B W 1994 *Custer's Last Stand: the anatomy of an American myth.* University of Nebraska Press: Lincoln, Nebraska.

Dixon, N 1994 *On the Psychology of Military Incompetence.* Pimlico: London.

Estcourt, A J B 1854 'Return of casualties, from 22nd October to 26th October 1854, both days inclusive', *The London Gazette—Extraordinary, November 12th 1854,* 21624: 3459

fFrench-Blake, R L V 1974 *The Crimean War.* Leo Cooper: London.

Freeman, P 2001 'Introduction: issues concerning the archaeology of battlefields' *in* Freeman, P W M & Pollard, A (eds) *Fields of Conflict: progress and prospect in battlefield archaeology.* BAR: Oxford.

—— forthcoming 'An archaeological reinterpretation of the events at the Battle of the Balaklava/Charge of the Light Brigade, 1854', *in* Babits, L, Scott D & Orr, D (eds.) *Method and Topics in Historical Archaeology on Military Sites.* University of Florida Press: Orlando.

Gernsheim, H & Gernsheim, A 1954 *Roger Fenton: photographer of the Crimean War.* Secker & Warburg: London.

Gilchrist, M M, nd, *Louis Edward Nolan* http://www.silverwhistle.co.uk/crimea/louisnolan.html, accessed 23/5/08

Groth, H 2002 'Technological mediations and the public sphere: Roger Fenton's Crimea exhibition and "The Charge of the Light Brigade"', *Victorian Lit & Cult,* 30 (2002), 553–70

Hamley, E B 1891 *The War in the Crimea.* Seeley & Co. Ltd: London.

Harris, B 2001 *The Hole Family of Georgeham Parish, Devon: a brief history.* Georgeham PCC: Georgeham.

Harvey, D 1999 'Monuments to Courage', *The RUSI Journal,* 144 (1999), 91–2.

Hibbert, C 1961 *The Destruction of Lord Raglan: a tragedy of the Crimean War, 1854–55.* Longmans: London.

Houston, N M 2001 'Reading the Victorian Souvenir: sonnets and photographs of the Crimean War', *Yale J Crit,* 14 (2001), 353–83.

Howard, M 2002 *Wellington's Doctors: The British Army Medical Services in the Napoleonic Wars.* Spellmount: Staplehurst.

Keegan, J 1991 *The Mask of Command.* Penguin: London.

—— 1994 *A History of Warfare.* Pimlico: London.

Massie, A (ed) 2003 *A Most Desperate Undertaking: the British Army in the Crimea, 1854–56.* National Army Museum: London.

Mawson, M H (ed) 2001 *Eyewitness in the Crimea: the Crimean War letters of Lieutenant Colonel George Frederick Dallas.* Greenhill Books: London.

Murray, R H 2004 *VIII King's Royal Irish Hussars 1693–1927.* Naval & Military Press: Uckfield.

Osgood, R 2005 *The Unknown Warrior: an archaeology of the common soldier.* Sutton: Stroud.

Pillenger, D & Staunton, A 2000 *Victoria Cross Presentations and Locations*. Military History Society: Maidenhead.
Russell, W H 1855 *The War: from the landing at Gallipoli to the death of Lord Raglan*. Routledge: London.
Small, H 2007 *The Crimean War: Queen Victoria's War with the Russia Tsars*. Tempus: Stroud.
Strauss, J 2004 'Heroism of the Light Brigade Still Shines', *Daily Telegraph*, 25 October 2004.
Thomas, D 1974 *Charge! Hurrah! Hurrah! A Life of Cardigan of Balaklava*. Routledge & Kegan Paul: London.
Vaughan, D C 1990 *'Newport First Stop': 100 years of news stories*. Privately published: Newport.
Whinyates, F A 1884 *From Coruna to Sevastopol*. W H Allen & Co: London.
Wood, E 1895 *The Crimea in 1854 and 1894*. Chapman & Hall: London.
Woodham-Smith, C 1953 *Theirs to Reason Why*. Constable: London.

FORTIFIED HOMESTEADS: THE ARCHITECTURE OF FEAR IN FRONTIER SOUTH AUSTRALIA AND THE NORTHERN TERRITORY, CA. 1847–1885

NICOLAS K GRGURIC

Abstract

This paper investigates the use of defensive architectural techniques by civilian settlers in frontier South Australia and the Northern Territory between ca. 1847 and 1885. Four sites were analysed, three of which are located in South Australia and one in the Northern Territory. This study takes a new approach to the archaeological investigation and interpretation of Australian rural buildings, one that identifies defensive strategies as a feature of Australian frontier architecture. These structures represent physical manifestations of settler fear and Aboriginal resistance. Over time, however, the folk stories attached to these structures have also come to play a significant part in Australia's frontier mythology. They are shown to form one component of a wider body of myths which serve the ideological needs of the settler society, justifying its presence by portraying the settlers as victims of Aboriginal aggression.

Introduction

Scattered across Australia's landscape, close to her capital cities and sometimes far off the beaten track, lie memorials of long-forgotten conflicts. When first built, these memorials were not intended or expected to become what they did: their construction was simply the physical expression of the fear felt by some of the colonial settlers of Australia. Over time, however, the stories attached to these structures have come to play a significant part in Australia's frontier mythology. These structures are the fortified homesteads of the Australian colonial frontier: this frontier is defined here as any area where colonial settlers were using the land for agricultural, mining and/or livestock, whilst Aboriginal people were still maintaining their traditional life-ways in the area.

All of the structures investigated within this research are associated with a myth of having been designed for defence against Aboriginal attack. A definition of 'myth' which can be applied here is that of myths as, '. . . stories drawn from a society's history that have acquired through persistent usage the power of symbolising that society's ideology and of dramatising its moral consciousness' (Slotkin 1993: 5). As well as providing a starting point for archaeological investigation, the myths associated with these sites are worthy of analysis in themselves in order to understand their role in the construction of Australia's identity, and of her collective and individual 'memories' of the frontier.

 DOI: 10.1163/157407808X382764

The aim of this paper is to investigate four issues: whether defensive architecture was used by civilian settlers on the South Australian and Northern Territory frontiers; the nature of frontier conflict in these regions; to what extent historical archaeology can test myths about civilian use of defensive architecture on the South Australian and Northern Territory frontiers; and the significance of these myths to past and present identity construction.

The Influence of Fear on Architecture

Frontiers have a different architecture to more settled areas, a topic that has been studied for several decades. As early as the 1950s, Frank Roos Jr described the protective value of the North American log cabin, block houses, and a grand fortified structure called *Campus Martius*, which,

> [although it displayed] . . . little of New England's influence except in the interiors, . . . might readily be called a descendant of the medieval fortified town, appearing here in the wilderness centuries after its prototypes on the continent (Roos 1953: 4).

More recently, Alison Hoagland studied the radical differences between United States military forts on the coast and those on the inland frontiers. The inland forts became more like villages in plan, often even without stockades. Hoagland attributed this to an unconscious expression of the fort's commanding officers, who revealed their ties to the eastern establishment from which they drew comfort in their unfamiliar and hostile environment (Hoagland 1999: 216, 215). Blair St. George examined the adaptation of 'bawns' (fortified houses traditionally built by English settlers in 17th century Ireland) to frontier New England in the United States (1990: 242), as an architectural source upon which the English settlers of New England drew. Margot Winer's (2001) study of building phases at the late 18th and 19th century English settlement on the East Cape of South Africa was significant in that it showed some striking similarities between the process in South Africa and that identified through the sites investigated in Australia. Even in the 20th century, architecture of fear can still be observed in the example of fortified houses and communities in modern Johannesburg in South Africa (Bremner 1999: 'B2').

Material Culture and Mythology

Myths are not naturally occurring. They are created by particular groups for particular reasons (Yentsch 1988: 7; Lydon & Ireland 2005: 3). When groups have something to gain from the propagation of a particular myth, they want people to believe that myths *are* naturally occurring, as such belief strengthens the validity of the myths and hence the intrinsic values and ideological purposes they are designed to spread and fulfil (Shackel 2001). 'Memory', in the form of myths, can add authenticity to a group's claims or objectives (Bodnar 1992: 14). For example, Anderson (1983) and Bhabha (1990) point out how an engineered historical consciousness is often made to seem natural as a means of instilling nationalistic values in society, such as 'roots, stability, boundaries and belonging' (Bender, 2001: 5). The customisation of the frontier and indigenous people by settler societies for their own ideological use has been discussed both in the United States and in Australia (Rubertone 1994: 32; Broome 1996: 55). Rubertone also demonstrated the important fact that archaeology has the potential to redress this situation, and thereby provide different interpretations of indigenous history, and in particular, indigenous responses to colonialism that are often unrecorded in written sources (Rubertone 1994: 32).

One of the determining factors for how material culture of mythic significance is remembered is of course which group comes to dominate the myth-making/remembering. Conversely, what the subordinate groups choose to do about the domination of these myths can also affect how a site is remembered (Shackel 2001: 3). The collective memory of a particular site may be in a constant state of flux, but there are other possibilities. Subordinate groups can attempt to subvert the dominant memory, or compromise it, trying to have their agenda become part of a 'multivocal history'. Other subordinate groups can fail to have their story remembered, and others still are not interested in having their story told at all.

Myths are also used to develop a sense of nostalgia about the past that legitimises the heritage of the myth-making group (*ibid.*). This strengthens that group's place and rights in the world: myths can be used to enhance the prestige and authority of certain groups (Lydon & Ireland 2005: 4). For settler societies, for example, myths associated with 'pioneer' struggles legitimise the right of the non-indigenous people to be there. Even when the sites used in this legitimisation are examples of invasion and conflict (such as fortified structures), the myth-makers still manage to turn them into sites they can be proud of.

Site Selection and Research Methodology

The site selection process began by finding examples of sites that had an associated myth about their use as defensive structures. This was usually found in local histories (e.g. Dolling 1981), more general histories of the frontier (e.g. Reynolds 1987) and books about frontier conflict (e.g. Connor 2002). The reference to their defensive nature was often minor, sometimes no more than a sentence such as, '. . . its two-storeyed walls complete with gun-slot loop-holes against Aboriginal attack' (Dolling 1981: 213). These words, though few, say more than the fact that a particular building has apertures in its walls. They imply that the building was deliberately fortified. They imply that the local Aboriginal people were considered hostile and that the settlers feared them as a source of attack. Overall, they imply that there was a state of racial conflict in the area. Any of these implications may be true or false, but all of them call for further investigation.

South Australia and the Northern Territory provide excellent case studies for a number of reasons. From 1863–1911, the Northern Territory was part of South Australia, being governed and administered from Adelaide (Barraclough 1994:113). This allows the process of colonisation to be followed from the south of the continent to the north under one state system. The dates of European settlement for the central portion of the continent cover a relatively long time span, commencing from the first official settlement of South Australia in 1836 until the 1880s/1890s, when the frontier had moved to the northern and central parts of the continent. This made it possible to compare the nature of frontier conflict over 50 years or so, as well as changing construction techniques and weapons technology over this time. South Australia and the Northern Territory also provided a wide range of terrains and environments in which to study frontier conflict, from wet and cold on the South Australian coast, to the temperate zones around Adelaide and northwards to the tropical north of the Northern Territory.

Each site was researched in the context of its particular region, allowing more localised information regarding frontier conflict and attitudes of settlers to be used when interpreting the myths (and therefore, more likely to have been known to the site's builders). By researching sites in different geographical regions, usually widely separated, the study was able to cover a relatively large area: if similar findings result in widely separated regions, then they are likely to apply at least generally to the geographical 'spaces' between them. The four regions selected were the area around Kingston in the south east of South Australia, metropolitan Adelaide, in particular the southern suburb of O'Halloran Hill, the western side of the lower Eyre Peninsula and the northern portion of the Northern Territory (in particular the Katherine area; see fig 1).

In the Kingston region, the site investigated was Mount Benson Homestead (ca. 1847), which has what may be an embrasure for defence against Aboriginal attack (e.g. Barrowman 1971: 52, 56: Fig 2). A door taken from Avenue Range Station which is currently in the Kingston museum was also given special attention due to its uniqueness. This door has a small aperture cut into it, supposedly to permit one to fire through (e.g. Banks 1970: 8; Barrowman 1971: 52; Fig 3).

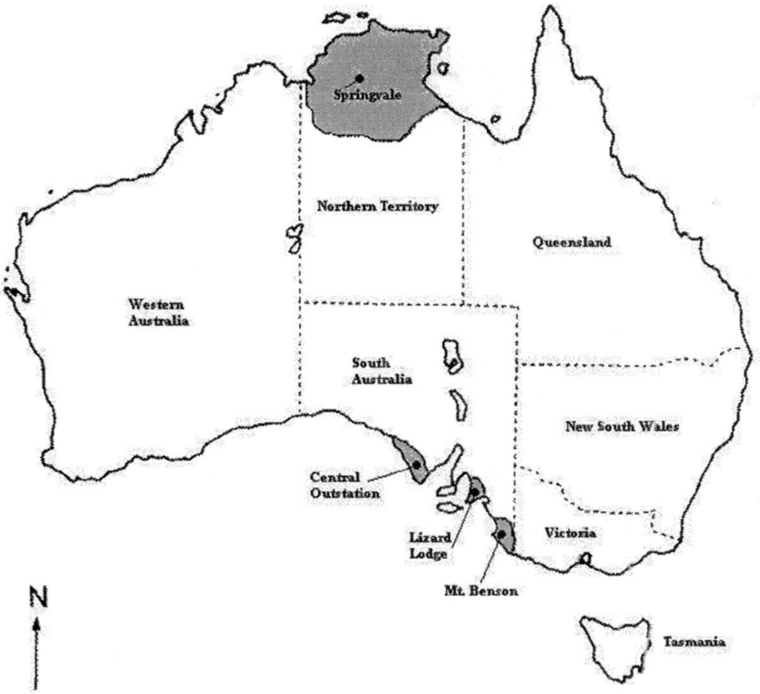

Fig. 1. Map of Australia showing the location of the sites investigated and the general regions, shaded grey.

In the Eyre Peninsula, the site investigated was a dwelling near Sheringa (ca. 1856), whose 'tiny windows' may have been built as a defence against Aboriginal attack (Baillie 1978: 134; Fig 4). This structure formed part of an outstation for a group of runs owned by Price Maurice.

In the O'Halloran Hill area, the site chosen was an outbuilding known as the 'coach-house' at Major T. S. O'Halloran's homestead, 'Lizard Lodge'. This structure is also very well preserved and appears to have been built between 1851 and 1855. It has what may be embrasures to protect the Major's family from Aboriginal attack (Dolling 1981: 323; Fig 5).

The site investigated in the Katherine region was Springvale Homestead. This pastoral station was established in 1879 and was only the second station to be established and stocked in the Northern Territory. It has a well-preserved store building that may have doubled as a fort in case of Aboriginal attack (Norris 1976: 78), as well as a well preserved homestead building, which may also have been built with defence in mind (The Architects Studio 2000: 5; Fig 6).

Fig. 2. View of the rear of the dwelling at Mount Benson. The embrasure can be seen just to the left of the right hand chimney.

Of equal importance to the archaeological investigation was the historical research. The purpose was to determine how far historical records supported the belief that a structure was built for defence. The aim of this component was to find information about each site's history, as well as that of the surrounding region; it was a search for information about race relations in the region prior to, and at the time of, the site's construction, as well as any other social factors which may have led to the site being built with defence in mind. This included such things as the attitude of the builder/owner regarding Aboriginal people and the builder/owner's past experiences with Aboriginal people.

The findings of both the historical research and archaeological fieldwork for a site were carefully compared in order to make an assessment of each site's functionality as a defensive structure. Even so, however, the results may be open to other interpretations and criticisms, the only possible exception being if primary source material securely identifies a site as a defensive structure.

When analysing a civilian site's supposed defensive functionality, it must be remembered that they were built by civilians and not military engineers, and they were not likely to have been as experienced or proficient as military builders, which can be manifest as poor design for functionality. Imperfect design could on its own cause them to be deemed non-defensive. This underlines the importance of historical evidence in the analysis, as the historical

Fig. 3. Door taken from James Brown's Avenue Range station, near Kingston South East. Brown's station was established in the late 1840s. The label attached to the door reads, 'Door from old 'Keilira', opening specially made by James Brown for the use in many raids on the Aboriginals of his day.' View of interior side of door. This door is currently on display in the Kingston South-East branch of the National Trust museum.

Fig. 4. Western side of the 'Men's Hut' at Central Outstation. This photograph, taken in 1970, shows the appearance of this side of the building before the collapse of a large portion of the wall. Three rectangular embrasures are clearly visible, evenly spaced along the wall. Today only the leftmost one remains. From Baillie, 1978: 134.

Fig. 5. The eastern side of the coach-house, showing the 2 embrasures as narrow vertical slits in the wall on each side of the chimney.

Fig. 6. Extant structures of Springvale Station. The store is at left, the dwelling at right. The dense trees behind the store mark the sloping bank of the Katherine River. Facing north east. 2004.

data associated with a site may provide a motive for building a site defensively that outweighs the design flaws.

Results and Discussion

Rural Architecture in Colonial Australia—Typical versus Fortified

One aspect of style, as Burke pointed out, is identification through 'differentness' (Burke 1999: 25). By comparing the design of the sites investigated here with the 'typical' (and non-defensive) design of Australian rural architecture of the period, it is possible to more clearly identify the way that defensive sites were modified, and thus different from, the typical design, forming a style of their own. This is useful because it helps both to deduce the intended tactical role of the structures investigated here, and to provide a basis for comparison, independent of historical evidence, against which other civilian sites can be compared to help identify whether or not they are examples of defensive architecture.

Not surprisingly, colonial builders in Australia were influenced in their building styles by those which had been long-established back home in Britain. The basic type of country cottage which influenced the colonial builders, both

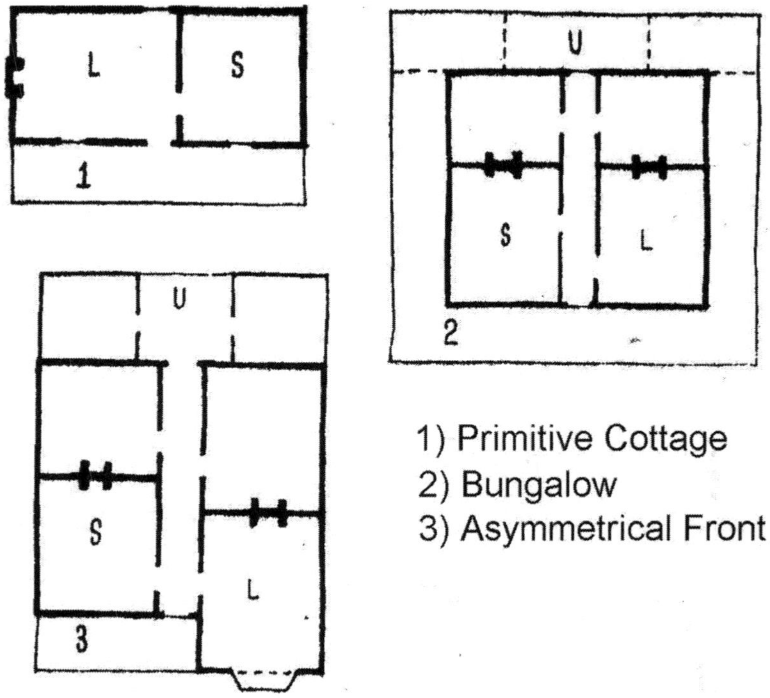

Fig. 7. Principal dwelling plan types used in colonial Australia. After Boyd, 1961: 9.

those in town and in the country, dated back to the late 18th century. Those cottages found in the Scottish highlands and the west coast of Wales were particularly influential to Australian designs (Pikusa 1986: 19).

Turning first to dwellings, during the period under investigation here (ca. 1847–ca. 1879), all dwellings were based on three basic plans. These were the primitive cottage; the bungalow; and the asymmetrical front (Boyd 1961: 8–10 Fig 7).

All three of the dwellings investigated (i.e. Mount Benson, Central Outstation and Springvale) appear to have been based on the primitive cottage plan, though in the more elaborate form of a complex of cells. The primitive cottage, in its most basic form, was characterised by one room, the living room/kitchen, being slightly longer than the other. One small window was placed either side of the door and a fireplace and chimney stood at the far end of the living room/kitchen. The side walls were blind (Boyd 1961: 8). This type of plan is also characterised by its additive quality. That is, its open-endedness allowed additional cells to be added to the sides or rear to suit the particular circumstances (Cox & Lucas, 1978: 14). This can clearly be seen in the examples of Central Outstation and Springvale (Figs 8 & 9 respectively). The Central Outstation men's hut uses the primitive cottage plan, but with the addition of an extra room on one of its short sides and an extra fireplace. Springvale's dwelling represents a more elaborate version of the cellular plan, with a main section of three rooms, once again all in a row, and still with the fireplace on one of the short ends. The other dwelling investigated here, Mount Benson, looks as though its plan could have been taken directly from Atkinson's 1826 book of practical advice to new settlers in the Australian colonies (Atkinson 1975 [1826]). The significant characteristic of this plan, and one which is mirrored in the Mount Benson dwelling, is the positioning of a fireplace in the rear wall, as well as on one of the short sides, as with the primitive cottage (Fig 10).

What is most noticeable about the 'typical' linear cell plans is the general absence of windows and doors in the rear wall. Even when present, there are fewer windows and/or doors in the rear wall than in the opposite (or front) wall. This is a feature of Australian vernacular cottages that comes from their British antecedents and is therefore not in itself part of a defensive design. The original reason for the lack of windows in the rear wall has its origins in the cottages of the northern hemisphere, which were generally sited so that the openings were on the southern side, protected from the prevailing northerly winds (Pikusa 1986: 19–20). The same procedure for siting was followed in Australia, although the building's orientation was often altered depending on the particular direction of the prevailing wind. It appears that, both in the British and Australian cottages, the only time a rear door *was* included in the plan was if there were buildings at the rear of the dwelling such as a

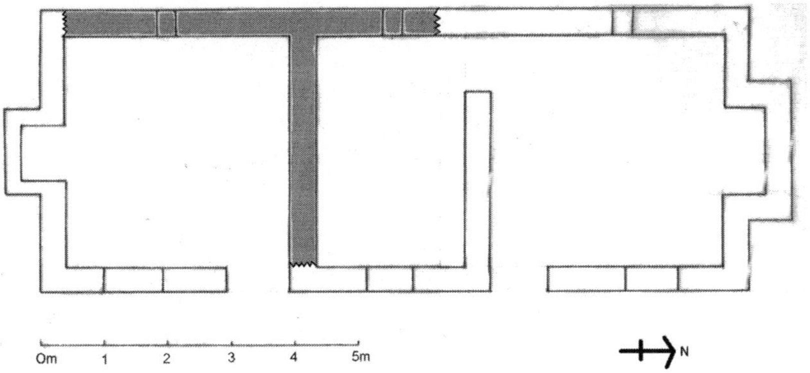

Fig. 8. Plan of the Men's Hut at Central Outstation. Grey-shaded portions are reconstructions of collapsed wall sections.

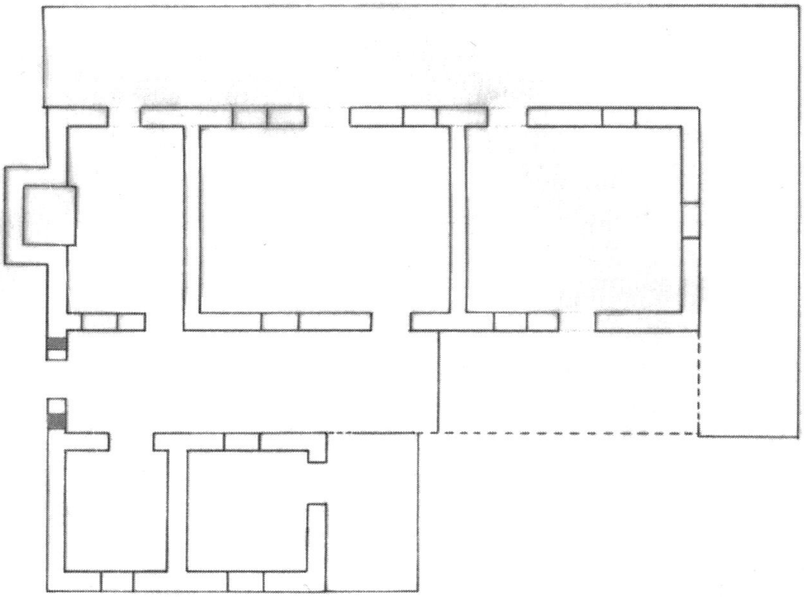

Fig. 9. Plan of the dwelling at Springvale showing original layout. The two embrasures are shown shaded grey, either side of what was the rear door to the yard.

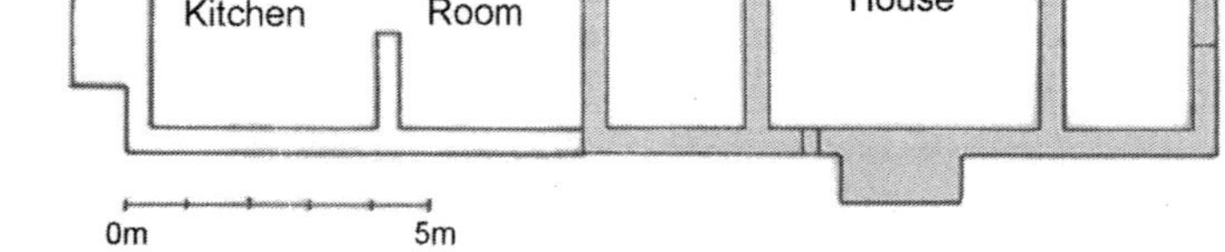

Fig. 10. Reconstruction of Mount Benson homestead at the time of the dwelling's construction, based on archival and archaeological evidence. The grey-shaded portions indicate stone construction, non-shaded portions indicate oak construction. The embrasure can be seen to the left of the fire place in the central room of the stone section.

wash-house, storage shed, privy or chicken house (Pikusa 1986: 23). Otherwise they were not considered necessary.

Thus, all of the dwellings investigated here generally conformed to the typical primitive cottage plan, particularly in their lack of windows or doors in the rear walls. The Springvale dwelling has a single door in the rear wall of the complex, because it was required to provide access to the outbuildings and yard. Today, there is also a small window in the rear wall of the Mount Benson dwelling; however, this is located in a section which was constructed later. The dwelling in its original configuration evidently did not have any windows or doors on this side.

The significant difference between the typical design, and those investigated here, is the existence of one or more small apertures, located in the rear wall of the dwelling. Only a single source of those provided a precedent for the adoption or function of such features, *The Australian Homestead* by Cox & Stacey (1972). Cox and Stacey mention that when defence against bushrangers or Aborigines was needed, wooden shutters were used instead of window panes and 'gun holes' (embrasures) were incorporated into the walls (1972: 14). The lack of references in the majority of the architectural literature suggests that such apertures were not a part of the usual cottage plan, either in Europe or Australia. Rather, they appear to have been incorporated when deemed necessary according to local situations. Therefore, these apertures constitute an important and significant modification to the Australian vernacular, and one which has hitherto been overlooked in the architectural literature.

The other two types of rural buildings investigated here were the coach-house at Lizard Lodge and the store at Springvale. It is rather difficult to describe the typical coach-house, since the actual function (or functions) of that at Lizard Lodge is unclear. In terms of its general design, it appears to have been heavily influenced by the English 'bank barn' (Bell 1997): it is built into a slope, with upper and lower levels. It is also common for traditional bank barns in England to have narrow apertures located in the upper level which splay outwards on the interior. These features in English barns are interpreted as providing ventilation for perishables such as bulk grain or fodder (Brunskill 1974: 141). As a result, when it comes to outbuildings (as opposed to dwellings), it is more challenging to distinguish between defence and ventilation.

Since the presence of apertures in an outbuilding is not in itself diagnostic of defensive nature, the only way to determine such a structure's defensive construction is through supporting evidence. Apart from documentary sources, the best test is to determine whether there is a feature (or features) that would render the construction of ventilation apertures superfluous or non-functional. This was the method adopted with the Lizard Lodge coach-house.

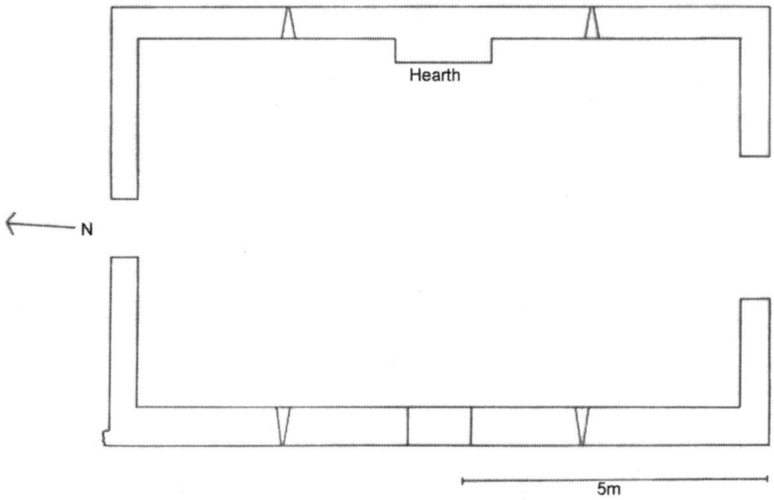

Fig. 11. Plan of the upper ground floor of the coach-house at Lizard Lodge, showing the two entrances, window, and position and dimensions of embrasures.

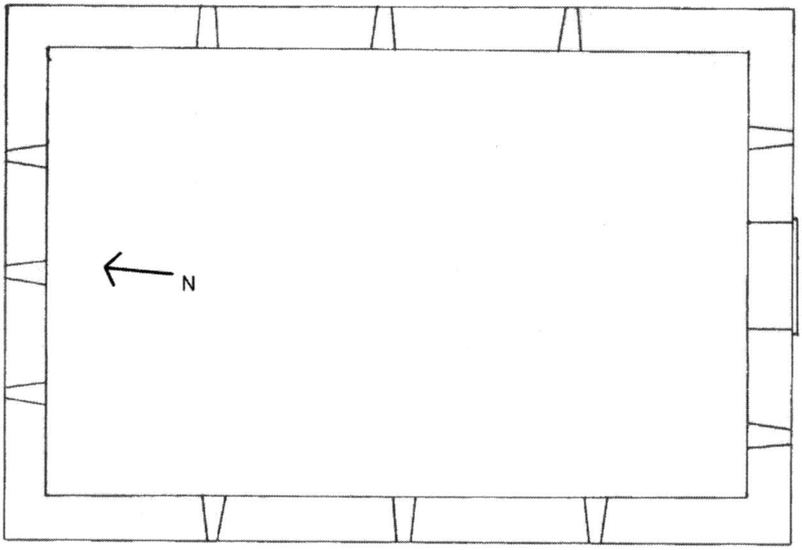

Fig. 12. Plan of the upper level of the store at Springvale, showing the position and shape of embrasures.

If this can be demonstrated to be the case, then providing there is supporting documentary evidence for a motive, the apertures can be fairly confidently interpreted as embrasures. However, there is always the possibility that the apertures of some outbuildings were designed to have a dual function for ventilation and defence should the need arise. When this is the case, it is almost impossible to state for certain whether such a structure was built to serve a defensive role, even as a secondary function. In such a case, the primary documentary evidence may be considered strong enough to interpret such a structure as defensive.

Defensive Strategy and Tactics

A common characteristic that all the dwellings shared was that their front facades were not designed any differently to non-defensive buildings, yet all had defensive embrasures built into their rear walls. This is very significant to Australian frontier construction techniques because it provides clues as to the intended tactical roles of these buildings as defensive structures.

As discussed above, the lack of doors or windows in the rear wall of these dwellings was not an indication of defensive construction, and was based on British antecedents. The standard rural dwellings of Britain were perfectly suitable for direct translation into Australia (with the addition of verandas), but proved unsuitable when the occupants feared attack. The dwellings investigated here show that, although these settlers did not feel the need to modify the vernacular design drastically to deal with the threat of attack, they evidently felt anxious about having no way to see if a threat was approaching from the rear of their dwellings. The evidence from these sites shows that one way this was achieved was by building one or more embrasures in the rear wall.

Being primarily domestic structures, it is easily appreciated why the settlers preferred to keep conventional windows in the front and sometimes side walls, rather than have small embrasures as the only source of light and air. Their intention was not to turn their dwellings into dark forts, but rather to have the added ability for the occupants to keep an eye on the rear of their dwellings and, in the event of an attack, have a firing position from which the defender would be practically invulnerable to Aboriginal weapons. The existence of conventional windows elsewhere in the building may at first glance appear to defeat the purpose of embrasures in the rear wall; it would have been just as likely that attackers would approach from the front of a building, or go around it. However, it was usual for dwellings during this period to have sturdy wooden shutters (Cox & Stacey 1972: 14; Cannon 1973: 30). These could be locked in the event of a threat, or at night time, and could also have

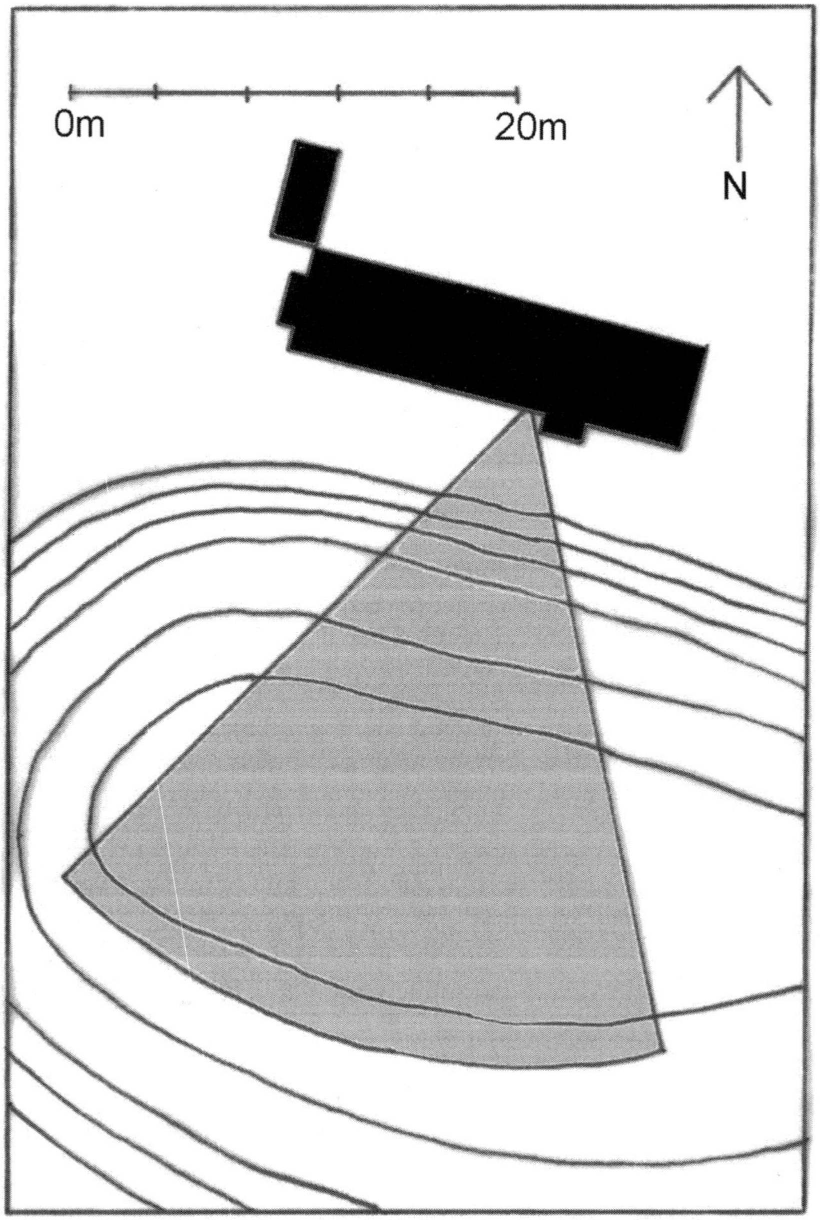

Fig. 13. Diagram showing arc of fire available to defenders on the southern side of the dwelling at Mount Benson. The contour lines represent an evidently natural mound located immediately to the rear of the dwelling. The length of the embrasure's arc shows the maximum distance one can observe and fire on an attacker approaching from the south. Contour intervals: 0.25 m.

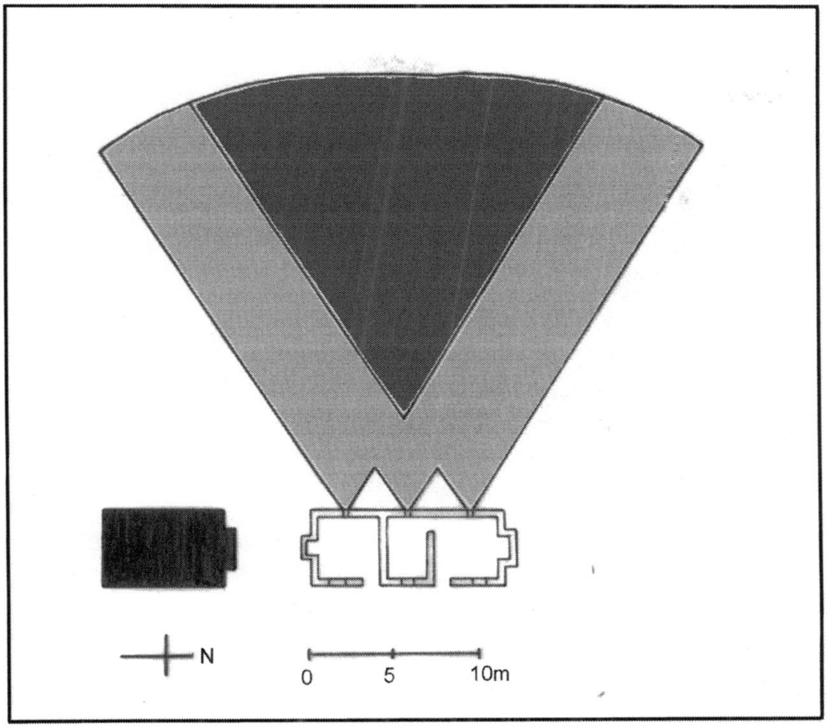

Fig. 14. Plan showing the arcs of fire provided by the three embrasures in the Men's Hut at Central Outstation, shown extending out to an arbitrary distance of 25 m. The dark grey portion shows terrain able to be covered by all three embrasures simultaneously. Shown to the left is an approximate reconstruction of the position and dimensions of the other structure which once stood on the site, based upon photographic evidence, but of which no trace remains today.

embrasures built into them, thereby rendering a dwelling very secure and well-designed as a defensive structure. Unfortunately, no original joinery survived at the sites investigated, and thus no physical evidence for such shutters.

The tactical role of these 'fortified' dwellings is therefore quite straightforward to deduce. In the event of a threat, these dwellings were designed to be 'battened down'. By doing so, they changed function from home to fort, and with embrasures in what would usually be blank walls, allowed the occupants to remain relatively safe, as well as be able to defend themselves.

The siting of the dwellings may also have borne a relation to their tactical role. To the rear (i.e. embrasured side) of all three dwellings were features that could be regarded as potential targets for Aboriginal attackers. In the case of the Mount Benson dwelling, this was a large fenced paddock which was probably used to keep sheep in; in the case of Central Outstation,

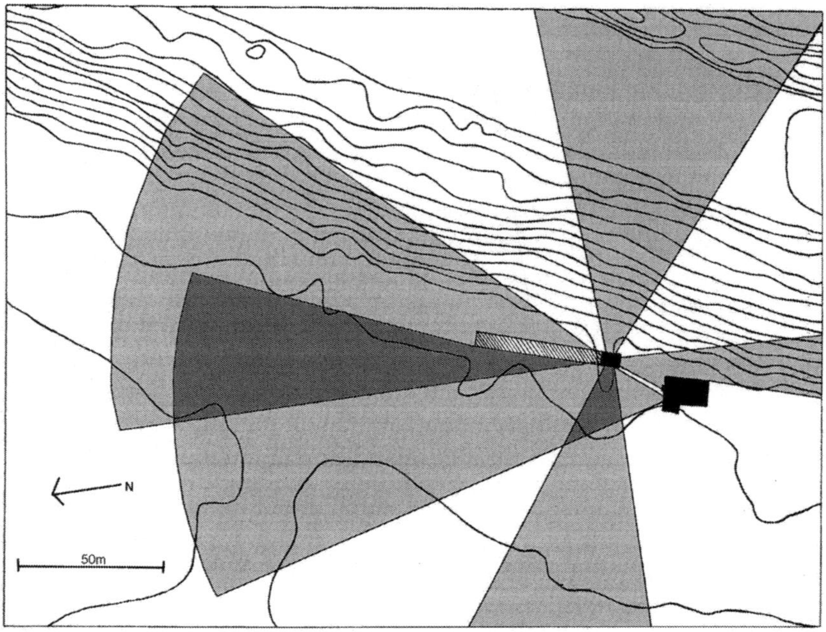

Fig. 15. Diagram showing the arcs of fire offered by the embrasures in the dwelling and store at Springvale, shaded grey. The darker grey areas indicate ground covered by embrasures of both the store and the dwelling. The diagonally-hatched area shows the approximate area covered by the original shed-line.

there were sheep yards to the rear of the fortified dwelling; and in the case of Springvale dwelling, the store was located to its rear. Therefore, it is possible that the embrasures were built into the rear walls facing these potential targets to keep an eye on them and drive off any attackers with gunfire from the safety of the embrasures. Another example of defensive siting in the cases of Springvale and Mount Benson is the location of the structures atop a steep river bank (as in the case of both of the Sprinvale structures investigated) or a hill (as in the case of the Mount Benson dwelling). This helped to provide better observation of any potential threats (Cox & Stacey 1972: 9; Taylor 1988: 24). With the case of the store and dwelling at Springvale, the two structures also appear to have been positioned in a manner that allowed them to mutually support each other.

As for the two outbuildings investigated, the Lizard Lodge coach-house and Springvale store, these appear to have been intended to be used slightly differently in the event of a threat. Although the primary function of the embrasured room in the coach-house is uncertain, it appears to have been

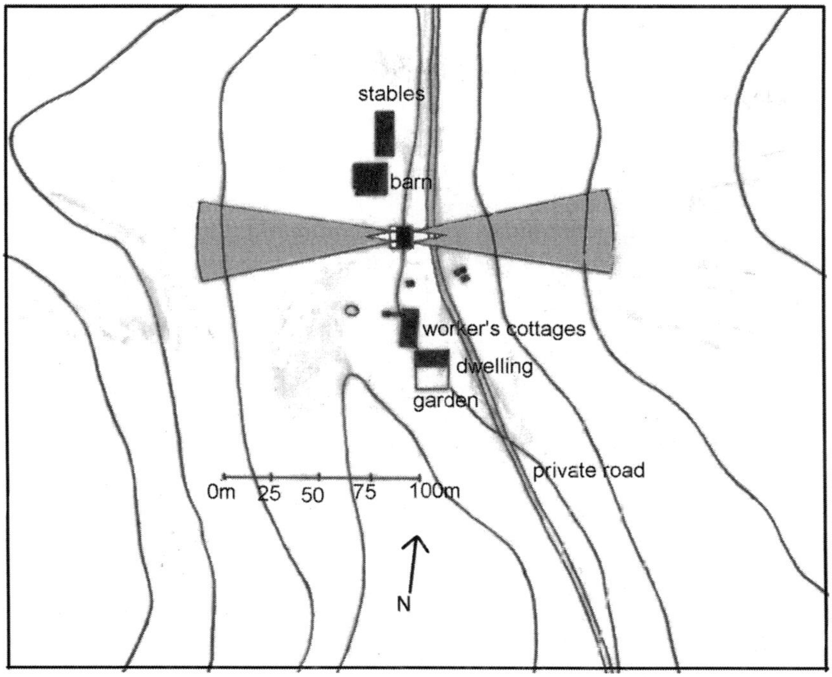

Fig. 16. Reconstruction of Lizard Lodge homestead at the time of the completion of the coach-house (ca 1852). The arcs of fire offered by the coach-house's embrasures are shown shaded grey. The arcs have been extended out to 100 m, this being the maximum effective range of the type of firearms it is believed would have been used at the time (i.e. Smoothbore longarms).

designed to function as a refuge for those around the homestead in the event of an attack. It was positioned in the centre of the homestead complex, though retaining clear fields of fire and vision on the embrasured sides. This central positioning was possibly designed to allow it to be the same distance from either end of the homestead complex, so that wherever one was at the time of the threat, the coach-house was not too far away.

The store at Springvale homestead was designed primarily for use as a store. This is evident from the fact that the embrasures probably doubled as ventilation apertures, since two of them are inaccessible as embrasures. However, that it was designed to be functional as a defensive structure is evident from its overall secure design, with no windows or apertures in the ground floor, yet with accessible apertures which could function as embrasures around all four sides of the loft, and no windows. It seems most likely that the tactical role of the store was for it to be 'garrisoned' in order to defend its contents, in the event of an attack upon the homestead.

Were their Precautions Justified?

> [Fear] is a complex feeling of which two strains, alarm and anxiety, are clearly distinguishable. Alarm is triggered by an obtrusive element in the environment, and an animal's instinctive response is to combat it or run. Anxiety, on the other hand, is a diffuse sense of dread and presupposes an ability to anticipate. It commonly occurs when an animal is in a strange and disorientating milieu, separated from the supportive objects and figures of its home ground. Anxiety is a presentiment of danger when nothing in the immediate surroundings can be pinpointed as dangerous. The need for decisive action is checked by the lack of any specific, circumventable threat (Tuan 1979: 5).

The above definition explains the possible mental process of the builders and also what must have been the atmosphere in which the settlers lived. It evokes the feelings of alarm and anxiety that evidently pervaded the minds of these frontier settlers. One could argue that, since no evidence was found of direct attack upon the sites investigated here, the defensively-built structures were never 'put to the test' through being attacked, and therefore the builders' precautions were unjustified. However, just as strong a counter-argument is possible that it was *because* the structures were built defensively that they were not attacked. This was certainly the case with regards to American Indians and U.S. Army forts (Hoagland 1999: 218) and the Aborigines and Fort Dundas in the Northern Territory (Connor 2001: 68, 73). Both American Indians and Australian Aborigines, when confronted with defensive structures, chose to avoid direct attacks on prepared positions, and instead waited for opportunities to pick off isolated individuals or groups away from the forts (Hoagland 1999: 218; Connor 2001: 68; 73). A further consideration is that, although a concerted attack upon one of these buildings would probably have been recorded in police or newspaper reports, small 'scares' may have gone unrecorded. Similarly, the firing of a shot or two from the embrasures at Aborigines who approached too close to the dwelling may have been commonplace and so not recorded, even though such an action would technically constitute the use of the structures in their defensive role. Furthermore, there is the unfortunate fact that, with the exception of Springvale, none of the station journals which recorded the day to day happenings are known to have survived. Such documents may have been invaluable in shedding light on the construction of the buildings and the frontier conflict events which occurred around them.

Although it is true that there is no evidence that the particular buildings investigated here were ever attacked, there *is* ample evidence for Aborigines attacking buildings within South Australia and the Northern Territory, and elsewhere in Australia. For example, between 1842 and 1851, the South Australian Police Commissioner's reports and the Adelaide press contained at least 27 reports of rural settlers being attacked, or threatened with attack, in their dwellings.

An apparent pattern is that buildings were often only built defensively *after* the initial settlers had been the target of Aboriginal resistance, and after they had already built non-defensive dwellings. When the runs were initially taken up, the settlers evidently did not seem to have anticipated much or any Aboriginal resistance to their presence, and hence did not think it necessary to build defensively. Often, the defensively designed structures were built in later developmental stages (e.g. Lizard Lodge), after a change in ownership of properties (e.g. Mount Benson), or during the later expansion of runs (e.g. Central Outstation). The irony is that by the time such structures *were* built, the most intense period of conflict had already passed, although this fact was, of course, unknown to the settler. This does not, however, mean that such structures were any less functional, or built without real justification. It was simply a case of the settlers learning from experience. Therefore, such defensively designed structures can be seen as part of a colonising learning-curve, a physical expression of the settler's 'coming of age' in the Australian frontier environment as they came to terms with the true nature of the frontier and their position within it. A close parallel with this kind of process is observable in the case of the settlers of the East Cape of South Africa in the 1830s, as identified by Winer (2001). There, as in the sites investigated here, fortification was not used by civilians until *after* the peak of frontier conflict (Winer 2001: 264–66).

What does this reveal about the Nature of Australia's Frontier?

These sites reveal that the frontier was a place of open conflict and fear. Fear of Aboriginal attack may have caused the settlers to fortify their buildings, but this very specific fear of attack was only one aspect of the general atmosphere of fear that pervaded the lives of both sides, settlers and indigenous people. The ample historical evidence for actual violent conflict, even if not directed against the specific structures investigated here, but against the individuals who had the structures built, their employees, their neighbours and others in the region, tells us that conflict was present and the fear that naturally goes with conflict was particularly strong. This is reflected in the fact that it caused the builders to modify normal construction techniques and designs to help address their fear. These structures also highlight the existence of an active and effective Aboriginal resistance in the regions studied. This may not have been effective enough in the long run to prevent the loss of their land, but it was effective enough to cause the settlers to take extra measures to deal with it.

The existence of these civilian-built structures also tells us something about the extent of protection (or lack thereof) that was afforded to the settlers by the government, as represented by the police, the military, and the so-called 'Protectors of Aborigines'. The government was evidently unwilling, unable, or particularly poor at preventing frontier conflict in the study regions; the settlers evidently did not consider that they could rely for protection on the government. This shows that often the civilian settler really was the 'front line' agent of colonial invasion and, through being the one who settled on the land and then proceeded to fortify and defend it against its traditional owners, was the one who actually 'conquered' it.

The findings also tell us a great deal about how the nature of the frontier affected the mindset of the settlers who built these structures. Each of the builders (Gifford, Maurice, O'Halloran and Giles) had a documented history of experiencing suffering and/or violence at the hands of Aboriginal people prior to the construction of their fortified buildings. The fact that these fortified structures were built in the wake of frontier conflict experience tells us that the settlers were evidently significantly affected by their previous experiences. This trauma, brought about by the nature of Australia's frontier (with its inter-racial violence), thus manifested itself in the construction of fortified buildings. This is demonstrated in all of the sites investigated here.

The structures, and the histories of the people who built them, also demonstrate the harsh reality of colonialism and the way it was carried out in Australia. The structures represent physical examples of the process of colonisation, a process which involved a society of strangers appropriating vast tracts of land for no other reason than capitalistic gain and displacing the previous occupants with little or no regard for their welfare and no compensation. With perhaps the exception of South Australia's Prussian settlers (see Jenkin 1989: 99–118), these settlers did not emigrate order to escape persecution, but to become wealthy. As often as not, the speculators who took up pastoral runs did not even live in the colony, residing instead in England and administering their pastoral interests through managers and agents in the colony. If they did live in the colony, it was usually in a capital city.

These structures, or more particularly the situations that gave rise to their fortification, also tell us about the serious inter-cultural misunderstandings that often existed between Europeans and Aborigines on the Australian frontier. Initial contact between the newly-established settlers and the local Aborigines was usually friendly if the Aborigines had not had much previous experience with Europeans. This was because the settler often unwittingly complied with the traditional Aboriginal custom of reciprocity (Elkin 1974: 363). The settler, upon meeting the local Aborigines who came to his/her dwelling, would initially, out of hospitality and optimistic goodwill, provide them with some meat, damper and tobacco (Franklin 1976: 28). The Aborigines, on the other hand, would have regarded the settler's provision of these things as his/her obligation. In return, the Aborigines allowed the settler to live in their country and often even provided male settlers with women. When, however, the Aborigines continued to carry out the reciprocity custom by taking what they needed of the settler's livestock, the communication breakdown became apparent, as the settler's concept of property and capital clashed with the Aboriginal concept of shared use of the land's resources. Eventually, after becoming frustrated and angered at the continual slaughtering of livestock and Aboriginal demands for flour, and tobacco, the settler invariably adopted a policy of keeping the Aborigines from approaching the property and took up arms against them (Franklin, *op cit*). Naturally, the Aborigines also took up arms, both to defend themselves and to punish the settler for breaking their laws. The attacks upon settler buildings in this context were launched in response to the settler's refusal to comply with Aboriginal laws. Aboriginal objectives were either to procure the food which they saw due to them, punish the settler through violence, or a combination of the two. All this is represented in the fortification of these buildings.

As a final point, it must be understood that although these structures are described as 'defensive'—and so they certainly were to those who lived in them—in the broader context of colonisation, these buildings were just as much *offensive* constructions. They were built on land belonging to Aboriginal people who were openly and demonstrably hostile to European society; land which the settlers occupied without the Aboriginal owners' permission or any consultation (the offensive nature of U.S. Army forts in the American West has also been noted, see Hoagland 1999: 218). The very fact that the settlers felt the need to construct these buildings in such a way demonstrates this.

What does this reveal about the Myths associated with these Sites?

Stanner's concept of 'the great Australian silence' (Stanner 1974: 18–29) appears to apply to the history of some of the sites investigated in this research: in some cases, the story about a structure's defensive nature is completely omitted (e.g. Forrest 1985). Although it has been claimed that this 'silence' is less true of local histories because they are

> the product of informed local history knowledge and completely at odds with the received wisdom of a twentieth-century white historical silence (Foster et al. 2001: 9),

it has also been pointed out that

> local history is not to be trusted because rural communities put a great deal of effort into covering up a past of violence and expropriation that was often uncomfortably recent in terms of family and community memory (Haggis 2001: 92).

At first glance, these two views appear diametrically opposed, but the results of this research have shown how both can actually betrue within the context of one site, and how this ties in with settler identity construction and social memory.

There are evidently two ways that local history information about fortified homesteads is used in the construction of Australia's settler identity. One is to ignore it entirely; the other is to mythologize it. The purpose the first option achieves is to omit evidence of conflict and thus create the illusion that the land was either unoccupied by Aboriginal people or settled without any interference from the Aborigines. Essentially, this option seeks to remove the Aboriginal factor. In both of these cases, these myths create a stark separation between those who are the 'insiders' (the European settlers) and those who are the 'outsiders' (the Aborigines) in settler culture, a phenomenon also identified in commemorative activities at United States battlefield sites (Linenthal 1991: 216).

The second option, that of mythologizing the conflict, while in a way acknowledging a prior Aboriginal presence on the land, also portrays the settler as a victim of violent 'savages', intent on murdering the settler in their own home. In this light, the Aboriginal threat is portrayed as one which the settler has to contend with as a hindrance to his/her heroic effort to farm the land and 'civilise' it.

Local histories are, in fact, the source of many of the myths about civilian use of defensive architecture. However, there are also exceptions to this within local histories, where defensive architecture has been played down or omitted altogether, such as Peter Forrest's book, *Springvale's Story* (1985). Furthermore, local histories associated with the sites investigated here have been found to include mentions of civilian use of defensive architecture while completely overlooking the frontier conflict and the causes that led to its construction (e.g. Baillie 1978: 134; Dolling 1981: 272; 313).

Settler societies are notorious for developing 'narratives of reversal' when it comes to the subject of settler/indigenous conflict and fear. Indigenous people are portrayed as the invaders and the settlers as the defenders (Curthoys 2003: 193). Whereas the myths associated with civilian use of defensive architecture make specific mention of the need for settlers to defend themselves against Aboriginal attack, no mention is made of the Aborigines' motives for attack. This lack of the explanation of a motive can only lead the average receiver to regard the 'aggressive' actions of the Aborigines as those of 'savages'. To omit Aboriginal grievances and denigrate them thus has served an important role in settler identity construction, that of removing settler guilt and facilitating the process of colonisation. Furthermore, this reversal of roles, casting the indigenous defender as aggressor and the invading colonist as defender, also serves the very important purpose of constructing a past that 'allocates the land as won through suffering, and therefore as theirs' (Curthoys 2003: 199). The 'self-chosen white victim finds it extremely difficult to recognise what he or she has done to others' (*ibid.*), and this is exactly what settler identity construction has traditionally been designed to do, since it serves to turn people's minds away from the dark truths of the foundations of their society and keep people proud of their whiteness and the nation that it forged.

The structures investigated here have, through their associated myths, evolved in their meaning to become just as much monuments as purpose-built statues. Gazin-Schwartz and Holtorf pointed out that

> [i]f we are interested in what monuments mean, it is our task as archaeologists to study the complete history of monuments rather than restrict our interests to the motivations that led to their first construction (1999: 16).

Monuments are meant to create consensus and stability. The durability of landscape and the monuments placed in it, makes them effective symbols for the sustaining of values over long periods (Foote 1997: 33). This is precisely how the structures investigated here have been used by settler society mythology. Like monuments in general, the mythic interpretation of structures by settler society is designed to 'make it worthwhile to be a descendant' (Greenbie 1981: 247).

Conclusion

Gazin-Schwartz and Holtorf wrote that

> when [mythology] is analysed (as archaeological materials have to be analysed), it sometimes does provide plausible interpretation for those materials, whether or not they can prove unbroken continuity of transmission (1999: 5).

This research not only demonstrated the truth of this statement through analysis of several examples of myths relating to fortified homesteads, but went further, analysing the material of the myths in close conjunction with archaeological analysis of the physical materials upon which the myths were founded. In all of the case studies presented here, in-depth analysis of the veracity of the myths using a combination of archaeological and historical data showed that the myths did more than provide a *plausible* interpretation of the material culture, but also provided an accurate interpretation of it.

Historical archaeology can thus be used very effectively to test the veracity of defensive architecture myths. Through a combination of archival research and a structured archaeological investigation of the material remains, this research has shown that the methods adopted here can be used to address the confusion that exists regarding what constitutes examples of civilian use of defensive architecture in the Australian frontier context.

Bibliography

Anderson, B 1983 *Imagined Communities: Reflections on the Origins and Spread of Nationalism.* Verso: New York.

Atkinson, J 1975 [1826] *An Account of the State of Agriculture and Grazing in New South Wales.* Sydney University Press: Sydney.

Baillie, P 1978 *Port Lincoln and District: A Pictorial History.* Lynton Publications: Blackwood, South Australia.

Banks, J 1970 *Kingston Flashbacks (Part 1).* Ladies Auxilliary of Kingston District Soldiers' Memorial Hospital: Kington, South Australia.

Barraclough, G 1994 *The Times Concise Atlas of World History.* Harper Collins: London.

Barrowman, A 1971 *Old Days and Old Ways.* A H Barrowman: Robe, South Australia).

Bell, P 1997 *Heritage Study of Glenthorne CSIRO Field Station.* Unpublished report.

Bender, B 2001 'Introduction', in Bender, B and M Winer (eds.), *Contested Landscapes: Movement, Exile and Place.* Berg: Oxford.

Bhabha, H (ed.) 1990 *Nation and Narration.* Routledge: London.

Blair St. George, R 1990 'Bawns and beliefs: architecture, commerce and conversion in early New England', *Winterthur Portfolio*, 25 (1990), 241–87.

Bodnar, J 1992 *Remaking America: Public Memory, Commemoration, and Patriotism in the Twentieth Century.* Princeton University Press: Princeton, New Jersey.

Boyd, R 1961 *Australia's Home.* Melbourne University Press: Melbourne.

Bremner, L 1999 'Crime and the emerging landscape of post-apartheid Johannesburg', *in* Judin, H & Valdislavic, I (eds.) *Blank—Architecture, Apartheid and After.* David Philip: Cape Town.

Broome, R 1996 'Historians, Aborigines and Australia: writing the national past', *in* Attwood, B (ed.) *In the Age of Mabo: History, Aborigines and Australia*, 54–72. Allen & Unwin: Sydney.

Brunskill, R W 1974 *Illustrated Handbook of Vernacular Architecture.* Faber & Faber: London.

Burke, H 1999 *Meaning and Ideology in Historical Archaeology: Style Social Identity, and Capitalism in an Australian Town.* Kluwer Academic/Plenum Publishers: New York.

Cannon, M 1973 *Life in the Country: Australia in the Victorian Age: 2.* Thomas Nelson Ltd: Melbourne.

Connor, J 2002 *The Australian Frontier Wars: 1788–1838.* University of New South Wales Press: Sydney.

Cox, P & Stacey, W 1972 *The Australian Homestead.* Lansdowne Press: Melbourne.

Cox, P & Lucas, C 1978 *Australian Colonial Architecture.* Lansdowne Editions: Melbourne.

Curthoys, A 2003 'Constructing National Histories', *in* Attwood, B & Foster, S G (eds.) *Frontier Conflict: The Australian Experience.* National Museum of Australia: Canberra. 185–200.

Dolling, A 1981 *A History of Marion on the Sturt. The Story of a Changing Landscape and its People.* Peacock Publications: Frewville, South Australia.

Elkin, A 1974 *The Australian Aborigines.* Angus & Robertson: Sydney.

Foote, K E 1997 *Shadowed Ground: America's Landscapes of Violence and Tragedy.* University of Texas Press: Austin.

Forrest, P 1985 *Springvale's Story and Early Years at Katherine.* Murranji Press: Darwin.

Foster, R, Hosking, R & Nettelbeck, A 2001 *Fatal Collisions. The South Australian Frontier and the Violence of Memory.* Wakefield Press: Kent Town, South Australia.

Fox, R A, Jr 1993 *Archaeology, History, and Custer's Last Battle.* University of Oklahoma Press: Norman.

Franklin, M 1976 *Black and White Australians.* Heinemann Educational Australia: South Yarra, Victoria.
Gazin-Schwartz, A & Holtorf, C 1999 'Introduction', *in* Gazin-Schwartz, A & Holtorf, C (eds.) 1999 *Archaeology and Folklore.* Routledge: London. 4–21.
Greenbie, B B 1981 *Spaces: Dimensions of the Human Landscape.* Yale University Press: New Haven.
Haggis, J 2001 'The social memory of a colonial frontier', *Australian Feminist Stud,* 16 (2001), 91–99.
Halls, C 1974 *Guns in Australia.* Paul Hamlyn: Sydney.
Hoagland, A 1999 'Village constructions: U.S. Army forts on the Plains, 1848–1890', *Winterthur Portfolio,* 34 (1999), 215–37.
Kammen, M 1991 *Mystic Chords of Memory: The Transformation of Tradition in American Culture.* Alfred A. Knopf: New York.
Jenkin, G 1989 *Calling Me Home.* South Australian College of Advanced Eduction: Adelaide.
Kenzle, S 1997 'Enclosing walls in the northern San Juan: sociophysical boundaries and defensive fortifications in the American Southwest', *J Field Archaeol,* 24 (1997), 195–210.
Linenthal, E T 1991 *Sacred Ground: Americans and Their Battlefields.* University of Illinois Press: Urbana & Chicago.
Lydon, J & Ireland, T 2005 *Object Lessons: Archaeology & Heritage in Australia.* Melbourne Scholarly Publishing: Melbourne.
Macintyre, S 2003 *The History Wars.* Melbourne University Press: Carlton, Victoria.
Murray, T 2004 *The Archaeology of Contact in Settler Societies.* Cambridge University Press: Cambridge.
Norris, K 1976 *Australia's Heritage Sketchbook.* Books for Pleasure: Sydney.
Paisley, F 2003 'White settler colonialisms and the colonial turn: an Australian perspective', *J Colonialism & Colonial Hist,* 4 (2003), Introduction.
Pikusa, S 1986 *The Adelaide House, 1836 to 1901.* Wakefield Press: Netley, South Australia.
Reynolds, H 1981 *The Other Side of the Frontier.* History Dept, James Cook University: Townsville, Queensland.
—— 1987 *Frontier.* Allen & Unwin, Sydney.
—— 1998 *This Whispering in our Hearts.* Allen & Unwin: St. Leonards, NSW.
—— 2001 *An Indelible Stain? The Question of Genocide in Australia's History.* Penguin: Australia.
Roos, F 1953 'Ohio: architectural cross-road', *J Soc Architect Hist,* 12 (1953), 3–8.
Rubertone, P 1994 'Archaeology, colonialism and 17th-century Native America: towards an alternative interpretation', *in* Layton, R (ed.) *Conflict in the Archaeology of Living Traditions.* Routledge: London. 33–45.
Ryan, L 1996 *The Aboriginal Tasmanians.* Allen & Unwin: St Leonards, NSW.
Shackel, P (ed.) 2001 *Myth, Memory, and the Making of the American Landscape.* University Press of Florida: Gainesville.
Slotkin, R 1993 *Gunfighter Nation.* Harper Perennial: New York.
Stanner, W E H 1974 *After the Dreaming.* The Australian Broadcasting Commission: Sydney.
Taylor, P 1988 *Station Life in Australia, Pioneers and Pastoralists.* Allen & Unwin: Sydney.
The Architects Studio 2000 'Springvale homestead, Katherine, Northern Territory. Conservation plan'. The Architects Studio, Darwin.
Tuan, Y 1979 *Landscapes of Fear.* Pantheon Books: New York.
Windschuttle, K 2002 *The Fabrication of Aboriginal History, Volume One Van Dieman's Land, 1804–1847.* Macleay Press: Sydney.
Winer, M 2001 'Landscapes, fear and land loss on the nineteenth-century South African colonial frontier', *in* Bender, B & Winer, M (eds.) *Contested Landscapes: Movement, Exile and Place.* Berg: Oxford.
Yentsch, A 1988 'Legends, houses, families, and myths: relationships between material culture and American ideology', *in* Beaudry, M (ed.) *Documentary Archaeology in the New World.* Cambridge University Press: Cambridge. 5–19.

LANDSCAPES OF THE BATTLE OF THE BULGE: WW2 FIELD FORTIFICATIONS IN THE ARDENNES FORESTS OF BELGIUM

DAVID G PASSMORE[1] & STEPHAN HARRISON[2]
1. School of Geography, Politics and Sociology, Newcastle University, Newcastle upon Tyne, NE1 7RU, UK
2. School of Geography, Archaeology and Earth Resources, University of Exeter, Cornwall Campus, Penryn, Cornwall, UK
Corresponding author: d.g.passmore@ncl.ac.uk

Abstract

This paper presents the results of a reconnaissance survey of battlefield archaeological features that are associated with the early stages of the German Ardennes offensive in December 1944, and which have been well-preserved in the post-war forests in the St. Vith–Schöenberg area of eastern Belgium. Field survey of the location, planform dimensions, (unexcavated) surface relief and orientation of forest-floor earthworks over a total area of ca. 1.4 km^2 has recorded 116 discrete and well preserved features that have been provisionally assigned to a threefold typology encompassing large emplacements, rectilinear entrenchments and circular and sub-circular entrenchments/shell craters. The form and disposition of these remains are considered in the context of field fortification doctrine, documented accounts of combat in the area and the terrain and landscape setting. It is to be hoped that the work will stimulate a wider awareness of the value of recording and managing the region's WW2 battlefield heritage in the face of future development pressures, and especially the immediate threat posed by mechanised forestry operations.

Introduction

The landscapes and physical remains of 20th century military conflicts are attracting increasing interest from archaeologists (e.g. Holyoak 2001; Saunders 2002; Schofield 2001; 2005; Schofield *et al.* 2002), the heritage sector (Bull & Panton 2001), military geographers (Woodward 2004) and geoscientists (Rose & Pareyn 1998; Doyle 2001; Doyle *et al.* 1997; 2001; Everett *et al.* 2006; Rose *et al.* 2006). In Western Europe, the battlefields of World War I and their extensive and well-maintained network of memorials have a particularly high-profile, although it is only in comparatively recent times that these areas have been the focus of controlled archaeological investigations (Saunders 2002). The study and experience of these landscapes is locally facilitated by the deliberate preservation of trench systems and cratered landscapes impacted by shell and mine-explosions for purposes of commemoration and remembrance (e.g. Bull

 DOI: 10.1163/157407808X382773

& Panton 2001; Gough 2007), while ongoing geological and archaeological study is promoted by the frequently excellent sub-surface preservation of deep bunker and tunnel systems (e.g. Doyle *et al.* 2001).

Elements of static defensive lines established prior to and during World War II have also locally survived in the present landscape of Western Europe. These include the concrete bunkers, gun emplacements and anti-tank defences built along the English Channel coastlines of England (Lowry 2004) and NW France (Zaloga 2005; 2007), the Maginot Line along the Franco-German border (e.g. Allcorn 2003) and Germany's 'West Wall' defences established during the 1930's and subsequently reinforced during the war (Short 2004). Also well-documented are many instances of extant military installations associated with air and naval warfare (e.g. Holyoak, 2001; Mallmann Showell 2002; Williamson 2003). In general, however, the mobile character of combat in the European theatre rarely permitted the development of extensive networks of trench and bunker systems, and military doctrine was adapted to emphasise the importance of temporary and discrete 'foxholes' or weapons emplacements (Rottman 2004; 2005). These relatively small-scale field fortifications and their associated artefacts have typically been removed or rendered invisible by post-war rebuilding, landscaping or the resumption of agriculture and hence have received little attention by the archaeological or heritage community.

Exceptionally, however, forested landscapes that have escaped intensive management since WW2 may still preserve field fortifications and shell craters associated with contemporary combat. One such area is the forested upland terrain of the Ardennes in the border region of Belgium, Germany and Luxembourg (Fig. 1); this region was the focus of the last major German offensive in the West in December 1944 and is notable as a marked—albeit temporary—setback for the Allied advance into Germany. Commonly known as 'The Battle of the Bulge', the campaign has generated a wealth of published military history (e.g. Cole 1964: Reynolds 1999; Whiting 2001; Zaloga 2003) and is a popular destination for organised battlefield tours and reunions for combatants from both the US and Germany. Numerous museums, memorials and static displays of armoured vehicles and weapons that participated in the campaign form a popular focus for visits, but battlefield guidebooks and popular media (including televised documentaries) also attest to the local survival of artefacts and earthworks in parts of the landscape that were forested during 1944 and have been maintained as woodland to the present day (Cavanagh 2001; Tolhurst 1999). These include parts of the contemporary front line along the Schnee Eifel, just inside the German border, and areas in the vicinity of key battles at Hollerath, Bastogne (Foy) and St. Vith in Belgium (Fig. 1).

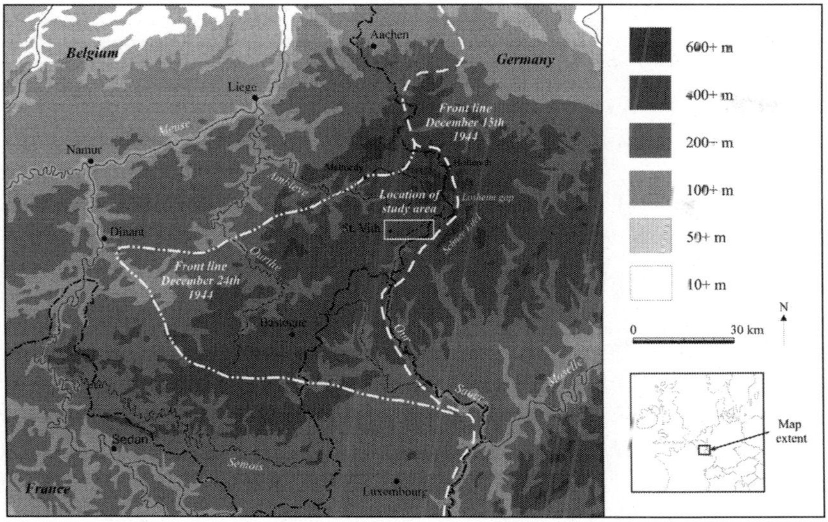

Fig. 1. Topographic map of the Ardennes region showing location of study area and front line configurations on the 15th and 24th December, 1944.

The fortuitous preservation of this battlefield evidence offers the potential to gain a uniquely detailed insight into troop dispositions and their relationship to terrain and the course of battle. It also constitutes a rare opportunity to experience the scene of combat in a landscape setting that is likely to have been very similar to that of late 1944; in this respect, these places may convey a particularly strong sense of past events amongst visitors with a knowledge of the local history, and especially veterans and those connected with former combatants (e.g. Bell 1997; Saunders 2004; Schofield 2005). In view of the potential significance of these landscapes, it is perhaps surprising that—at least to the authors' knowledge—there has been no published attempt to conduct a systematic survey or analysis of these battlefield remains. This paper makes an attempt to initiate such an investigation by presenting the results of a pilot study in the St. Vith–Schöenberg area of eastern Belgium. This part of the battlefield lay on a critical axis of advance for the German offensive, and here we present an overview of field evidence with the aims of (i) establishing a baseline survey of the disposition, morphology and surface relief of field fortifications in two localities within the study area; (ii) relating the pattern and character of field fortifications to published accounts of US Army units and dispositions in the study area over the period between 17 and 21 December, 1944; and (iii) briefly considering the prospects for further study regarding the archaeology, military geography and heritage management of WW2 battlefields in the Ardennes forests.

Background to the Study Area and the 1944 Offensive

On two occasions during the Second World War, the Ardennes uplands of Belgium (Fig. 1) were the scene of major armoured offensives by the German army. The 1940 campaign proved to be a spectacular success and was a key factor in deciding the Battle of France. In late 1944, by contrast, Operation *Wacht am Rhein* (which translates as 'Watch on the Rhine'), more commonly known as the 'Battle of the Bulge', was conceived in very different circumstances with the intention of reversing the Allied advance across NW Europe following the Normandy landings on 6 June 1944. *Wacht am Rhein* followed a pause in the advance of Allied armies against the western flanks of Germany in the face of stiffening German resistance and an over-extended logistical system (Cole 1964; Reynolds 1999). The offensive planned to deploy three armies comprising 9 Panzer Divisions with over 1,400 tanks under the command of Field Marshal Model to penetrate the American front in the Ardennes and Luxembourg, and then hinging on the right flank to cross the Meuse river south of Liège and exploit the port of Antwerp (Fig. 1). The aim of this was to isolate the British and Canadian 21st Army Group and the American 9th Army from the remainder of the Allied front, thereby prompting large-scale surrender and depriving the Allies of their most crucial port (Reynolds 2002). Launched on December 16, 1944, the Battle of the Bulge was the largest and most fiercely fought battle on the Western Front following the Normandy breakout. It was, however, ultimately a failure for the German Army, falling well short of its planned objectives (Fig. 1), while the diversion of units away from the Eastern Front only served to considerably weaken it ahead of the massive Soviet winter offensive which was launched on January 12, 1945 (Cole 1964).

Although very different in their outcomes, both Ardennes offensives were notable in achieving the element of complete surprise against weakly deployed Allied opposition. In both cases this reflected the Allied assumption that the Ardennes presented terrain that was unsuited to rapid and large-scale movement of armoured forces. The eastern Ardennes uplands that form the border between Belgium and Germany are characterised by dissected plateaus and north-easterly trending ridges formed in Devonian sandstones, quartzites, limestones and shales with gently rounded summits rising to around 600–650 m (Fig. 1). The valleys which cut through these hills are deeply incised with narrow floodplains and these are liable to flood during periods of heavy rain and snowmelt.

The St. Vith–Schöenberg area lies immediately west of the junction between the heavily-forested Schee Eiffel ridge and the relatively open, rolling terrain of the Losheim Gap to the north (Fig. 1). The lower relief and limited forest cover of the Losheim Gap offered some of the more traversable terrain in the region and was an important point of entry to advancing German forces in both 1940 and 1944. In December 1944, St. Vith constituted a critical road junction west of the front line and its capture was assigned to the 18 *Volksgrenadier* Division, part of the LXVI Korps, Fifth Panzer Armee (Quarrie 2000). Access to St. Vith lay through the valley of the River Our, including the river crossing at Schöenberg, and the forested Prumerberg heights overlooking the eastern approaches to the town (Fig. 2). The attack began at dawn on 16 December and by the morning of the following day, the 293 and 294 *Volksgrenadier* regiments had converged on Schöenberg, cutting off the US 106th Infantry Division's 422nd and 423rd Regiments and elements of their supporting artillery (589th, 590th and 592nd Field Artillery Battalions) on the slopes of the Lindscheid hills (Quarrie 2000). Leading units of the 294 *Volksgrenadiers* advanced on St. Vith but were halted at the Prumerberg heights by a hastily assembled force mainly comprising men of the 168th Engineer Combat Battalion and several howitzers, anti-tank guns and bazookas under the command of Lieutenant-Colonel Thomas J Riggs (Whiting 1969; Tolhurst 1999).

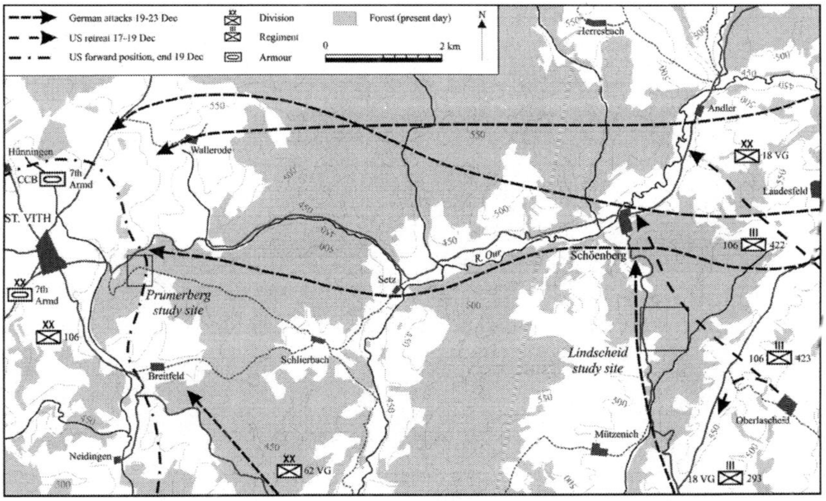

Fig. 2. Map of the St Vith / Schöenberg area showing main axes of German attacks between the 19th–23rd December, axes of local retreat by elements of the 422nd and 423rd regiments, US 106th Infantry Division, and the main US forward position on the night of 19th December, 1944 (after Zaloga 2003 and Tolhurst 1999). Also shown are areas of modern forest cover and the locations of the study sites at Prumerberg (Fig. 5) and Lindscheid (Fig. 6).

Over the course of 18–19 December, the isolated US units at Lindscheid attempted to break out of their encirclement to the west before being ordered to retake Schöenberg. This attack failed and, exhausted and running low on ammunition, the troops surrendered to the *Volksgrenadiers* late on 19 December. Meanwhile, the US forward positions immediately north and east of St. Vith were reinforced by elements of the 7th Armoured Division's Combat Command B and succeeded in holding the line until a concerted German assault on 21 December. During this attack, the Prumerberg defenses were finally breached by the 294 *Volksgrenadier* regiment and St. Vith was captured during the night of 21/22 December (Quarrie 2000).

Study Sites

The study site at Prumerberg encompasses 1 km^2 of woodland at the western end of a ridge of ground rising to 525 m and overlooking St. Vith 1 km to the west (Figs. 2 & 3). The ridge is traversed by a W-E road that links St. Vith with Setz and Schöenberg. On December 17, 1944, this location was chosen by Lieutenant-Colonel Riggs to mount a stand against the advancing *Volksgrenadiers* and the subsequent actions are commemorated today by a roadside memorial to the men of the 168th Engineer Combat Battalion (Fig. 3). Riggs deployed his forces in a skirmish line astride the St. Vith–Setz road (Tolhurst 1999) where troops could command good visibility for some 1 km east along the road, and also across open ground to the south-east (currently the site of Fahrfeld farm; Fig. 3). An aerial photograph taken on 12 August 1944 (US 7GP/2858–3020) reveals that Fahrfeld farm did not exist at this time, and that the extent and boundaries of the contemporary woodland cover were the same as those at present. However, clear felling of forest in 2007 has opened up an area of ground on the northern side of the road (Fig. 3).

The study site at Lindscheid extends over 0.4 km^2 on the south-east facing slope of the Lindscheid hills 2 km south of Schöenberg above the River Ihrenbach, a small tributary of the River Our (Figs. 2 & 4). This area is also forested, with the exception of small clearings flanking the Schöenberg–Bleialf road. During the fighting for Schöenberg in late December 1944, this area was occupied by the US 106th Infantry Division's 423rd Regiment (3rd Battalion) and the 589th Field Artillery Battalion (Tolhurst 1999).

Methods

Fieldwork at Prumerberg and Lindscheid was conducted during the summer of 2007. Forest floors in these areas exhibit little natural relief at the scale of field fortifications and hence dug features were readily identified (Figs. 5 & 6).

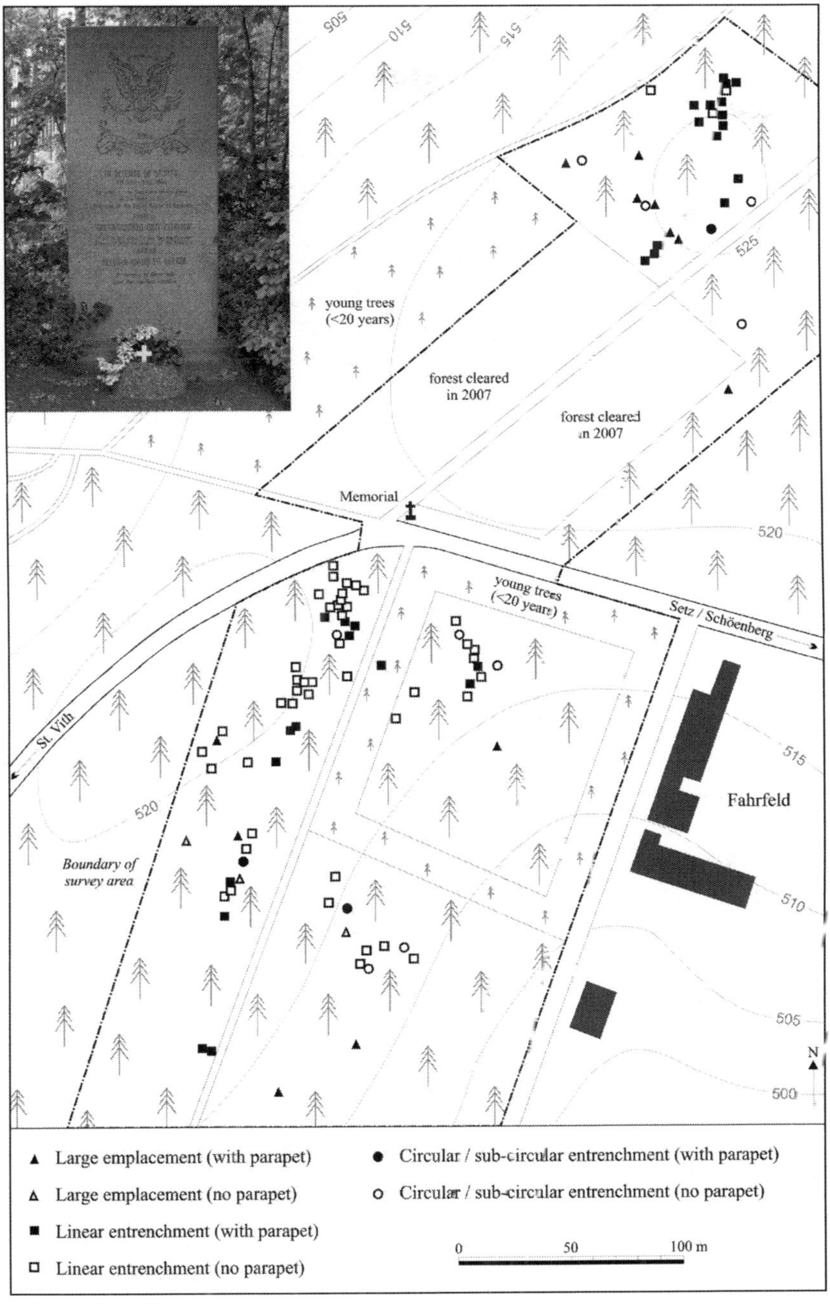

Fig. 3. Map of the Prumerberg study site showing location of all field fortifications recorded in this study. Also shown (inset) is the memorial to the 168th Engineer Combat Battalion. For location of study site see Fig. 2.

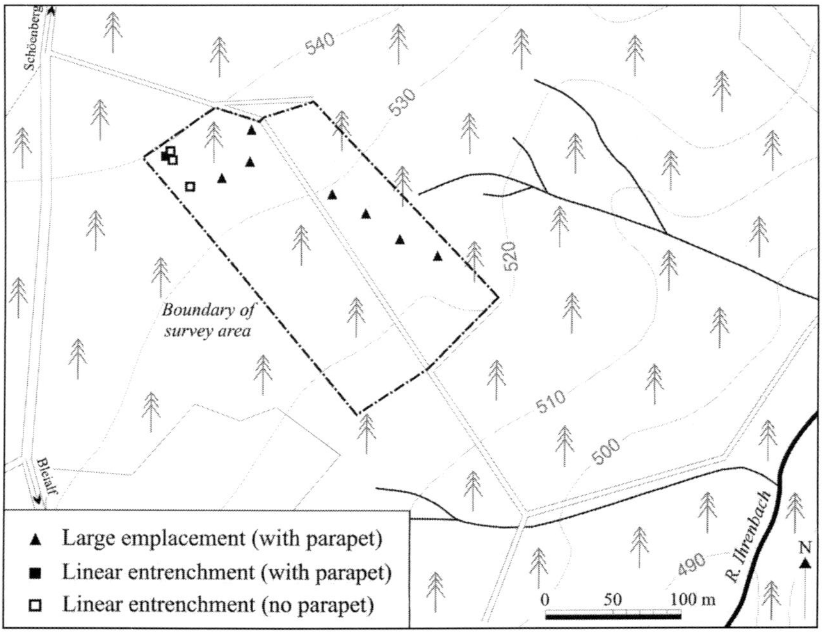

Fig. 4. Map of the Lindscheid study site showing location of all field fortifications recorded in this study. For location of study site see Fig. 2.

Survey commenced in the vicinity of identified features and was terminated in all directions when features were no longer in evidence. All features identified in the survey areas were located relative to road junctions using a laser rangefinder and measured for a- and b-axis length, a-axis orientation and maximum (unexcavated) depth to ground surface or, where present, the top of adjacent parapets. Development of a simple typology of features was made on the basis of planform dimensions and was informed by reference to field fortification terminology and specifications set out in US War Department *Field Manual FM5–15 (Field Fortifications)* published in February 1944 (Table 1). No attempt was made to excavate or disturb the ground surface in or adjacent to any of the features.

Results

A combined total of 116 discrete and well-preserved dug features were recorded in the study sites with an a-axis range of 9.4–1 m and an unexcavated depth range of 1.8–0.2 m (Table 2). The vast majority of features (105) were located at the Prumerberg study site where they flank NE-SW orientated forestry tracks up to 250 m to the north and south of the St. Vith–Setz

Fig. 5. Example of a large field fortification with a prominent berm at the Prumerberg study site near St.Vith (see Figs. 2 and 5 for location).

Fig. 6. Cluster of small linear entrenchments at the Prumerberg study site near St.Vith (see Figs. 2 and 5 for location).

Table 1. Dimensions for selected field fortifications specified by US War Department Field Manual FM5-15 Field Fortifications (1944) (see text for details).

Type	Diameter (cm)	a-axis (cm)	b-axis (cm)	Min. firestep depth (cm)	Parapet depth (cm)	notes
Infantry emplacements (hasty)						
One-man foxhole	–	107	61	122	15	a-axis parallel to front
Two-man foxhole	–	183	61	122	15	a-axis parallel to front
Prone shelter (individual)	–	183	61	61	15	not intended as a fire trench
Covered observation post	–	168	152	183	46	a-axis parallel to front; timber / earth cover
Infantry weapons emplacements						
30cal (light) horseshoe (first stage)	–	244	152	30	15	b-axis parallel to front
30cal (light) horseshoe (final stage)	–	229	198	122	15	a-axis parallel to front
30cal (light) two-man foxhole	–	183	61	122	15	two offset two-man foxholes
30cal (heavy) horseshoe	–	213	183	122	15	a-axis parallel to front
30cal (heavy) two-man foxhole	–	183	61	122	15	three two-man foxholes in T-shape configuration
30cal AA	122	–	–	91	15	all-around parapet
60mm mortar	–	152	122	107	15	a-axis parallel to front
60mm mortar two-man foxhole	–	183	61	122	15	two offset two-man foxholes
81mm mortar	–	183	122	137	15	a-axis parallel to front
Rocket launcher	91	–	–	91	15	plus 2 foxholes

Table 1. (*cont.*)

Type	Diameter (cm)	a-axis (cm)	b-axis (cm)	Min. firestep depth (cm)	Parapet depth (cm)	notes
37mm AT gun (circular-type)	335	–	–	76	76	all-around parapet
37mm AT gun	–	853	305	76	76	a-axis parallel to front; three-quarter parapet & ramp
57mm AT gun	–	564	610	61	91	fan-shaped emplacement with access ramp
105mm (M3) howitzer (circular-type)	579	–	–	61	76	includes access ramp
Field artillery emplacements						
Open pit ammunition shelter	–	229	168	122	30	horseshoe parapet
50cal AA	274	–	–	76	30	all-around parapet
105 & 155mm howitzers	732	–	–	61	46	Fan / circular emplacements with parapet and special trenches for shelter, ammunition, etc

	Prumerberg	Lindscheid
All recorded features		
Area surveyed	1 km^2	0.4 km^2
No of features	105	11
Long-axis (max-min)	7.2–1 m	9.4–2.3 m
Long-axis (mean)	2.9 m	5.2 m
Depth (max-min)	1.6–0.2 m	1.8–0.5 m
Depth (mean)	0.6 m	1.0 m
A/B ratios (max-min)	2.66–1.02	2.88–1.02
A/B ratios (mean)	1.58	1.66
Large emplacements		
No of features	15	7
Long-axis (max-min)	7.2–3.7 m	9.4–4.5 m
Long-axis (mean)	5.7 m	6.8 m
Depth (max-min)	1.6–0.8 m	1.8–0.9 m
Depth (mean)	1.22 m	1.3 m
A/B ratios (max-min)	1.60–1.02	1.59–1.02
A/B ratios (mean)	1.27	1.29
Rectilinear entrenchments		
No of features	78	4
Long-axis (max-min)	5.4–1.0 m	2.7–2.3 m
Long-axis (mean)	2.4 m	2.5 m
Depth (max-min)	0.9–0.2 m	0.6–0.5 m
Depth (mean)	0.45 m	0.53 m
A/B ratios (max-min)	2.67–1.22	2.88–1.80
A/B ratios (mean)	1.72	2.31
Circular / sub-circular entrenchments		
No of features	12	–
Long-axis (max-min)	3.1–1.3 m	–
Long-axis (mean)	2.42 m	–
Depth (max-min)	1.0–0.2 m	–
Depth (mean)	0.6m	–
A/B ratios (max-min)	1.17–1.03	–
A/B ratios (mean)	1.12	–

Table 2. Summary of field fortification dimensions for Prumerberg and Lindscheid study sites

road (Fig. 3). However, it is also noted that recent mechanised woodland clearance over the past 20 or so years, and especially in 2007, has occurred in the area immediately to the north of the trunk road over an area that amounts to approximately one-quarter of the survey site. Newly cleared forest has been machine-felled that has disturbed the forest floor to the extent that no field fortifications were evident. Only 11 features were recorded at Lindscheid where they form a localised cluster astride a forest track that branches off the Schöenberg–Bleialf road (Fig. 4).

Figure 7 shows the combined assemblages of dug features at Prumerberg and Lindscheid are characterised by a wide range of a- and b-axis dimensions that only rarely correspond closely to FM5–15 field fortification specifications. However, it is recognised that field manuals and contemporary doctrine were intended as guidelines only and that the nature and configuration of field fortifications will have varied according to unit practice (Rottman 2005) and in response to terrain, ground conditions and the perceived level and imminence of threat. Furthermore, features will have been subject to some degree of degradation over the past half-century and this will have acted to lower the surface relief of parapets, partially infill excavations and soften the edge definition (see Figs. 5 & 6). We also accept that the differentiation of field fortifications from shell craters may be difficult to resolve without recourse to archaeological excavation. Accordingly, the following analysis has adopted a threefold generic classification of features on the basis of overall size and shape as reflected in a/b ratios and is intended only as a provisional assessment of their possible origin and function.

(i) *Large Emplacements*

Large emplacements have a-axes between 9.4–3.7 m in length and are generally sub-rectangular or sub-circular in plan (e.g. Fig. 5). Of the 22 examples recorded, all except 3 have prominent berms or parapets and these account, at least in part, for the comparatively high internal depth measurements (between 1.6–0.8 m, Table 2). Parapets generally achieve near-complete enclosure of the internal emplacement, being punctuated by an access slot or ramp. The largest examples of this category were recorded at the Lindscheid study site where they constitute 7 of the 11 features identified (Fig. 4). Large emplacements most closely approximate the field manual guidelines for field artillery emplacements, especially 105/155 mm howitzers, 57 mm anti-tank (AT) guns and, to a lesser extent, 37 mm AT guns (Figure 7), although there is little consistency in the study area examples which span a wide range of a-axis and a/b ratio dimensions.

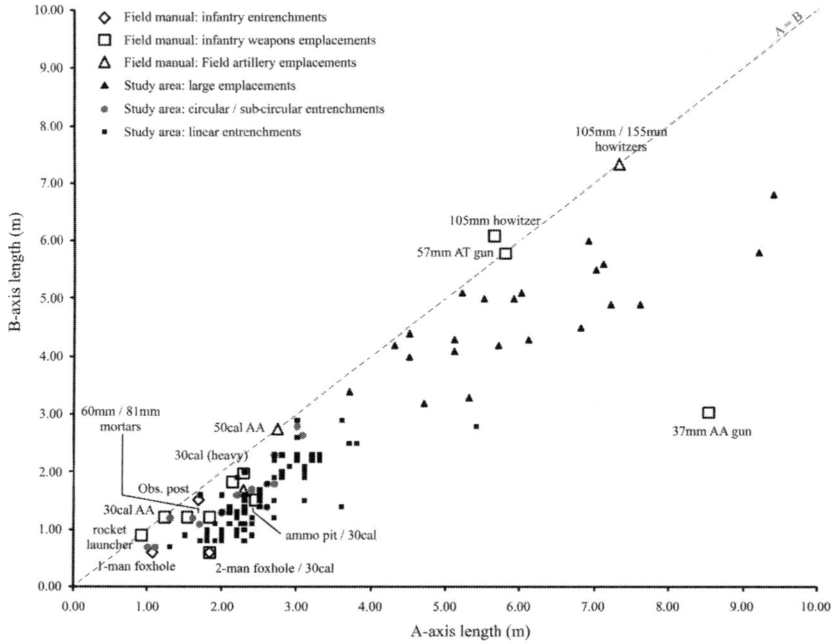

Fig. 7. Plot of A and B axis length for (i) recorded field fortifications at Prumerberg and Lindscheid, and (ii) examples of field fortifications as specified in US War Department Field Manual FM5–15 Field Fortifications (1944) (see text for details).

(ii) *Rectilinear Entrenchments*

Rectilinear entrenchments account for 82 of the total features recorded in the study area and all except 4 examples are located in the Prumerberg study site (Figs. 3 & 6; Table 2). One example exhibited an a-axis length of 5.4 m, but in general these features are less than 4 m in length and are differentiated on the basis of their broadly rectilinear planforms with a/b ratios in excess of 1.20 (Table 2). Depth recordings indicate that these features are shallower than the large emplacements (depths range between 0.9–0.2 m) and fewer than half of the examples were associated with subdued parapets. Where present, parapets are generally evident on one side of the entrenchment only. Rectilinear entrenchments are typically clustered within or near the regulation planform size range of infantry weapon emplacements (e.g. mortar and both light and heavy machine guns) and infantry entrenchments (e.g. two-man foxholes, prone shelters and observation posts; Fig. 7; Table 1).

(iii) *Circular and Sub-Circular Entrenchments / Shell Craters*

A total of 12 circular and sub-circular entrenchments / shell craters have been differentiated at Prumerberg on the basis of their planform morphology and a/b ratios of less than 1.2 (Table 2). Their a-axes range between 3.1–1.3 m and depths span a similar range to rectilinear entrenchments (1.0–0.2 m). Only 3 examples exhibited discontinuous parapets (Fig. 3). These features also cluster within the regulation planform size range of infantry weapon emplacements and infantry entrenchments (Fig. 7), but they include smaller examples that may represent one-man foxholes or rocket (bazooka) emplacements as well as shell-craters.

Rose diagrams showing a-axis orientation for features with a/b ratios greater than 1.2 are plotted in Figure 8. At Prumerberg this accounts for a total of 77 large emplacements and rectilinear entrenchments and here there is a general trend in orientation to the NE-SW, but with some features aligned broadly parallel to the St. Vith–Setz road (Fig. 3). Only 8 features at Lindscheid exhibit rectilinear planforms and here there is little evidence of a preferred orientation (Fig. 8).

Discussion

US Defensive Positions at Prumerberg

The disposition of field fortifications at Prumerberg is likely to have been initiated as the skirmish line established by Lieutenant-Colonel Riggs on the morning of 17 December (Tolhurst 1999), and may have been augmented by subsequent consolidation and the arrival of some reinforcements from the 7th Armoured Division later that afternoon. The positions are arrayed across a frontage of some 500 m where they occupy the undulating crest of a NE/SW ridge and the forward slopes that dip gently towards the southeast (Fig. 3). Linear entrenchments that comprise the majority of features are interpreted as two-man (or larger) foxholes that were broadly orientated to defend an attack from the southeast along the axis of the St. Vith–Setz road. These positions are typically disposed as mutually supporting clusters with individual features spaced between 1–10 m apart. In the northern extent of the study area, a cluster of linear entrenchments is located immediately behind the crest line on the reverse slope and may have been sited to provide flank protection or perhaps as a sheltered aid post or other non-firing position. Six of the 15 large emplacements at this site also cluster in the northern part of the study area in a linear array extending from the ridge crest some 60m down

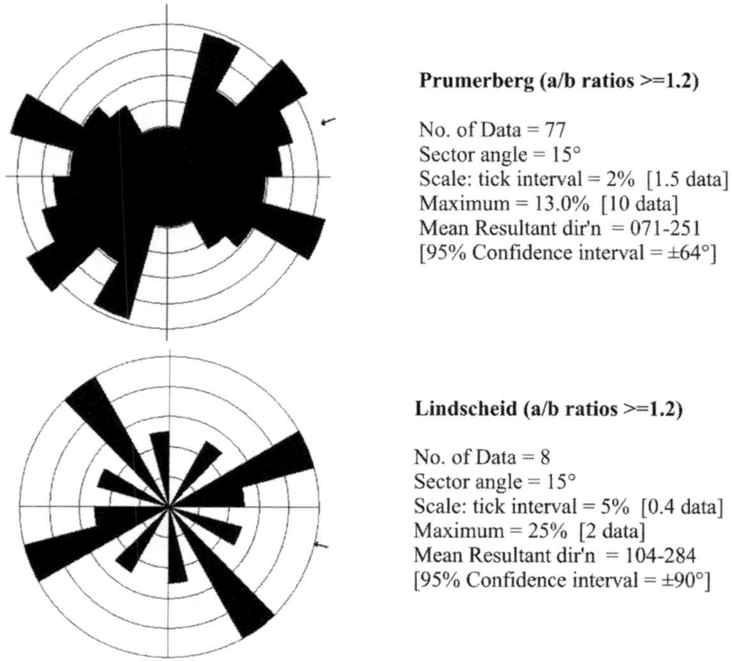

Fig. 8. Rose diagrams and summary of A-axis orientation for selected field fortifications at Prumerberg and Lindscheid (where ratio of A/B axes is equal or greater than 1.2; see text for details).

the gentle reverse slope to the northwest. Those emplacements without line-of-sight to the southeast may have housed mortars offering local fire support. The remainder of large emplacements evident at Prumerberg are distributed throughout the skirmish line; these are frequently positioned along the forward margin of the position facing the line of expected attack, but in contact with supporting positions not more than 40 m distant. Although it is difficult to ascribe a specific function to these large emplacements, it would seem likely that at least some examples mark the position of crew-served weapons requiring line-of-sight to the front (including heavy machine guns, 37 mm AT guns and bazookas) and described as being present by Whiting (1969) and Tolhurst (1999). Larger artillery pieces are unlikely to have been located within this front line sector but some local tank support at Prumerberg has been reported by Tolhurst (1999).

Estimates of initial US troop numbers at Prumerberg vary between 300 (Quarrie 2000) and 500 (Whiting 1969), but may be reviewed by attempting a first approximation of troop numbers based on surviving field fortifications at the locality. For hastily prepared defences, US doctrine generally preferred the use of two-man rather than one-man positions in order to allow for mutual support (Rottman 2005), and this is consistent with the pattern of fortifications at Prumerberg where nearly 90% of features have a-axes that equal or exceed the 1.8 m specified for two-man foxholes and larger positions (Tables 1 and 2). Table 3 provides an estimate of troop numbers based on a simple correlation of a-axis dimensions with the likely number of occupants, and this gives an approximate total of 239 soldiers at Prumerberg on the assumption that all positions were simultaneously occupied. It is accepted that these numbers are liable to be over-estimated where foxholes were dug to provide shelter for troops manning heavy weapons in the large emplacements, and for cases where shell craters have been interpreted here as foxholes. However, it is also noted that approximately one-quarter of the skirmish line at Prumerberg has been disturbed by woodland clearance (Fig. 3) and hence troop numbers will be under-estimated by a similar magnitude. This analysis would suggest that the field fortifications at Prumerberg are broadly consistent with the accounts of troop numbers given by previous authors; however, given that the numbers are liable to have been reinforced to some extent over the period between 17 and 21 December, we suggest that the initial deployment of engineers in this locality is perhaps likely to have been closer to Quarrie's (2000) estimate of 300 troops.

A-axis size (m)	Estimated no. of troops in occupation	No. of positions	Total no. of troops
Prumerberg			
1–1.4	1	5	5
1.5–3	2	66	132
3+	3	34	102
			Total: **239**
Lindscheid			
1–1.4	1	–	–
1.5–3	2	4	8
3+	3	7	21
			Total: **29**

Table 3. Estimated number of troops occupying surviving field fortifications at Prumerberg and Lindscheid study sites (see text for details)

For units at company strength of around 200 men, contemporary field manuals recommended a dispersal frontage of no more than 500 yards (457 m) in heavily wooded terrain (FM 7–10–44); at Prumerberg, troop numbers in the order of 250–300 occupied a frontage of some 500 m and hence lie comfortably within these guidelines. The depth of the skirmish line, at around 100–120 m, is significantly lower than the recommended (company-strength) maximum of 500 yards for open terrain (FM 7–10), but is likely to have been configured so as to occupy the forward slopes lying between the ridge crest and a forward line just inside the woodland margin to the southeast (at the present site of Fahrfeld farm) (Fig. 3). A compressed depth of sector is also consistent with field manual guidelines (e.g. FM 7–15 and FM 7–20) that specified close defensive fire positions in wooded areas with restricted observation and lines of fire. Accordingly, and allowing for the expedient nature of the initial deployment, the general pattern of field fortifications at Prumerberg appears to broadly conform to US doctrine for defensive operations in wooded terrain during the later stages of the war. Indeed, the position was of sufficient strength to resist 4 days of probing attacks by the *Volksgrenadiers* (albeit with the aid of artillery support from the rear) until succumbing to a large-scale German assault on 21 December. Accounts of this attack describe it as being preceded by intense artillery fire (Quarrie 2000), although comparatively few dug features at Prumerberg may be readily interpreted as shell craters (Table 2). During field survey of the 105 recorded features in this locality only 7 were tentatively interpreted as shell craters, and these may also have been degraded foxholes. These results are likely to reflect, at least in part, a high proportion of incoming artillery shells detonating as tree-bursts rather than impacting the ground surface. Further exploration of this issue will require a more extensive survey coupled with excavation of selected dug features.

Field Fortifications at Lindscheid

Field fortifications in the Lindscheid study area are relatively few in number but include the largest examples of emplacements identified in this study (Table 2; Fig. 4). A total of 7 large emplacements at this site lie close to a forest track that branches off the Schöenberg–Bleialf road along a general NW-SE alignment and are typically spaced some 20–30 m apart (Fig. 4). Also present is a cluster of 4 linear entrenchments located at the NW end of the emplacement group. No features at Lindscheid were interpreted as shell craters and, notwithstanding the possibility of tree bursts (see above), there is no evidence of this area as having been the focus of artillery bombardment. Tolhurst (1999) describes the woods on the eastern side of the Schöenberg–Bleialf road as being occupied by elements of the 106th Division and its supporting artillery; in particular, this locality is known to have been the temporary site for batteries of the 589th Field Artillery Battalion prior to their withdrawal through

Schöenberg on 17 December. The 589th FAB was equipped with 105 mm howitzers and it is perhaps most likely that the Lindscheid fortifications reflect an associated battery position. Troop numbers for this position can be estimated at 29 using the criteria developed in Table 3 and are well below the typical battery complement of around 100 troops. However, in temporary positions it is possible that the gun crews (numbering 10 per gun) were dug in within their emplacements rather than nearby foxholes.

Summary

In the final analysis, these fortifications may be viewed as an unusually detailed record of the improvised battlefield response of troops and their commanders to a confused and rapidly unfolding tactical situation. Analyses of these engagements and the wider campaign suggest that the stubborn defence of St. Vith not only caused serious delays to the advance of the Fifth Panzer Army, but also prevented the local road network being used to relieve and by-pass stalled spearheads of the Sixth Panzer Army to the north (Zaloga 2003). At the time, however, the men engaged in tactical battles in the forests around St. Vith and Schöenberg probably had little appreciation or understanding of the larger strategic-scale development of the offensive. The scale issues that follow from the impact of tactical operations on overall strategy are further explored in Harrison and Passmore (2008). At the local scale, however, and following the discussion by Freeman (2001), the battlefield landscapes of the Ardennes forests can be argued to provide a very immediate example of the unique contribution that archaeology can offer to the exploration of the extremes of human experience.

It is therefore unfortunate to report the evidence of extensive local disturbance of forest floors within the area of battlefield remains at Prumerberg (and immediately adjacent to the memorial to the 168th Engineer Combat Battalion) by recent (ca. 2007) mechanised felling operations. It is concluded that there is an urgent need both to establish the scale and character of this archaeological resource before it is further disturbed or permanently lost, and to develop frameworks that can secure—where possible and appropriate—the future management of this heritage resource.

Conclusions

Reinforced concrete structures associated with static WW2 defensive positions in Western Europe have frequently survived in the modern landscape and are proving an increasingly well-studied aspect of the military and cultural heritage of this period. Yet the key battles of the Western European theatre were typically fought beyond these fixed emplacements and the field evidence of these relatively mobile engagements is rarely preserved and documented. The results of a reconnaissance survey in 1.4 km^2 of the Ardennes forests in the St. Vith–Schöenberg area have demonstrated, however, that temporary field fortifications and shell craters have locally survived in woodland that has escaped intensive post-war management. A total of 116 discrete features have been identified which in their disposition correspond well to documented accounts of US defensive actions during the early days of Germany's last major offensive in the West in December 1944. Although these earthworks have experienced some level of post-war degradation they remain readily identifiable on the forest floors. However, the study has not attempted to disturb or excavate any features and this, in combination with the tendency of troops to depart from contemporary field manual specifications for field fortifications, renders it difficult to evaluate the function of the recorded earthworks. Nevertheless, variations in the size and to some extent the orientation of features suggests that simple foxholes may be differentiated from larger pits that probably served as heavy weapons emplacements and(or) observation posts. They also permit a first approximation of troop numbers.

This baseline archaeological audit thus provides an illustration of the potential for such studies to explore the hurried deployment of field fortifications in the face of unexpected and imminent threat, while also serving to inform a comparison of battlefield remains with military unit histories, contemporary military doctrine and published accounts of the local conduct of battle. It is to be hoped that the work will stimulate a wider awareness of the value of recording and managing the region's WW2 battlefield heritage in the face of future development pressures, and especially the immediate threat posed by mechanised forestry operations.

Acknowledgements

The authors wish to thank the anonymous reviewers of the manuscript for their helpful and stimulating comments.

References

Allcorn, W 2003 *The Maginot Line 1928–45*. Osprey: Oxford.

Bell, M 1997 'The ghosts of place', *Theory & Society* 26, 813–36.

Bull, N and Panton, D 2001 'Conservation of historic battlefield terrain: drafting the Vimy Charter', *in* Freeman, P W M & Pollard, A (eds.) *Fields of Conflict: Progress and Prospect in Battlefield Archaeology*. BAR International Series 958, 269–74. Archaeopress: Oxford.

Cavanagh, W C C 2001 *A Tour of the Bulge Battlefield*. Pen and Sword: Barnsley.

Cole, H M 1964 *The Ardennes: The Battle of the Bulge*. Washington: Office of the Chief of Military History, Department of the Army.

Doyle, P 2001 'Geology as an interpreter of Great War battle sites', *in* Freeman, P W M & Pollard, A (eds.) *Fields of Conflict: Progress and Prospect in Battlefield Archaeology*. BAR International Series 958, 237–52. Archaeopress: Oxford.
Doyle, P & Bennett, M R 1997 'Military Geography: terrain evaluation and the British Western Front, 1914–1918', *Geog J* 163 (1), 1–24.
Doyle, P, Bostyn, F, Barton, P & Vandewalle, J 2001 'The underground war 1914–18: the geology of the Beecham dugout, Passchendaele, Belgium', *Proc Geologists Assoc* 112, 263–274.
Everett, M E *et al.* 2006 'Geophysical investigation of the June 6, 1944 D-Day invasion site at Pointe du Hoc, Normandy, France', *Near Surface Geophysics*, 4(5), 289–304.
Field Manual FM 5–15; Field Fortifications (1944). US War Department.
Field Manual FM 7–10; Infantry Rifle Company, Infantry Regiment (1944). US War Department.
Field Manual FM 7–15; Heavy Weapons Company, Rifle Regiment (1942). US War Department.
Field Manual FM 7–20; Rifle Battalion (1942). US War Department.
Freeman, P 2001 'Introduction: issues concerning the archaeology of battlefields', *in* Freeman, P W M & Pollard, A (eds.) *Fields of Conflict: Progress and Prospect in Battlefield Archaeology*. BAR International Series 958, 1–10. Archaeopress: Oxford.
Gough, P 2007 'Contested memories, contested site: Newfoundland and its unique heritage on the Western Front', *The Round Table* 96 (393), 693–705.
Harrison, S & Passmore, D G in press 'The Ardennes campaigns of 1940 and 1944: some theoretical considerations on the role of topography', *in* Nathaniel, P *et al.* (eds.) *Military Geology and Geography; History and Technology*. Nottingham: LQ Press.
Holyoak, V 2001 'Airfields as battlefields, aircraft as an archaeological resource: British military aviation in the first half of the C20th', *in* Freeman, P W M & Pollard, A (eds.) *Fields of Conflict: Progress and Prospect in Battlefield Archaeology*. BAR International Series 958, 253–64. Archaeopress: Oxford.
Lowry, B 2004. *British Home Defences 1940–45*. Osprey: Oxford.
Mallmann Showell, J P 2002 *Hitler's U-Boat Bases*. US Naval Institute Press.
Quarrie, B 2000 *The Ardennes Offensive; V Panzer Armee, Central Sector*. Osprey: Oxford.
Reynolds, M 1999 *Men of Steel: I SS Panzer Corps, The Ardennes and Eastern Front 1944–45*. Spellmount: Staplehurst.
Rose, E P F & Pareyn, C 1998 'British applications of military geology for 'Operation Overlord' and the battle in Normandy, France, 1944', *in* Underwood, J R, Jr. & Guth, P L (eds.) *Military Geology in War and Peace*. Geological Society of America Reviews in Engineering XIII, 55–75. Boulder: Colorado.
Rose, E P F, Clatworthy, J C & Nathanail, C P 2006 'Specialist maps prepared by British military geologists for the D-Day landings and operations in Normandy, 1944', *Cartographic J*, 43 (2), 117–143.
Rottman, G L 2004 *German Field Fortifications 1939–45*. Osprey: Oxford.
—— 2005 *US World War II and Korean War Field Fortifications 1941–53*. Osprey: Oxford.
Saunders, N J 2002 'Excavating memories: archaeology and the Great War, 1914–2001', *Antiquity* 76, 101–8.
—— 2004 *Matters of Conflict: Material Culture, Memory and the First World War*. Abingdon: Routledge.
Schofield, J 2001 'D-Day sites in England: an assessment', *Antiquity* 75, 77–83.
—— 2005 *Combat Archaeology: Material Culture and Modern Conflict*. Duckworth: London.
Schofield, J, Johnson, W G & Beck, C M (eds.) 2002 *Matériel Culture: The Archaeology of Twentieth Century Conflict*. Routledge: London.
Short, N 2004. *Germany's West Wall: The Siegfried Line*. Osprey: Oxford.
Tolhurst, M 1999 *St. Vith: US 106th Infantry Division*. Battleground Europe Series (Battle of the Bulge). Cooper/Pen & Sword: Barnsley.
Whiting, C 2001 *Decision at St. Vith*. Spellmount Ltd: Staplehurst.
Williamson, G 2003 *U-Boat Bases and Bunkers 1941–45*. Osprey: Oxford.
Woodward, R 2004 *Military Geographies*. Blackwell: Oxford.
Zaloga, S J 2003 *St. Vith and the Northern Shoulder 1944: Battle of the Bulge Pt. 1*. Osprey: Oxford.
—— 2005. *D-Day Fortifications in Normandy*. Osprey: Oxford.
—— 2007. *The Atlantic Wall (1)*. Osprey: Oxford.

ARCHAEOLOGICAL INVESTIGATION OF MILITARY SITES ON INCHKEITH ISLAND

TONY POLLARD & IAIN BANKS

Abstract

In August 2001, a programme of survey and trial excavation was carried out on the island of Inchkeith in the Firth of Forth in Scotland. The work was carried out as part of the first series of the BBC TV series *Two Men in a Trench*, and examined the WWII defences, together with some of the Victorian defences and a midden that probably dates to the 16th century.

Introduction

During the last two weeks of August 2001, five small trenches were excavated on Inchkeith in the Firth of Forth (Figures 1 and 2); each trench targeted a specific feature of the island's military archaeology. Trench 1 was excavated in the base of an impressive rock cut ditch, which delineated the southern side of the Victorian fort located on the southern tip of the island. This trench revealed shallow soil deposits covering the flat bottom of the rock cut ditch and some later modification to the stone built caponier attached to the fort itself. Trench 2 was a half-section through earth and rubble deposits that filled a sunken concrete feature that had served as a battery command post. Excavation revealed that much of the fill was formed from demolition debris, possibly from the roof of the structure, while the concrete walls of the command post were still adorned with stencilled notices which provide some insight into its function. Trench 3 was cut across a section of a fire trench which occupies a cliff top on the eastern side of the island. Excavation revealed two phases of trench digging—the first and most complex possibly created during the late 19th century, while the second may date to World War II. Trench 4 was placed across a cut terrace, also on the eastern side of the island, and revealed an iron gun mounting set into a concrete base. This feature relates to a gun used for artillery practice during the first decade of the 20th century. The fifth and final trench on the island took the form of a cleaned back section face across a shell midden deposit on the beach on the north easterly shore of the island. A small column sample recovered a variety of marine shells and also the leg bones of a small horse. This shell midden was the same feature located by Grieve in 1870 and probably relates to the 16th century occupation of the island.

 DOI: 10.1163/157407808X382782

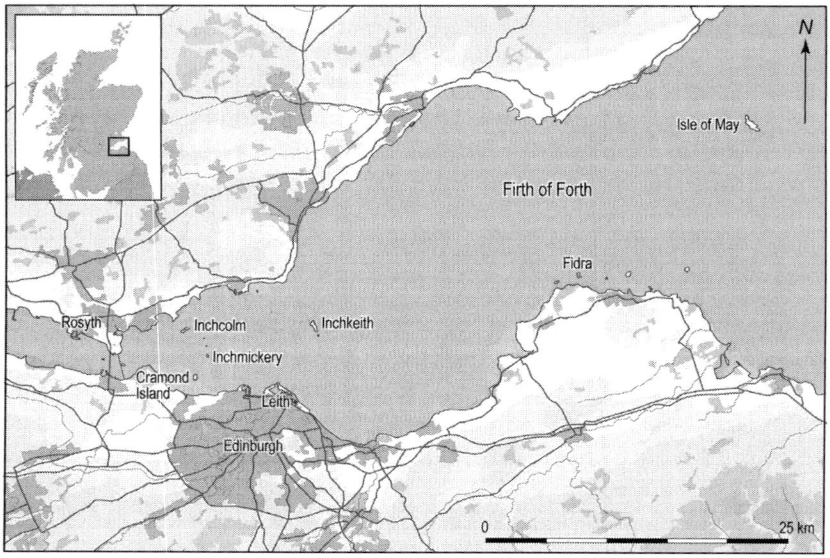

Fig. 1. Islands in the Firth of Forth

Project Background

The archaeological investigation reported here formed the basis for one episode of *Two Men in a Trench*, a six part television documentary series focusing on military and battlefield archaeology. The programmes were made by London based independent production company, Optomen Television Ltd, under commission from BBC2. The series was accompanied by a book (Pollard & Oliver 2002), which presented summaries of the projects to a non-academic audience. The aim of this paper is to provide a more detailed report on the Inchkeith project, and it is intended that the other projects will receive the same treatment in due course.

Historical Background

Since Roman times, the Firth of Forth (Figure 1) has been an important anchorage and commercial harbour, with its deep water channel and proximity to Edinburgh providing an obvious focus for maritime activity, serving as a vital off-loading point and sheltered anchorage for ships plying trade routes through the North Sea and the Baltic. It was also to serve as an important naval anchorage, a role that was formalised in the early 20th century with the creation of the naval dockyards at Rosyth. These factors made the Forth a site of considerable strategic importance during times of war. In the

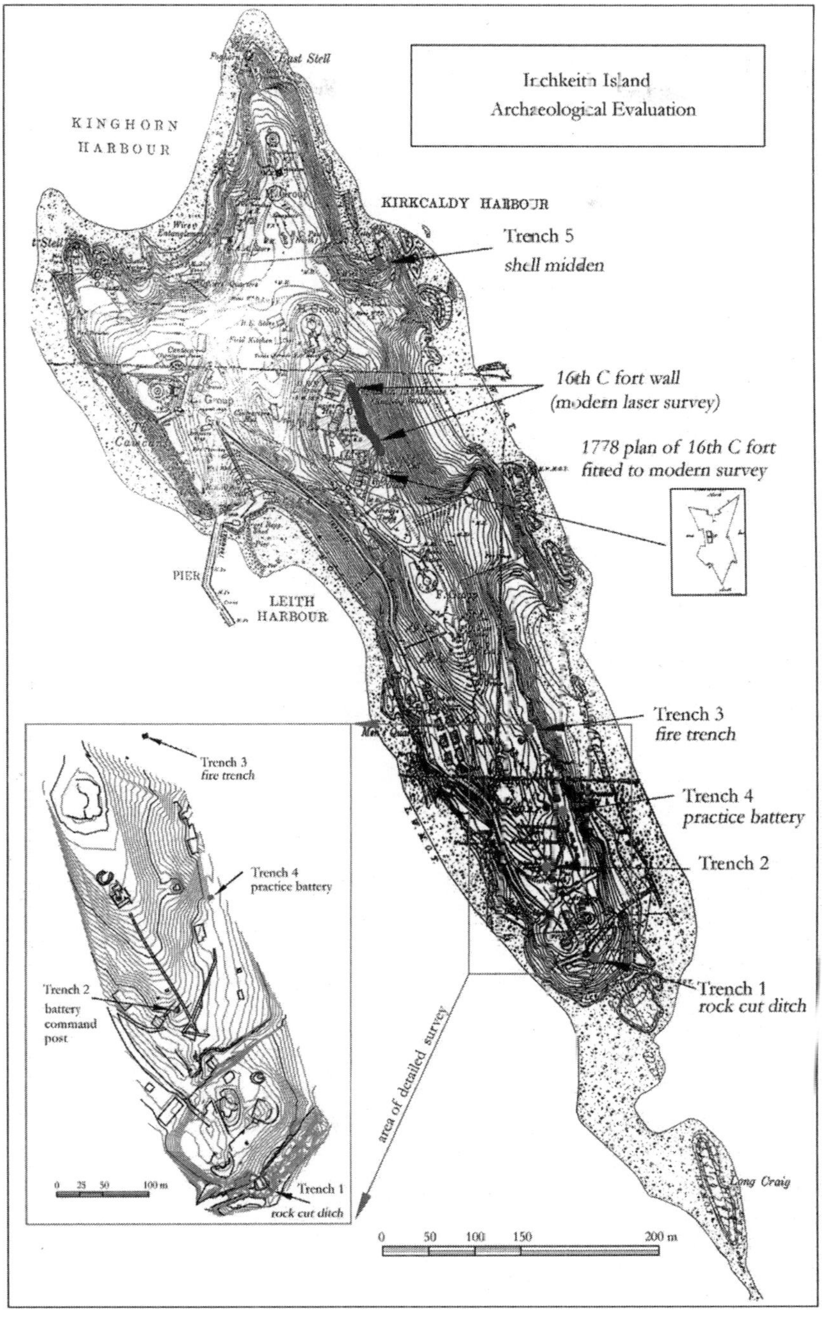

Fig. 2. Ordnance Survey map showing installations and trench locations

early 16th century, King James IV ordered a tower to be constructed on the island of Inchgarvie and, up until World War II, there were continued episodes of fortification. The islands also served other functions. It was to Inchkeith that James IV exiled two babies with a mute woman and her two young children to see which language they would speak; according to Pitscottie, they too grew up mute. During his reign the island was also used as a place of isolation for victims of syphilis and plague, a role that was reprised in 1799 when a Russian fleet off-loaded plague victims, most of whom were buried on the island.

The first fort was built on the island of Inchkeith by the English in the mid-16th century, after beating the Scots at the Battle of Pinkie in 1547. During the regency of the Mary of Guise, following the death of her husband James V in 1542, Leith had become a French enclave (see Pollard, this volume) and in 1549 the fort on Inchkeith, garrisoned by English and Italian troops, was taken by storm by a French and Scottish amphibious force. Despite later attempts to retake it, the fort was to remain in French hands until the Treaty of Edinburgh of 1560 saw the departure of French troops from Scotland. Little of this early fort (Figure 2) survives today, following its slighting in 1567 and because the area of the fort was taken over by the Northern Lighthouse Board in the 19th century. A vestigial stretch of wall can still be seen at the top of the cliff on the eastern side and a possibly later gateway bearing the arms of Mary Queen of Scots still stands within the complex of lighthouse buildings.

The centuries following this French adventure saw continuing fortification of the Firth of Forth. In 1656, a citadel was constructed at Leith during the Cromwellian period. The Napoleonic period saw the creation of gun batteries at several locations, including Inchcolm in 1795 and Inchgarvie in 1806 (Saunders 1984) and a Martello tower at Black Rocks, Leith in around 1812 (Smith 1985).

Following the Crimean War in the 1850s, Anglo-French relations reached a new low and the threat of invasion from the Continent was once again taken very seriously. Although the War Department focused its attentions on the south of the British Isles, the most likely target of any sea-borne attack, there were moves to increase the defensive capabilities of coastal military installations further north. In 1858, the report of the Committee of Home Defences included a proposal dating from 1855 for the siting of two heavy gun batteries on Inchkeith, allowing interlocking fire with a third battery at Kinghorn on the Fife coast (Smith 1985). This proposal was acted upon, and in 1861 plots of land on the island were purchased from the Buccleuch Estate for the purpose of constructing three forts, known as east, west and south, while land at Kinghorn was purchased in 1863. However, work on the forts was delayed, perhaps due to lack of funds, but the threat from France was also reduced by her humiliating defeat in the Franco-Prussian War of 1870–71.

By the late 1870s, however, there was increasing concern over a potential alliance between France and Russia, and this was reflected in the War Department's purchase of the entire island of Inchkeith in 1879. By this time, those tasked with defending the British Isles fell into two schools; those who saw the Navy as the first and last line of defence, the so-called 'Blue Water School', and those who placed more reliance on coastal defence and the role of land forces in the face of a landing invasion force. This latter group clearly had the upper hand in 1888 when a National Defence Bill was drawn up to speed the mobilization of ground troops, including the militia and volunteers, as it was realised that the Royal Navy could not stand up to both superpowers coupled with advances in high velocity propellants that made earlier ships obsolete (Saunders 1989). By 1889, however, the Naval Defence Act signalled victory for those supporting the Navy, with the construction of no less than eight new battleships, 38 cruisers and various other types. There was also a parallel increased awareness of threat posed by maritime raiders on commercial ports, including the Forth and the Tyne, and in 1878 calls for the former's defence reached such a pitch that the ambitious programme of defence construction first proposed 20 years previously was put into action and building work began on Inchkeith.

After a number of conflicts in Europe and beyond, it had been realised that earthen glacis slopes fronting concrete barbette gun positions were a much more effective form of defence against the ever-improving destructive power of high explosive artillery shells and the increasing accuracy of long-range, high angle fire than castle-like stone defences. In short, what had been bomb proof in the 1860s was far from such by the 1880s (Saunders 1989, 195). In the British Isles, this pragmatic shift in tactical philosophy was given further impetus by the outcome of the British Navy's bombardment of the barbette and glacis parapet artillery defences at Alexandria, Egypt in 1882. This heavy bombardment from the sea was later found to have caused relatively little damage to the fortifications and the guns within them. Barbette emplacements provided small, low-lying targets while the carefully angled earth slopes which fronted them caused incoming shells to ricochet over their targets. The effectiveness of this type of fortification was to be tested at Inchkeith in 1884, when the western fort was subject to heavy bombardment from the sea during a well-publicised experiment. A variety of weapons, including artillery and machine guns were fired from HMS Sultan (which had seen action at Alexandria) at one of the barbette emplacements (No. 2 battery in the western fort—Plate 1), which was provided with wooden cut outs to stand in for the gun crew. The results were somewhat inconclusive, with the jamming of guns on the ship

Plate 1. West fort taken from east, Victorian structure with later additions

reducing the effectiveness of the fusillade; though some hits on the dummy crew and the emplaced gun were recorded (a full report on the experiment can be found in document WO 396/2 in the National Archives).

The forts (Figure 2) were designed by Colonel John Yarberry Moggridge, and included glacis parapets and concrete barbette emplacements along with vaulted casemated barracks, narrow ditches and musketry caponiers. These latter elements at least in general appear to be much in keeping with the designs adopted by the 1859 Royal Commission (Saunders 1989, 202). The casemates and tunnels which are a characteristic of the forts give them an almost subterranean character, with magazines located deep within a system of chambers and corridors. At the south fort at least, the chain driven hoist used to carry ammunition from the magazines up to the guns can still be seen today (Plate 2).

The construction contract for Inchkeith went to Messrs. Hill & Co. of Gosport, who in the 1860s built the Royal Commission forts in the Solent. The work itself, which must have been arduous to say the least, was carried out by gangs of navvies working 14 hours a day, 6 days a week (Smith 1985, 92). Construction of the three forts on Inchkeith was completed in 1880 but they were not armed until the following year, when four 10-inch rifled muzzle loading guns were mounted, one each at the east and west forts and two in the south fort.

Plate 2. Ammunition hoist in south fort

As the 19th century drew to a close, there had been a dramatic shift in strategic importance from the south of Britain, which had been the natural target for French raiders, to the north-east where the threat was now more likely to come from the direction of Russia. As early as 1882, the Morley

Committee recommended that the defences of the Forth be upgraded once more, as it had also done for the ports on the Clyde, the Tay and for Aberdeen. The form of this upgrade would be the establishment of an inner line of defence, with guns to be mounted on Inchmickery and Leith Tower. By 1884, however, the proposed inner line had shifted further to the west, to North and South Queensferry. The Forth was further protected from attack by the laying of underwater mines, which was well underway by 1887, when a report quoted the sum of £6,937 having been spent on the programme with a further £19,163 required to complete the task (Smith 1985, 95).

The importance of the Forth further increased with the completion of the rail bridge in 1890, and by 1902, the proposed inner and outer line of defence had been established; the inner was served by batteries not only at Queensferry, which had been constructed by 1901, but also on Inchgarvie, the island which supported a leg of the bridge. By the turn of the century, Germany was providing yet another threat, with fears of invasion reaching almost fever pitch. In response to this, a series of enquiries was set up to assess the potential threat of invasion, and as a result of the first of these, held in 1903, the go-ahead was given for the construction of a naval dockyard at Rosyth, to the west of the bridge. Until then, there had been no Royal Navy base further north than the Medway, but with the rapid growth of the German High Seas Fleet and the threat this posed to the North Sea, this situation was no longer tenable. Not only was Rosyth to be Scotland's first naval base, but it was to become the most important in the British Isles. Following an announcement in Parliament by Balfour in March 1903, work on the base began in 1909 and it was proclaimed fully operational in 1916, by which time it was to serve as home port for the British Home and Grand Fleets, although the latter was to have a northern base at Scapa Flow.

The forts on Inchkeith were regularly re-armed as new types of guns were introduced. By 1891, the muzzle loaders in the west and east forts had been replaced by 6-inch breech loaders (BLs). These were mounted on disappearing carriages which after firing dropped the guns into a pit and allowed the most precarious operation for a gunner, reloading, to be carried out under cover. In 1892, a 9.2-inch gun was mounted between the lighthouse and the east fort and the same year, two 4.7 Quick Firing guns (QFs), with their rapid rate of fire most suited to defence against fast-moving cruisers and torpedo boats, were mounted in new emplacements to the north and south of the lighthouse (Smith 1985, 97). The last of the muzzle loaders were removed from the south fort in 1899 and replaced by a pair of 6-inch BL Mark VII guns.

Just ten years after their completion, guns were being mounted outside the forts, which may suggest that they were already regarded as redundant. These external batteries, along with those retained in the three forts, were to provide the basis for the six battery groups which were in place by the end of the 19th century and were to serve through both world wars. This expansion reflected a more holistic approach to the defence of the Forth and the abandonment of the self-contained principal. Installations became interactive rather than self-reliant. The batteries were part of a greater whole, each an element of what was to become known as 'Fortress Forth'.

In January 1900, these were given the following designations: A group (south fort), B group (to north of A group), F. group (between B group and lighthouse), H group (east fort), L group (west fort—Plate 2) and M group (northern tip of island). At the time of the outbreak of World War I, the only fort to have serviceable guns in place was the east fort (H group), which by then housed a 9.2-inch BL Mark X, as did battery groups B and F. Hostilities soon brought about a change to this situation, however, and in February 1915, two 4.6-inch BL Mark VII guns were mounted in the south fort (A group) and two in M group. One of these latter pair was soon thereafter moved to the west fort (L group) and the armament of this emplacement was bolstered further by the addition of two further 6-inch BL Mark VII guns, which had been received in September 1916.

The lighthouse was constructed in 1803 inside the remains of the original 16th century fort on the highest point of the island (a position which could compromise all of the forts should it be taken by an invader). The lighthouse was permanently manned up until the 1980s when it was automated.

With the move outside the forts came the need for accommodation blocks and barracks. By 1891, the small village of houses that served as the main quarters, and included married quarters, had been constructed across the terrace in the south eastern part of the island (Plate 3). This situation remained little changed until at least 1910, but some time after then but before 1919, a substantial barrack complex was constructed on the low lying ground to the west of the lighthouse and to the east of the west fort. The pre-fabricated facilities included latrines, officer's quarters a Garrison Institute and even a YMCA hut, both of the latter providing recreation facilities, food and basic home comforts prior to the foundation of the NAAFI in 1921. This complex was augmented and in part replaced by the final phase of accommodation construction on the island, which is shown on a map entitled *Layout of Hutting*, dating to 24 January 1939 (WO 192/251). The main expansion was to the north, where 15 living huts were built in addition to two huts specifically for the use of the Royal Engineers, a Sergeant's Mess, latrines and urinals, an Infantry cookhouse and a Royal Artillery cookhouse (Plate 4—WWII aerial photograph).

A further four accommodation huts for the Royal Artillery, along with ablutions and latrines, were also built at this time on the southern part of the

Plate 3. Huts on west side of island, harbour in background and west fort

island, just to the north of the south fort. Just a little further to the north, the pre-existing men's quarters area was extended with the addition of three more huts, one each for the infantry, the Royal Engineers and the Royal Artillery.

In general, these later buildings have not survived at all well. The core of the accommodation complex in the north part of the island is partially upstanding, but the buildings are undoubtedly in a dangerous condition. Those furthest to the north and south have been entirely demolished. At the extreme southern end of the island, the only building relating to the Second World war phase of construction that has survived to any extent is the latrine block, but even this only survives as a collapsed (?demolished) structure. The older stone-built structures have generally fared better, especially in the area of the original Men's Quarters. However, none of these buildings has intact roofs and serious decay and collapse must eventually result while they are left in this condition.

World War II was to the most intensive period of military activity for the Firth of Forth. Batteries were re-equipped and new ones created, while the outer line of defences pushed as far east as Fidra, where a 6-inch battery was in place by 1941. Batteries on the north and south shores and on most of the islands bristled with guns and lights of various kinds. New batteries were created at sites such as Charles Hill, a former militia camp and north shore

Plate 4. 1941 aerial photograph taken from south (courtesy of Royal Commission on the Ancient and Historical Monuments of Scotland)

anchorage point for the World War I anti-submarine boom, where in early 1940 a twin QF 6-pdr 10 cwt gun was mounted, along with three searchlight emplacements and the requisite engines. The anti-torpedo boom was upgraded and an anti-coastal motorboat boom extended along the top of it (Heddle & Morris 1997). This boom, which passed through Inchcolm and terminated at Cramond, lay to the east of the Rosyth boom, laid in 1938. At Cramond on the south shore, the World War I defences were upgraded and new guns installed, along with new light installations to cover the south channel. Fixed torpedo tubes were in place at Burntisland and Methil. As always, the latest technology played a role and an experimental ASDIC (anti-submarine detection indicator loop) was put in place off the Isle of May. Airfields on both sides of the Firth took on a new importance and on 16 October 1939, Spitfires from RAF Drem and RAF Turnhouse engaged German bombers over the Forth, a landmark combat that heralded the beginning of the air war over Britain.

Inchkeith saw its most intensive period of active service during the early years of World War II, when it served as HQ for 505th (Forth) Coast Regiment RA. At the height of its service, the island was host to a garrison of almost 600 men, hence the need for the extended accommodation facilities described above.

No reference to the island's role in WWII can go without reference to the notorious events of 21 February 1940, when an Admiralty trawler strayed dangerously close to a minefield. Unable to raise the vessel by radio, the gunners in the southern battery fired a practice round across the boat's bow. Like a skimmed stone, the round bounced on the surface of the water and hurtled on to Leith, where it crashed through the wall of a tenement before coming to rest in a garden shed. Fortunately, no one was injured, and in some re-tellings of what is locally remembered as the 'Battle of Salamander Street,' the projectile was mailed back to the garrison on the island (Pollard & Oliver 2002, 305).

In 1943, with the war entering a new offensive phase, the defences of the Forth were reduced, in an exercise known as 'Operation Floodtide' (Heddle & Morris 1997). The inner defence line, including Cramond, Inchcolm and Charles Hill, was stepped down and the equipment placed on a care and maintenance basis. The garrison on Inchkeith, which had continued to serve an important training role, was reduced and many of its gunners went on to serve in North Africa (Grant, pers comm). Unlike the majority of other installations, Inchkeith remained in active service in the years following World War II and provided a training facility during the period of National Service, with the final programme of disarming taking place in 1953.

Documentary Sources

Historical research plays an essential role in any attempt to understand historic military sites and every effort was made to consult as many of the available sources as possible, however limited. A number of informative works on the history of the Forth defences have appeared over the last twenty years (e.g. Saunders 1984; Smith 1985; Heddle & Morris 1994); relatively few additional original documents relating to the 20th century use of the island came to light during the project. From World War II, the most notable documents are probably the standing orders which give details of the garrison disposition, procedures for stand-to in the case of emergency, disposition of weapons and so on. Among this limited batch of documents are also the army's own history of the occupation and development of the island, beginning in 1879 with the purchase of the island by the War Department.

Aerial photographs take on a special resonance in the case of 20th century military sites, as many of the photographs were taken for military reasons by both the Royal Air Force and the German Luftwaffe. The photographs taken of Inchkeith by the RAF in 1941 (Plate 4) show an island densely populated by semi-subterranean fortifications and more traditional buildings—the majority of the latter represented by barracks and other garrison facilities for the hundreds of men stationed on the island in the early part of World War II.

It is fortunate that early 20th century detailed plans survive for at least the south fort on Inchkeith survive, having originally been produced by the Fortification Design Branch (presumably part of the War Department). These are not original blueprints but were created as record plans in 1901 and provide not only detailed plans of the battery as it appeared then but also notes on changes made to the structure as far back as 1898.

Perhaps the most important cartographic document is a highly detailed Ordnance Survey map of Inchkeith Island, which was originally drawn up in 1891 (Figure 2). The published map was then updated and re-issued on at least two later occasions in 1909/10 and in 1919. There are, however, examples of the 1910 map with hand-drawn alterations made in 1915. This map was designed for military use and shows the various fortifications and other installations on the island in some detail. Reference to this map, which essentially shows the development of fortifications and facilities from the 1880s up to the immediate aftermath of World War I, alongside the study of the 1941 aerial photographs, has provided vital information on the function and chronology of features investigated as part of this project. Some plans relating to World War II do exist, including the plan of new accommodation blocks drawn up in January 1939. More may come to light as researchers continue to take an interest in the military history of the area. A more fragile resource, however, and just as important as the consultation of documents, is the testimony of ex-military personnel who were actually stationed on the island during World War II: most notable for this project was Dr Douglas Grant, formerly a Captain in the Royal Artillery, who provided much in the way of personal insight which would otherwise have been unavailable. It is worth considering that this is a resource that diminishes annually, and within a couple of decades will have been lost unless it has been recorded.

Fieldwork Results

Trench 1—rock-cut ditch (NT 2958 8224)

Three forts were constructed on the island in the late 1870s and early 1880s—each one self-contained and capable of defending itself in the event of either or both of its counterparts being overwhelmed by an enemy. The main function of the forts was to provide secure platforms for heavy artillery that served to protect the sea-ways of the Forth. Today, these forts are perhaps the finest examples of their kind in the British Isles, although there is some doubt as to how much of the original east fort survives. The most southerly of the forts (Figure 2) stands out as being easiest to understand and interpret as a standalone defensive work. The fort sits upon an island within the island, created by the cutting of two massive ditches through the living rock from sea to sea on both sides. These impressive features leave the fort alone on a slice of the island's southern tip. Two caponiers were built into the base of the ditches—one in each (Plate 5). These stone-built block houses would provide enfillading fire along the base of the ditches in the event of an incursion by enemy troops. Each caponier was connected to the fort itself via a tunnel and a staircase which were entirely subterranean.

Plate 5. Caponier in south fort, rock cut ditch (to left)

The excavation trench was positioned at the narrowing of the ditch created by the presence of the southern caponier and was approximately 4.4 m long by 1.5 m wide. Initial observation of the southern of the two rock ditches suggested that the ditch-bottom was heavily silted, and it was hoped that this material sealed surfaces of archaeological interest. In the event, however, there was little useful evidence from this trench. A door, which had clearly come from inside the caponier, lay to the southern end of the trench. There was also a concrete slab projecting into the north side of the trench for 2.14 m from the base of the caponier. Some damage had been caused to the southern edge of the slab, towards the centre of the trench. The concrete surface sat flush against the caponier wall and extended into the trench sections on both sides and, while it was presumed to run along the entire base of the caponier, it appeared to be of later date and not related to the original construction of the caponier. The bedrock, which occupied the southern half of the trench did not appear to be heavily weathered, perhaps because after the ditch was cut, there was little or no attempt to prevent its gradual silting up.

There was also a small rubble deposit that appeared to relate to a modification of the caponier, which included the blocking up of an opening, possibly a doorway, into its front wall. The blocked aperture on the outer wall appeared as a ragged, irregular repair, whereas inside the caponier the blocked hole was clearly a low, arched doorway. The opening was approximately 1.35 m in height on the exterior and 1.95 m high on the interior. Once the blocking had been completed the concrete slab was laid against the base of the wall, covering the lower part of the repair.

The internal face of the caponier was generally better made than the exterior, using larger, more regularly shaped blocks. The reason for the inclusion of a door in the front of the original caponier is unclear as it would appear to compromise unnecessarily the integrity of a structure already provided with concealed, internal access. The blocking up operation, when taken into account with the creation of the concrete slab, the relatively modern nature of the silt deposits and the un-weathered condition of the base of the ditch, suggests that the operation involved the clearing of earlier silt deposits and in so doing revealing the base of the wall and the ditch bottom in order to allow the repair to take place. This operation may have taken place as recently as World War II.

Why a caponier should have an obvious point of weakness such as a doorway built into it is uncertain. The doorway may have been created after the defensive role of the forts became less of a concern in the late 19th century, but there is no evidence for this. Alternatively, the doorway may have served as a form of emergency exit, should the fort fall to an overwhelming assault from the north side, or indeed be in danger of destruction from a magazine fire. In these circumstances, the doorway would allow escape into the southern ditch, and from there to the shore at either end of the ditch. Alternatively, it may have provided an emergency entry to men stationed in the concrete fire trench located to the south of the ditch. If their position was over-run, they would have no other means of entry into the fort as they fell back. It is pertinent to note here that a doorway also opens into the base of the north ditch, though this is located in the wall of the fort to the west of the north caponier. Today, this doorway is almost entirely blocked by silt and rubble and its relationship to the fort interior is uncertain—not all areas of the fort interior were explored because of health and safety considerations. It may be, however, that this north doorway served a similar function to its partner on the south side.

Trench 2—Battery command post (NT 2952 8234)

An almost completely buried concrete feature is situated on the ground sloping gently down and away from the island's centre toward the south fort (Figure 2). Although only the topmost semi-circular surface of the walling was visible, it was clearly the lining of what had been a subterranean or semi-subterranean construction dominating a significant field of fire or view point over the southern part of the island. The general appearance of the feature had initially suggested the remains of a machine gun nest, a number of which had been observed built into stretches of concrete fire trench. Reference to the 1891 OS map, however, showed the feature to be a 'B.C. Post (south)' [Battery Command Post].

The feature appeared to abut a larger, also subterranean or semi-subterranean bunker or building immediately to the north, which on the OS map was annotated as 'Telephone Room'. The feature was half sectioned along the north-south axis (Plate 6) to ensure that once the western half had been emptied, the relationship between the feature in question and the larger building it abutted would be revealed.

The fills of the feature consisted of a mixture of soil and building debris, demonstrating that it had been deliberately backfilled. Removal of the half-section revealed a circular depression in the centre of the concrete floor of the interior. Access to the feature appeared to have been from the surface via a narrow opening to the west, where the stumps of an iron ladder were also uncovered. No entry could be gained from the rectangular room-like bunker against which the post had been built. Visible on the inside of the southern wall of the post was stencilling in white paint which had

Plate 6. Battery command post from west

survived remarkably well given the combined actions of in-filling and erosion by weather. The stencilled lettering read:

TRAINING
PRACTICE AREAS
A1-224 30-275 degrees
2-229-329 degrees

This notice refers to two practice firing areas, each of which was defined by the numbers, which represent degrees and minutes from a compass and define the arc within which the two guns, denoted A1 and A2 could fire.

The excavated feature was positioned close to the two large gun emplacements of the island's south fort—and would have given its operators a clear view over the sea to the east and west. Although no longer extant, it is recorded that a painted panel bearing a picture of a cannon and 'A1 & 2' (Smith 1985, 93) ties in with the notice in the post and confirms that these were indeed the guns in question. This panel sat above the inscription 'VR' and '1880', which can still be seen on the arched entrance to the south fort. The final piece of evidence lay in the interpretation of the circular depression in the centre of the concrete floor. This had been the setting for a range-finding device used to sight and monitor the fire from the gun emplacements. Presumably, instructions from this position would have been passed forward to the gunners via a telephone controlled from the 'telephone room' behind the post.

The feature itself had a diameter of approximately 2.2 m and a depth of 1.3 m. The stencilled wall to the south was flat, while the walls to east and west were gently curved. Both curved walls ended in square terminals, giving the feature—when viewed from above—a penanular or 'horseshoe' shape. The stump of an iron fitting survived on the eastern-most square terminal—perhaps indicative of the anchoring for the roof or some other structure above ground level. The date of its burial is uncertain, but since the feature appears on a military map of the island made in 1891 and reappears on the 1910 update means that it was in use at least between these periods. Interestingly, the feature appears on the 1919 version but is not annotated, nor is the telephone room. The command post had definitely disappeared from view by the time of an RAF aerial photograph taken in 1941. This photograph also shows a number of accommodation blocks to the south of the features location. These were erected in 1939 and even if it was still in use by then they would have obscured the view from the post and so prevented it from serving its primary observational role. By that time the guns in the south fort (A group) were controlled from a fire control tower constructed on top of the fort itself.

Trench 3—Fire Trench (NT 2956 8240)

On the east-facing side of the island, there is a heavily silted and possibly back-filled trench complex hugging the contours of the cliff top (Figure 2 the trench can be seen as a dark shadow line on the right side of the aerial photograph—Plate 4). This trench was presumably part of a network designed to protect the island from a sea-borne assault from the east. In the event of enemy troops landing on the island as part of a wholesale invasion of the British mainland, Inchkeith's defenders would have sought to hold them at bay with small arms fire from this trench line.

The line of the trench is still clearly visible as a linear depression, which snakes around the contour at the cliff top, where it is generally cut into the base of a slope just before the edge of the cliff itself. However, there is considerable damage to the trench from erosion, in some places enough to suggest that eventually the remains of the trench in these areas will disappear entirely. Another preservation issue is created by rabbits, which have caused erosion through burrowing into the island's s friable, humic soils and are accelerating forward collapse of this fragile soil environment.

There were clearly three phases of the trench (Figure 4). The original feature was created by digging a wide trench through the natural soils, as deep

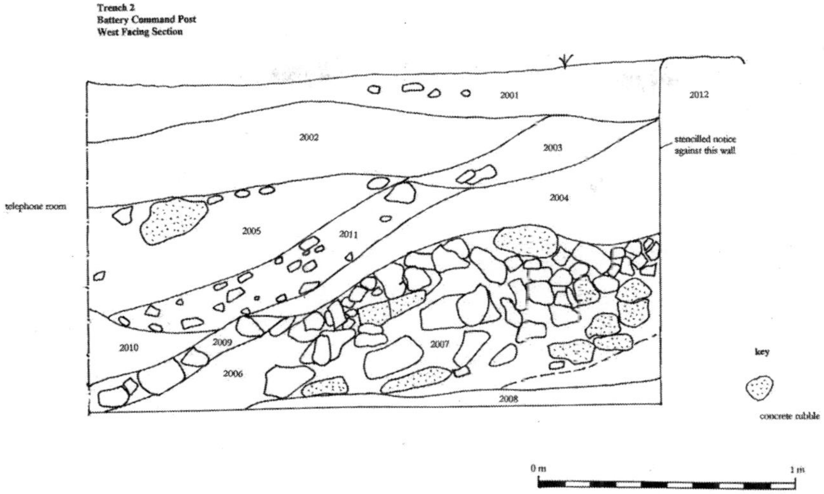

Fig. 3. West facing section through battery command post

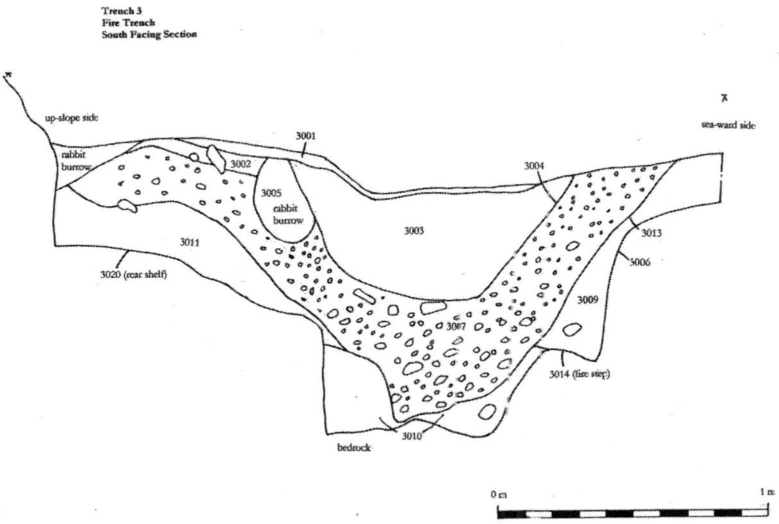

Fig. 4. South facing section through fire trench

as the presence of bedrock would allow. Against the seaward side of the trench, a firing step was created. Given that the height of the trench from the firing step to its present lip is only 0.5 m it seems highly likely that the effective depth of the trench was increased through the presence of a sand bag parapet built across the eastern lip. The rear of the trench, where it had been cut into the steep slope, took the form of a second step, or shelf, up to one metre wide. The function of this feature is less clear than the fire step, but given the unstable nature of the soils and steep slope to the rear of the trench, it may be an reinforcing feature designed to accommodate a secondary sandbag bulwark. The primary aim of this bulwark would not be to deflect bullets but to prevent tons of unstable earth from collapsing into the trench.

Over time the original trench was filled with natural silts. At a later date, the trench was re-cut and the soils that had filled the fire trench were partially removed. The new trench was not as impressive as the first and seems to have lacked a firing step, as the original feature remained buried within the seaward wall of the second trench. The wide shelf at the rear was partially uncovered but was now half as wide as in the original trench. This smaller trench was then back-filled with gravely material which included the tip of a pick-axe, probably broken in the original digging process, and sometime thereafter a rubbish pit was cut into the upper fill in this part of the trench.

According to map evidence, the first fire trenches were dug prior to 1891, as they are shown on the original Ordnance Survey of the island. The trenches at that time are short, discontinuous and are very few in number, apparently located at obvious points of weakness and where good fields of fire were available. Field observation has established that some of these stretches are actually constructed from concrete and include built-in machine gun positions. Machine guns appeared on Inchkeith at a relatively early date, with four .45 inch Maxim guns of unknown vintage being replaced by four .303 inch Maxim guns in 1899. The most substantial stretch of concrete fire trench dating from this time was located to the south of the south fort, outside the ditch, the shape of which it roughly mirrors in plan. Wire entanglements were placed in advance of most trenches to provide extra impediment to an attacking force (fig 2). The presence of these fire trenches is indicative of the late nineteenth century disillusionment with traditional forts. The replacement of the single shot rifle by the rapid fire magazine rifle, in the form of the Lee Metford, and the introduction of efficient machine guns in the 1880s altered infantry tactics dramatically. With the intelligent deployment of these light weapons, rapidly constructed fieldwork defences were capable of offering just as effective defence as the old style permanent forts (Saunders 1989).

By the time the OS map was revised in1910, more trenches had been created; most of them were apparently earth cut, but still of limited extent and discontinuous. One of these stretches appears to coincide with Trench 3. It was between then and the appearance of the 1919 map that the trenches were extended and, although not continuous by then, most of the island was encompassed by trench systems. Excavation of Trench 3 revealed the original creation of a complex trench, including a firestep and the later re-cutting of a silted trench. From the map evidence, the original trench was created sometime before 1910 and certainly after 1891. If the trench was dug not long before 1910, then it may still have been serviceable by the time of the First World War, as it was revetted and may have been reinforced with sandbag bulwarks. During World War I, the trench system was extended, incorporating already existing trenches such as that in Trench 3. A hand annotated version of the 1910 version of the OS map dated from 1915 shows the blockhouses or pill-boxes drawn on and labelled as 'already present'. These were therefore probably constructed at the start of the war and it does not seem unreasonable to see the major episode of trench digging to have taken place at the same time (although there is no attempt to show the extended system on this hand annotated map). Over the twenty or so years following World War I, the trenches, at least in some places, may have been allowed to silt up, as suggested by Trench 3. The second re-cut, through these silting deposits, created a simpler trench without a firing step and may date to the early stages of World War II, when the trench system was put back into use and can be seen on aerial photographs from 1941.

Pillboxes were the third type of defence to be added to the island outside the forts, in addition to the fire trenches and wire entanglements. These brick and concrete structures accommodated both riflemen and machine guns and are generally thought to have their origins in the blockhouses used by the British in South Africa during the Boer War. There is some similarity, however, between these and the earlier caponiers, the big difference being that the pill-box is a free standing structure whereas the caponier is integrated physically into a fort, those on Inchkeith being entered by tunnels in the forts. The original pillboxes were round, hence their name, but quickly developed into a multitude of styles. The pillboxes on Inchkeith sit forward of the previously existing trench systems and would provide strong-points around this discontinuous perimeter. It would seem likely that the major extension of this trench system took place not long after the pillboxes were built in order to provide an effective, defensible fall-back line. Obviously, there would never have been the number of men required to effectively man this entire system, but it would have allowed rapid deployment and gap-plugging while under cover from enemy fire from both land and sea. During the project, graffiti was observed in a number of the pillboxes, either scratched into the concrete or written in pencil (Pollard & Oliver 2002). Presumably created by soldiers on watch, most of this material relates to the early part of WWII and some of it was of a rather lewd nature.

Trench 4—Practice Battery (NT 2954 8236)

The guns in the south fort which were controlled from the excavated battery command post were set within substantial concrete emplacements—but not all of the guns were so well accommodated. The 1891 OS map shows what is marked as a 'former practice battery' on the south eastern edge of the island, to the east of the Command post (Figure 2). From the map, the battery appears to have consisted of eight guns mounted on an open terrace. Examination of the cliff top marked on the map revealed a series of terraces scalloped into the back of the hill, running in a line north to south. Closer investigation revealed at least two examples of metal gun mounts protruding through turf and vegetation in the centre of these features. Sweeps with the metal detector revealed further examples, one of which was entirely revealed by excavation.

Removal of turf and topsoil revealed a concrete slab into which a semicircular Vavasseur type gun mount had been positioned (Plate 7). The orientation of the mount clearly indicated that the guns had been positioned with their barrels pointing out to sea, with the mount allowing the gun to fire within an arc. The only document to refer to guns that may have been part of this battery is the War Office's own history of the works on Inchkeith (WO 192/251), which states that 'In August 1901 four 5-inch B.L. guns on Vavasseur carriages were received and mounted as a practice battery.'

The only practice battery shown on any of the maps of the island is the 'former practice battery' shown on the 1891 and 1910 maps, which by the time of the 1919 update has been relegated to 'Old Emplacements (practice battery)'. Given that the four guns noted above were not mounted until 1901, it seems possible that this battery was used sporadically over a number of years in the late 19th and early 20th centuries and that the term 'former' may be a bit misleading. The 1891 map shows a total of eight mounts, with the Vavasseur type clearly discernible as what is essentially a half circle. The four southern most examples are all of the same size, while the next pair to the north are slightly larger, possibly denoting a different size of gun. The pair to the far north are more rectangular in plan, with just a slight curve along the rear edge, and appear to be a different type of mount. The two buildings to the rear of the battery on the 1891 and 1910 maps are described as 'Ammunition Store' and 'Artillery Store' and probably relate to these guns. By 1919, however, by which time the battery appears to have fallen entirely out of use, the larger of these buildings, the 'Ammunition Store', has become a 'Guard Room'. In addition, only the four southern and the most northerly of the two more rectangular gun mounts are shown on this map, and it is tempting to regard the group of four as the mounts known to have accommodated the five inch

Plate 7. Vavasseur type gun mount exposed by excavation

guns in 1901. Metal detector survey suggests that the other mounts are still in place today, but by 1919 they had been out of use long enough to have attained their buried state and so were not shown on the map.

As suggested by the stencilled notice in the battery command post, practice firing played an important role on Inchkeith, and was not confined to the practice battery. In the 1880s, the island's guns were regularly used for training purposes by contingents of local Artillery Volunteer Units. The former artillery training facilities at Kircaldy, Burntisland, Kinghorn, Inverkeithing and Barry-Buddon, where a 64 pounder had been installed for training on heavy guns, became obsolete with the completion of the forts on Inchkeith (Guinan, 2001, 7). In addition to the four 5-inch B.L. guns installed in the practice battery in 1901, the four 6-inch B.L. Mk VII guns (A and M groups) were removed in 1907 to be replaced by four 6-inch B.L.C. guns specifically for practice purposes. These were, however, removed in November 1909 when the School of Gunnery moved from Leith to Broughty Ferry.

Trench 5—Shell Midden (NT 2928 8300)

Midden deposits were first identified on the eastern side of the island in 1870 by Grieve, who identified sheep, pig, cow, horse, rabbit and grey seal bones in the deposits as well as shells. A later visit in 1898 by a Dr T B

Sprague recovered deer-horn and bone implements from the island, although there is no clear evidence that they came from Grieve's midden; these were compared to material coming from late Mesolithic middens in Argyll (Munro 1908, 230). Since then, the location of this midden has been lost; in particular, a visit in 1973 found no sign of the midden (Mowat *et al.* 1973), so an attempt was made to relocate this feature as part of the project. The remains of the old landing place referred to in Grieve's original account were identified through the presence of well-worn slabs of stone sitting at the rear of the pebble beach. To the south-west of the landing place, the base of the slope had suffered from collapse and erosion, and in one of the exposed faces a deposit of marine shells was clearly visible as a white layer sealed within a darker soil horizon (Figure 2).

Closer examination revealed a deposit of oyster shells extending along the exposed section for around 2 m. Just above the midden deposit, at its eastern end, was an exposed animal long bone which at first was thought to be cow. The section face was hand-cleaned and recorded by photography and a measured sketch. A small column sample including shells and soil matrix, which included flecks of charcoal was removed for later analysis. The mammal bone and a number of closely associated smaller bones were removed by excavation, the long bone itself being at the point of falling out of the erosion face.

The midden deposit appeared to have built up on a sandstone outcrop which protruded from the erosion face at an angle. Given the rather acute angle of the slope upon which the midden is situated, it seems unlikely that the midden deposit extends into the hillside for much more than 1 m. In its original state prior to erosion, the midden may have been a much more substantial feature, but unfortunately much has been lost to the sea. Some 50 cm above the shell midden deposit was a compacted layer of water-rolled pebbles and stones. This represents a storm beach which post-dates the deposition of the midden material. Above the pebble layer were the remains of a stone wall, built onto what survives today as a narrow terrace; the relationship between the midden deposit and the wall remained uncertain because of the limited excavation.

The material removed from the midden was examined by Catherine Smith, of the Scottish Urban Archaeological Trust (SUAT), who identified the mammal long bone as the lower portion of the rear leg of a small horse or pony. Other bones recovered included part of the tail and several bones from one foot of the horse or pony. Bones from a rabbit and a chicken were also present. The marine shells included oysters (the predominant species), along with some limpets and periwinkles. No datable artefacts were recovered, but the presence of horse or pony, chicken and rabbit, certainly indicate a historic origin; the range of species is not consistent with the prehistoric dating ascribed by Munro (Munro 1908, 230). As it is located at the foot of the cliff immediately below the 16th Century fort, it is not unreasonable to suggest that the midden may represent food refuse deposited by the occupants of the fort, perhaps thrown over the cliff onto the beach below. Grey, one of the commanders of the English force besieging the fort in 1560, wrote:

> "There are 140 soldiers in the fort, besides 70 women, boys and labouring persons. They have no drink but water, wheat to serve 10 or 12 days, other victual, little or none. Their great relief is oysters and periwinkles, which they get at low water mark in the Isle, and fresh fish with angling roads" (Steuart, 1920, 74).

The limited menu described in this report obviously has some similarity to the contents of the midden. It is also interesting to note that the island was known by the French as the 'island of horses', as it was a favoured place for the secure pasturing of horses.

While the shell midden is obviously of some antiquity, there is at least one further midden on the island that relates to much more recent events. On the western side of the island are a series of cottages which served as garrison accommodation and were built during the late nineteenth century expansion onto the island away from the forts (Pl 3). Included within what is almost a small village was the cookhouse, which today still has the rusting oven in place. The cookhouse overlooks a sheer cliff that falls onto the beach on the western side of the island. It is against the base of this cliff that a substantial midden deposit accumulated as rubbish was thrown from the cookhouse. The midden is characterised by a steep soil talus which includes large quantities of animal bone and pottery sherds.

Due to the precarious nature of the deposit, which undergoes regular collapse, only a very cursory examination was possible. A number of pottery sherds were removed from the deposit, including fragments of white china plates, glasses and teacups. A few of the teacups displayed NAAFI stamps on their base, with one example showing the NAAFI crest on the side of the cup. An identical crest was observed on one drinking glass fragment. Numerous china fragments were also encountered on the pebble beach on the other side of the island where the older midden had accumulated. These also included fragments of teacups with NAAFI stamps, with several displaying the dates 1940 or 1941. These again appear to have been thrown over the cliff from the barrack blocks above.

Conclusion

The importance of military remains from recent periods has over recent years been acknowledged through the Defence of Britain project and the designation of sites in the Firth of Forth, such as the island of Inchkeith, as Scheduled Ancient Monuments. Intervention by archaeologists, however, although not unknown, is relatively rare in the case of these sites—at least within the British Isles. One of the aims of the project was to apply traditional archaeological excavation techniques in an attempt to more fully understand archaeological features, many of which also appear in historical documents and on maps. With minimal intervention being the constant aim it is believed that the project has achieved this aim and demonstrated that a similar marriage of archaeological data with historical research will be vital in any programme of future research.

Acknowledgements

The authors would like to thank Historic Scotland and Fife Council for their cooperation and the various permissions to carry out the works reported here. Doreen Grove at Historic Scotland guided us through Scheduled Monument Consent and Dave Easton of the Royal Commission for Ancient and Historic Monuments of Scotland shared his enthusiasm for military sites and guided us around the many aerial photographs of the Firth of Forth.

Sir Tom Farmer, owner of Inchkeith Island allowed us to spend two weeks on his property and Charlie Knolf, the island's one permanent resident, provided invaluable assistance throughout. Bill Simpson and the crew of the Seahunter provided safe passage for the archaeologists and television crew on a daily basis. Thanks also to our archaeological team Helen McQuarrie and Ross White.

Various specialists gave willingly of their time and expertise throughout the project: Norman Clark, John Dickson, Dr Douglas Grant, Nigel Harding, Olaf Kruger and Dr Catherine Smith.

Last but not least, our thanks to the television crew who shared the ups and downs of the project with the authors: Co-presenter Neil Oliver; Executive Producer Pat Llewelyn; Series Producer Ben Adler; Series Director Paul Ratcliffe; Assistant Producer Margaret Becket; Researcher Nick Angel; Production Manager Linda Stradling; Production Coordinators Ben Motley and Richard Herd; Sound Recordist Rex Phillips; Cameraman Richard Hill; Camera Assistant Patrick Acum; Runner Caroline Stopp.

References

Grieve, D 1873, 'On the discovery of a kitchen midden on Inchkeith', *Proc Soc Antiq Scot* 9, 452–55.

Guinan, A 2001 'Chapter 10: the Coast Artillery', *The Scottish Artillery*. Unpublished draft manuscript.

Heddle, G & Morris, R 1997, 'Charles Hill Gun Battery', *Tayside & Fife Archaeol J* 3, 207–15.

Mowat, R J C, Campbell, J B & Morrison, I A 1973, 'Inchkeith midden', *Discov & Excav, Scotland*, 1973, 26.

Munro, R 1908 'On the transition between the Palaeolithic and Neolithic civilisations in Europe', *Archaeol J* 65, 205–44.

Pollard, T & Oliver, N 2002 *Two Men in a Trench: Battlefield Archaeology—the key to unlocking the past.* Michael Joseph, London.

Saunders, A 1984 'The defences of the Firth of Forth', *in* Breeze, D (ed.) *Studies in Scottish Antiquity presented to Stewart Cruden.* John Donald Publishers, Edinburgh.

—— 1989 *Fortress Britain.* Beaufort Publishing.

Smith, V 1985 'Defending the Forth: 1810–1910', *Fortress*, 89–102.

Steuart, A F 1920 'Inchkeith and the French occupation', *Trans Franco-Scottish Soc* 1914–18, 36–86, Edinburgh.

Appendix—List of Documents Consulted

Written Accounts

'History of the works on Inchkeith' War Office record. PRO ref WO 192/251

"B" Administration—5 Medical Arrangements & Sanitation. Refers to facilities on Inchkeith, typed and dated 26/3/31. Hand written notes dated 1932. Lists refuse chute near cookhouse west of island.

Standing Orders for Land Defence Scheme referring to Inchkeith. Typed but undated—WWII. PRO ref WO 192/251

Report on HMS Sultan artillery experiment at Inchkeith in 1884 with recommendations by Colonel H. Shaw RE dated 13/1/1885. Includes plan of Battery and tables. PRO ref WO 396/2.

Maps and Plans

WWII plan of structures (huts, batteries etc) on Inchkeith (extract) date and source unknown.

'C.A.S.L. Arcs of Search—Middle Line'. WWII map showing arcs of illumination from lights at Leith, Inchkeith and north shore of Forth, date and source unknown PRO Ref: 371/112054

1891 OS map of Inchkeith. Reduced from 1:200 scale? PRO ref not known.

1909/10 revised OS map of Inchkeith, hand drawn annotations and title Inchkeith A, M and H Group plan showing sites of proposed for engine rms (two) three combined B.C. and ELD post and four E.L. Empts. Dated 27/5/15 and 1/7/19 by hand. PRO ref 78/5159.

1919 revised OS map of Inchkeith , with hand drawn arcs of fire. Scale 1:2500. Printed at Ordnance Survey Office, Southampton 1919. PRO ref 192/251.

Arcs of lights on Inchkeith and east Forth. Undated WWII plan at 1/4" to mile, marked secret. PRO ref WO 199/1171

'Firth of Forth, Inchkeith Record plan of No. 3 South battery, 1 & 2 6-Inch BL guns mk VII'. South Fort plan. Stamped for return to Fortification Design Branch. Dated 10/6/01 by Colonel on the Staff District Engineer Scottish District.

'Layout of Hutting'. Inchkeith, scale 1:2500 Signed by Chief Engineer, Scottish Command 24/1/39. PRO ref WO 192/251.

Aerial Photographs

Oblique of north Inchkeith taken 2/10/41 sortie S309, frame 6961

Oblique of Inchkeith from south taken 2/10/42 sortie S309, frame 6959

Vertical of central Inchkeith taken 12/9/41 6759.B309 PRO ref WO 192/251

Vertical of north tip of Inchkeith taken 13/9/41 6757.B309 PRO ref WO 192/251.

Vertical of west Inchkeith taken 13/9/41 6760.B309 PRO ref WO 192/251.

Vertical of south Inchkeith taken 13/9/41 6758.B309 PRO ref WO 192/251

Oblique of Inchcolm from north, shows torpedo and shipping boom to south taken 2/10/41 sortie S309, frame 6965.

Oblique of Inchcolm from west taken 2/10/41 sortie S309, frame 6962.

Oblique of Inchcolm from south, shows boom running to Charles Hill taken 2/10/41 sortie S309, frame 6963.

Vertical of Donibristle airfield taken 28/3/46 108G.UK1326

WAR AND PLACE: LANDSCAPES OF CONFLICT AND DESTRUCTION IN PREHISTORY

JAMES E SNEAD[1]

Abstract

The concept of *place* has rarely been applied to the archaeological study of warfare. Given that cultural landscapes embody meaning, however, the idea that places can be the focus of competition makes it evident that they can also shape associated conflict. As archaeologists move toward a more nuanced study of conflict in the past, such considerations will take on increasing importance, although as of yet most such studies are heavily reliant on textual sources and overtly symbolic material culture. This paper presents a case study from Burnt Corn Pueblo, in the Galisteo Basin, New Mexico, USA, and argues that evidence for conflict there at the beginning of the 13th century CE can be usefully interpreted through Ancestral Pueblo concepts of place.

War and Place

War is the ultimate placemaker. Personal perceptions of battle typically focus on the human cost: lives lost, bodies maimed, families forever ruptured. In contrast, the relationship between warfare and the material world is envisioned largely in economic or strategic terms, such as capture of the enemy's resources or loss of our own, and familiar terms such as 'scorched earth' are understood in this light. Neither frame of reference covers the intentional demolition of features that have no military value. There is thus particular shock when warfare involves the destruction of cultural monuments and historical sites, and we struggle to explain them as a consequence of pique or malevolence. Despite the human suffering associated with the Balkan wars of the 1990s, some of the most enduring images of those conflicts relate to the

[1] The fieldwork on which this article is based is supported by the National Science Foundation, BCS 0352702 and conducted under permit from the Bureau of Land Management Paul Williams and Buck Dant play a critical role in this process. Support of the Department of Sociology and Anthropology and the College of Arts and Sciences at George Mason University is gratefully acknowledged. We also benefit from a long-term collaboration with the archaeology program at California Polytechnic University at Pomona under the direction of Mark Allen. My thoughts on these topics have benefited from conversations both recent and ancient with Mark Mike Bremer, Andy Darling, Timothy Earle, Michael Kolb, Steven LeBlanc, Steve Post, Douglas Schwartz, Linda Seligmann, Monica Smith, Julie Solometo, Susan Trencher, and the dozens of visitors who have come to Burnt Corn Pueblo while fieldwork was in progress or asked provocative questions during public lectures. A published report describing research to date with preliminary interpretations is in process (Snead and Allen n.d.)

 DOI: 10.1163/157407808X382791

obliteration of mosques and churches (see Chapman 1994). The cheers that were reportedly heard when artillery fire struck the famous Stari Most bridge in Mostar, Bosnia, obliterating a landmark that had no strategic significance, seem particularly disturbing.

Understanding the annihilation of cultural monuments as a mode of conflict engages the idea of *place*, a topic that has received little attention from archaeologists studying warfare in prehistory. Until recently, our preference was for ancestors uncorrupted by violence, what Lawrence Keeley has termed the 'pacified past' (1996). One legacy of this preconception is that the conversation about prehistoric conflict remains focused on conceptually remote 'core' issues, such as the presence/absence of war or its fundamental motivations (cf. Ember & Ember 1997; Ferguson 1997; Haas 1990; LeBlanc 2003; Otterbein 2004). With few exceptions, prehistorians have most directly been concerned with what warfare tells us about human society in general, rather than in the processes of warfare *within* particular contexts. Despite general calls for a social archaeology of war (i.e. Parker Pearson 2005:26), it is telling that recent literature exploring this topic is heavily focused on the 19th and 20th centuries, emphasizing memorabilia, monuments, and overtly symbolic material culture rather than the empirical remains of war itself (c.f. articles in Gilchrist 2003, Saunders 2002).

A central reason for limited research on issues of place in the context of war in prehistory is that place is fundamentally concerned with meaning, traditionally a difficult subject to approach through strictly archaeological evidence. It is also the case that anthropological concepts of place and landscape rarely address their role in conflict (e.g. Feld & Basso 1996; Myers 2000; Rodman 1992; Schama 1995; Stewart 1996; Torren 1999; Weiner 1991). Indeed, place can seem inherently benign, a serene ordering of the world in space and over time, a 'symbol of stability, a spatial and temporal anchorage' (Munn 1970:46).

Inevitably, however, the idea of place must be linked with exclusion. Place demands priority, ownership, and occupation. Since place is entwined with order, social, natural, political, it plays a central role in reifying that order, particularly in the face of dissident perspectives (cf. Ashmore 2002:1178; Snead 2008b; Tuan 1979). Western Apaches told Keith Basso of being 'shot' by stories related to places in the landscape and thus compelled to conform to the culturally-constructed ideals they embodied (1996:56). Since places are not only the result of history or 'dwelling', but are also established through intent (i.e. Bradley 1993:5), placemaking must be considered a competitive process.

The ultimate manifestation of the relationship between place and conflict is destruction. Recent literature on destructive war in 20th century contexts (e.g. Bevan 2007) links the obliteration of monuments to genocide, eliminating not only the present but also the past of a targeted community. Intentional destruction in pre-modern contexts presents a somewhat different problem, particularly since—in the absence of dynamite, a large labour pool and convenient landfills—places that were 'destroyed' must have remained visible and were thus places still, albeit with new meaning. Archaeologists are turning their attention to this particular sort of war, recently described as 'destructive conflict with profoundly political repercussions' (Arkush & Stanish 2005:22). Sharon Zuckerman, for instance, addresses the nature of 'destruction deposits' in the ancient Near East, describing the burning of Canaanite Hazor as 'a systematic annihilation campaign, against the very physical symbols of the royal ideology and its loci of ritual legitimation' (2007: 24). This evolution from the traditional, default interpretation that sites like Hazor had simply been 'sacked' illustrates the utility of a more nuanced approach to war, place, and destruction in the archaeological record.

The intent here is to examine prehistoric landscapes of war with an eye toward the role of place as a structuring element of conflict. This requires a shift away from causality, emphasizing context over comparison. The case study that follows, derived from the American Southwest in the late Pre-Columbian era, is particularly appropriate for such an exploration, given both the wealth of historical/ethnographic resources and a strong empirical base. What emerges thus pertains directly to our understanding of Ancestral Pueblo society, but demonstrates the relevance of place to examinations of warfare in archaeological cases broadly conceived.

Landscapes of War

If the organization of war is contextual, then landscape must be more than 'setting' for such violence. Michael Kolb and Boyd Dixon, for instance, argue that various features of the cultural landscape 'played an important role in defining the accepted *social parameters* of Hawaiian conflict' (2002:515 [emphasis added]). Mark Allen brings this line of reasoning to its logical conclusion, arguing that the defensive architecture of Maori *pa* had a profound impact on the organization of Maori polities. As Allen indicates, it is difficult to imagine any significant political integration in pre-contact New Zealand, given the structure of a purposefully balkanized landscape studded with strong points (Allen 1994).

The argument that landscape defines the social parameters of warfare can be taken one step further—a landscape of meaning can itself be a subject of competition. This is particularly compelling given the complex relationship between landscape and 'tradition' (i.e. Stoller 1980; Sahlins 1992:17). Legitimacy is a fulcrum of conflict, a pivot for social and political rationale. Human memory may be fleeting, but landscape—at least as socially constructed—is eternal, and thus a powerful guarantor of authority (c.f. Alcock 2002). This is particularly relevant in situations where writing systems are either absent or pertinent only to elite classes. In effect, landscape represents the only 'true' history, albeit mute in the absence of interpreters. Control of this resource, then, can be essential to establishing and maintaining authority, making landscape something to fight for.

The approach here is thus to invert the correlation of place and war, turning from places shaped by violence to conflict shaped by ideas of place. Sarah Tarlow describes the superimposition of a Viking ship-grave over a nearly-contemporaneous Christian cemetery on the Isle of Man as quite literally seizing the high ground:

> Violent action such as desecration is a trespass which implies not only antipathy toward the individual or group against which it is directed, but also for all their most profoundly held beliefs and principles, everything that they stand for (Tarlow 1997:33).

Our ideas of battlefields, as the most obvious 'places' of war, are also being reformulated (i.e. Blades 2003; Carman 1999; 2002; Pollard 2001; 2002). These components of the cultural and built environments are historically emplaced, and as such powerful 'signifiers' would be notable targets in a competitive arena.

Conflict and Place in Maya Landscapes

The complex relationship between war and place can be traced through various archaeological examples, with the Maya providing a particularly relevant case. Stereotypically, arguments over Maya conflict concern whether there were 'real' wars, with predatory armies on the march, or instead more ritualized, elite-driven battles with few casualties. Empirical evidence has been marshalled in favour of either argument. Apparent defensive walls are associated with some Maya cities (Demarest *et al.* 1997; Dahlin 2000; Webster 1976), but not all, and some traditional arguments about Maya fortification have recently been debunked (c.f. Callendar & Puhleston 1967; Webster *et al.* 2007). There is clear evidence for large-scale destruction, with palatial centres such as Aguateca showing signs of extensive burning (Inomata 1997). Warfare is also a central feature of Maya monumental imagery and texts, but the extent to which these sources are literal or metaphorical remains a matter of debate. We know that the Maya fought each other, but the how and why of it remains under review.

The Maya built environment reflects conflict in many ways, from the 'capture' of the sacred landscape by building structures atop earlier buildings—or over particular topographic and hydrological features (Demarest *et al.* 2003)—to the placement of victory stelae in the plazas of defeated enemies (i.e. Webster 2000:93). Particularly relevant for this discussion is evidence for the destruction of monumental architecture in different parts of the Maya lowlands that have been described as 'desecratory terminations' (Ambrosino *et al.* 2003: 112; see also Friedel *et al.* 1998; Mock 1998; Pagliaro *et al.* 2003; Brown & Garber 2003). Several of these authors argue that such targeted acts of demolition were attacks on the legitimacy and identity of the groups they represented (see also Webster 2000:87). They were, in essence, attempts to obliterate or reconfigure places and their associated meanings. David Friedel has described the process of re-shaping place at Yaxuná as

> 'a conscious and self-reflecting one, registering the history of intentions—one that we can indeed interpret as social history' (Friedel 1998:193).

The fact that the establishment of such history was hotly contested should alert us to the role of violence in the creation of that narrative.

Considering 'termination' in its various forms as a potent tool of warfare allows for a more nuanced understanding of Maya war as a whole. Ross Hassig has argued that aristocratic Mesoamerican societies were particularly reliant on supernatural sanction for legitimacy (1992:168), and the sorts of destruction documented at Yaxuná and elsewhere were clearly aimed at undermining such support. Re-conceptualizing the roles of war and place in archaeological settings mandates a substantive investigation of cultural context. It may well be possible to generalize about some of the processes involved, but it is in the realm of meaning that acts of destruction can be most productively situated.

For archaeologists, the Maya case demonstrates that it is possible to examine the relationship between war and place in empirical terms. Considering issues of place in the context of conflict seems particularly valuable in cases where the nature of warfare itself is in question or where societies do not appear to 'follow the rules' of resource-based conflict. Each of these variables plays a critical role in the more detailed case study that follows.

War and Place in the Ancestral Pueblo Landscape

The archaeological literature on warfare in the Pre-Columbian American Southwest has grown rapidly, making the region a significant 'test case' for empirical studies of conflict among small-scale village farming communities (e.g. Billman *et al.* 2000; Chenault & Motsinger 2000; Haas & Creamer 1993; Kuckelman 2002; Kuckelman *et al.* 2000; LeBlanc 1997; 1999; 2000; Rice & LeBlanc 2002; Turner & Turner 1999, Wilcox & Haas 1994; Wilcox *et al.* 2001). In recent years, this literature has incorporated more complex theoretical perspectives, particularly as archaeologists move from acknowledging conflict in Pueblo society toward trying to understand it (i.e. Kohler & Turner 2006; Lowell 2007; Plog 2003; Schaafsma 2000; Solometo 2006; Wilcox *et al.* 2006).

Ethnographic research indicates that life within the modern and historic Pueblo villages of New Mexico and Arizona is structured by an intricate cultural landscape invested with cultural, social, and ideological significance (Ortiz 1969; 1979; White 1942; 1962). For the Tewa and Keres of the northern Río Grande region, the land is defined both by the cardinal directions—including 'zenith' and 'nadir'—and by a zonal organization, with each village as the notional centre point of a set of concentric circles radiating out to the horizon, each bounded by cardinal hills and peaks (c.f. Snead 2008a). The founding of new villages requires building networks of shrines linked to a central shrine in the village centre that that both 'represents' and 'is' the place of origin of the Pueblo people (i.e. Ellis 1979:441, Whiteley 1988:126).

The primacy of place in the organization of cultural space in the pueblos has deep historical roots linked to legitimacy (i.e. Anschuetz 1998, Hegmon 2002). As Mark Lycett has noted, whenever new settlements were established, 'social space and claims of ownership or access were being remade just as physical space was being reconstructed' (2002:71). It is precisely this issue of contestation—or competition, and ultimately conflict—that provides the opportunity to bring ideas of war and place together in the Pueblo context.

Burnt Corn Pueblo

Burnt Corn Pueblo is an Ancestral Pueblo settlement in the Galisteo Basin of New Mexico, just south of the state capital at Santa Fe (Figure 1). The pueblo, situated within dissected terrain and open woodland, is the centre of a larger community made up of farmsteads, fields, work areas, and shrines. The environment is semi-arid, with seasonally-variable precipitation and few permanent streams. The author has been conducting fieldwork in the Burnt Corn community since 2000 as part of the Tano Origins Project, a multiscalar research program examining population movement and conflict in the region during the AD 1300s. As of 2008, 700 ha containing 231 sites had been intensively surveyed, with excavations conducted at five different sites and collections from other excavations in the region studied.

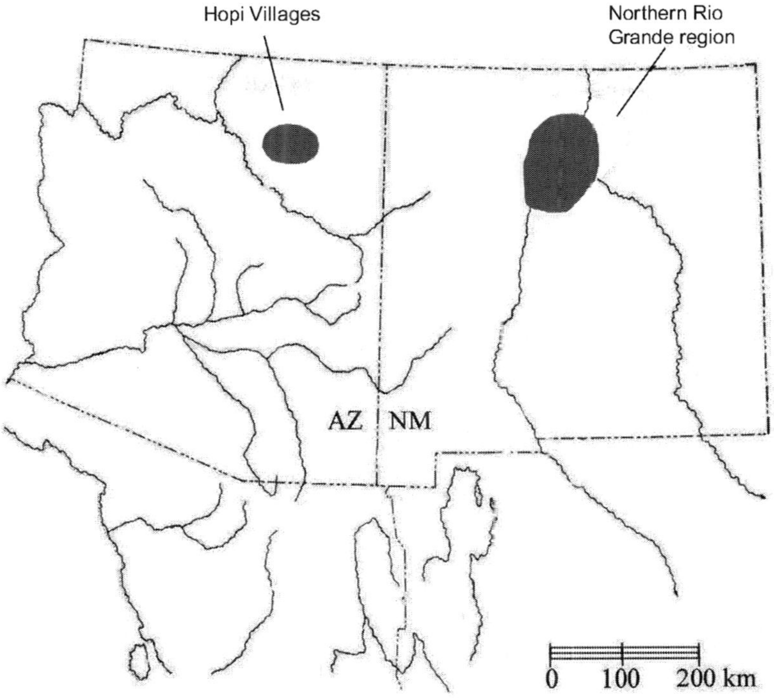

Fig. 1. Location map

Burnt Corn Pueblo itself consists of nine structures built of masonry and adobe dispersed along 300 m of ridgetop (Figure 2). Eight of these are a single story in height and contain 8–20 rooms each, sizes appropriate for housing three or four extended families. The ninth structure is a larger 'plaza pueblo,' consisting of 40–60 rooms arranged around an enclosed courtyard with some multi-story sections. This structure would have been partially residential as well, but probably also served as a community centre. The entire complex overlooks the floodplain of an intermittent stream. Tree-ring dating indicates that the pueblo was built between CE 1290 and 1302.

The founders of Burnt Corn organized their community with attention to several different variables. Appropriate terrain for dryland agriculture along the nearby drainages was obviously important, but the ridgetop on which the pueblo was built is also defensible, commanding wide views in all directions. The position of outlying structures along obvious routes into the community centre implies that they were built to protect these pathways (Snead 2008a: 92). Symbolic elements of the broader landscape were also in play. The eastern horizon is dominated by Petroglyph Hill, a major shrine of the period.

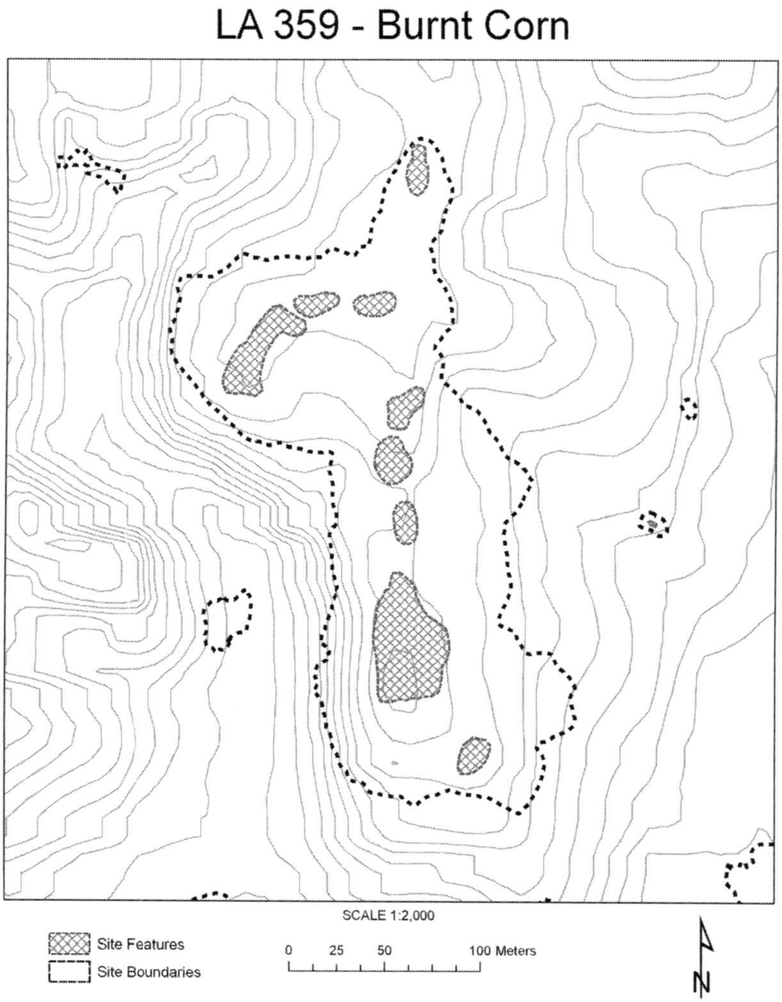

Fig. 2. Burnt Corn Pueblo—site outline

Burnt Corn Pueblo was also 'bounded' by constructed shrines, including an apparent centre shrine amidst the ridgetop structures, cupuled boulders on the periphery of the complex, and shrines away from the pueblo in at least some of the cardinal directions. It was thus established as a place within the context of pueblo tradition, with all the associations of permanence that such a designation implies. The cumulative effect of the system of peaks, shrines, and plazas surrounding Burnt Corn was that it had always been there, even if such a 'history' had been established within the living memory of its inhabitants.

What brings placemaking at Burnt Corn into sharp relief is the fact that the pueblo was completely destroyed by fire before the passing of a single generation. Seven excavation units in five different structures dispersed across the site contained—in varying frequencies—scorched plaster, carbonized roof timbers, and the ubiquitous charred corn cobs that give the site its name. The precise chronology and the absence of evidence for roof repair prior to destruction indicate that this event probably took place within 20 years of construction (following Crown 1991:305). The condition of the charred corn cobs suggested that they were burned within a few months of the harvest (R Ford, pers comm), all of which leads to the belief that the conflagration took place in the autumn, no later than 1320 CE. Destruction by chance event is unlikely. Forest fires can be discounted since the surrounding piñon-juniper woodland burns with low intensity. Regardless, the fuel load in the immediate vicinity of the pueblo would have been minimal given demand for firewood/construction material and constant foot traffic. Human accident can also be discounted. Although storage rooms filled with dry corn would have been a constant fire hazard, empirical evidence from other sites suggest that such fires rarely spread beyond their immediate vicinity.[2] The presence of corn drying on the roofs of several structures fuelled the flames, but none was present at the plaza pueblo, which nonetheless burned as well. Although excavations have yet to uncover any of the other signs of overt conflict present in warfare situations elsewhere in the Southwest (c.f., LeBlanc 1999), it is confidently asserted that Burnt Corn ended in an act of violence.

The initial interpretation of the destruction of Burnt Corn was that it represented a raid: enemies had caught the inhabitants unaware one autumn morning and left devastation in their wake. This assessment was based on expectations derived from theories of warfare, since raiding is what war in tribal groups is supposed to be (i.e. Haas & Creamer 1993). There is some ambiguity on this point, however, and as Steven LeBlanc has noted, other forms of conflict have been documented for small-scale societies (2001:30; cf. Wilcox & Haas 1994:235).

In fact, the empirical evidence from Burnt Corn raises troubling questions regarding a 'raid.' The destruction of so much architectural wood and corn seems remarkably wasteful if the attack was intended to capture economic

---

[2] At nearby Arroyo Hondo, burning was noticed in seven out of the 66 component I ground floor rooms, and these were distributed throughout the pueblo. This is a reasonable frequency for accidental fires dispersed over the forty years of the primary occupation. In contrast, 21 out of 53 component II rooms had been burned, and these were often clustered. It is thus argued that, while the evidence for component I is ambiguous, component II was ended by a violent event (Creamer 1993:13, 154).

resources, although it is impossible to determine whether the destroyed corn was simply the excess that could not be carried away (cf. LeBlanc 1999:82; T van Zandt, pers comm). It was also noted during the course of the 2002 field season that the sampled rooms were relatively empty, with little of the expected casual debris. Raiding implies sudden attack, and some signs might be expected of domestic life interrupted by the shouts of the enemy outside. The longer the evidence was considered, not only did economic raiding seem less likely, but it was clear that whatever happened at Burnt Corn was part of a process that was harder to classify.

Awat'ovi Events

What undoubtedly *did* happen at Burnt Corn was that a living place and its architectural manifestation were transformed within the landscape. This implies that destruction was the point, rather than a side-effect of another sort of conflict. In Pueblo tradition, the burning of Burnt Corn would have been more than the simple removal of a rival community. In the fire's aftermath, Burnt Corn had been 'replaced' by a landmark of an entirely different kind.

Violence against places would be entirely in keeping with Pueblo perceptions of landscape. As Hopi tales of the destruction of villages reveal (Malotki 2002), such events are precipitated by the moral failings of their inhabitants. Although disasters may be manifest as fire, flood, attack, or malevolent supernatural agency, they always reflect a breakdown of the social order. The Tewa and Keres ethnographic literature is replete with examples of catastrophe resulting from disobedience and disrespectful behavior (c.f. Harrington 1916:208; Parsons 1929:274; White 1935:184).

In Pueblo history, the most notorious episode of the intentional 'cleansing' of a threat to the moral order was the colonial-era destruction of the Hopi village of Awat'ovi. The residents of Awat'ovi had sought accommodation with the Spanish in defiance of other Hopis, and their community was attacked and burned by their neighbors in 1700 CE. Although the history of this episode is complex (cf. Whiteley 2002), in traditional accounts it was the corruption of Awat'ovi's residents, particularly as manifest by their partial adoption of Christianity and dalliance with colonial authorities, that mandated their obliteration. Awat'ovi was never rebuilt, its people either killed in the attack, massacred shortly afterwards (i.e. Turner & Morris 1970), or incorporated into other Hopi clans. The pueblo remains in ruins today. Archaeological investigations of Awat'ovi in the 1890s and 1930s (Fewkes 1893; Mongomery *et al.* 1949) documented a pattern of destruction broadly similar to that described by oral tradition.

An 'Awat'ovi event' offers a credible scenario for what occurred at Burnt Corn.[3] Visualized in terms of the logic of place, the teleology of conflict embodied in the post-destruction landscape also becomes clearer. Once memory about the events faded—and regardless of what actually took place—the most visible, empirical source of any related historical narrative would have been stark ruins on a ridgetop. From a Pueblo perspective, such a place must have come into existence because of a disruption in the social order, and the legacy of such a failure would have been visible for generations (Snead 2004). Whatever threat Burnt Corn may have represented to neighbouring communities in the western Galisteo Basin—access to land and resources, competing forms of political organization, ritual practices—had been eliminated, and in addition the place that it became supported the dominant narrative. No matter what the reality of the events, the tale left behind in the landscape was one that anyone passing by could discern for themselves.

Orayvi Events

Identifying an Awat'ovi event at Burnt Corn that reflects Pueblo concepts of place, morality, and violence accords with evidence from the site and the surrounding terrain as it is currently understood. To identify the culprits, however, leads once again to grapple with unpredicted patterns of empirical data. Without knowing more about the context of the destruction, our ability to impute motives and identify actors is weak.

The 2005 excavations exposed much more contiguous space than previous seasons, and again presented an absence of domestic debris in room contexts. Nearly all artefacts were found in the destruction layers rather than in other contexts. The floors of the completely excavated room A in unit 6, in fact, looked as if they had been swept clean, with hearths and vents tidily sealed by mud plaster (Figure 3). In most cases, debris from walls and roofs lay directly on these floors, implying that very little time had passed between the emptying of the rooms and destruction. The sample size remains small, but these patterns have significant implications for the last days of Burnt Corn Pueblo.

The possibility that the pueblo was intentionally prepared for destruction leads us to consider the scenario that the violence was conducted not by others, but by the residents of Burnt Corn themselves. Evidence pointing to such 'decomissioning' has been discussed by archaeologists working in the Southwest

[3] I am grateful to Mike Bremer, Forest Archaeologist for the Santa Fe National Forest, for suggesting this term.

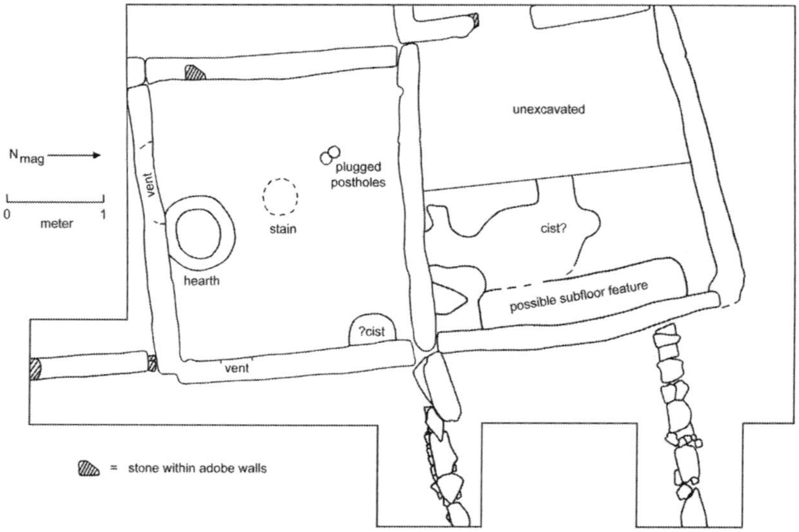

Fig. 3. Post excavation plan of Room A in Unit 6

for some time, usually in the context of particular structures or ritual facilities such as pithouses and kivas (cf. Cameron 1990:35; Chenault & Motsinger 2000:62; Walker 1998; Walker & Lucero 2000; Wilshusen 1986:251). That an entire pueblo might be decomissioned in this way is notable.

In the case of intentional decommissioning, the conflict faced by residents of Burnt Corn was not necessarily with neighbours, but perhaps among themselves. Pueblo society is notoriously rife with factionalism, evident both in historical ethnography and modern politics, and such internal animosity can lead to the sundering of whole communities. Such a process is implicated in the so-called 'Orayvi split', in which a long period of discord at the Hopi Third Mesa village of Orayvi culminated in 1906 with the departure of half the population and the founding of new villages elsewhere. Anthropologists have long argued about the causes of the Orayvi split, explaining it as an inevitable product of social fission (Titiev 1988), inequitable distribution of farmland (Levy 1992), or as an effort to disrupt the Orayvi ceremonial system in the face of its impending corruption (Whiteley 1988). Most important for the present paper, however, is that conflict *within* the community led to the destruction of the local order (Ellis 1979).

Orayvi was not burned, and remains a small village today, but there is evidence to suggest that such 'splits' occurred elsewhere (c.f. Ellis 1979), and in the Pre-Columbian era may have had more extreme consequences. The most specific case is that of Pot Creek Pueblo, which in Taos tradition was once shared by their ancestors and those of the nearby Pueblo of Picurís. In the face of division within their community, the different factions agreed to depart, leaving an empty and decomissioned Pot Creek behind them that, at least in part, was burned (M Adler, pers comm; Fowles 2004; Wetherington 1968).

Decomissioning is one facet of an 'Orayvi event' that may pertain to the abandonment of Burnt Corn. The pattern of systematic destruction, however, must be accounted for, particularly since it seems to have been relatively rare. In such drastic circumstances, the presence of a more sinister fellow-traveller of factionalism—witchcraft—must also be considered. In Pueblo history, witches were manifestations of social disharmony, and the few 19th century 'outbreaks' of witchcraft for which documentation exists were typically associated with hard times:

> Witchcraft accusation and sanctioning, may have played an important role in 'internal feuds' resulting in factionalism (Darling 1999:736).

His analysis also makes it clear that witch-killing was one of the most overtly violent Pueblo practices, involving torture, execution, dismemberment or other extreme treatment of the deceased 'witch.' Social stresses associated with witch trials may have promoted the depopulation of the associated villages, such as the Pueblo of Nambé, which was in severe demographic decline in the late 1800s and was also the setting for several witch executions. The ethnographic record details places associated with witches (Dumarest 1919:208; Lomatuway'ma *et al.* 1993:157; Parsons 1929:305), and accusations of witchcraft were used as justification for the destruction of Awat'ovi.

The possible association of archaeological evidence for village destruction and witchcraft has been explored by William Walker (1998). Most of these cases are explained by attacks from the outside. Burnt Corn would be one of the best potential instances of a witchcraft-related destruction carried out by people from *within* the community. Such a witchcraft-provoked Orayvi event would have represented an extremely difficult decision, since in the wake of the conflagration those who walked away would have faced an uncertain future.

It is at this juncture that the 'Awatovi' and 'Orayvi' scenarios come together. In both cases, a lived place is construed as a threat, and its replacement on the landscape becomes a morality tale brought about through destruction.[4] The annihilation of the Hopi village of Pivanhonkyapi was ordered by its own chief, who thus 'purged the dark hearts of his people' (Malotki 2002:115), but at great cost.

---

[4] Whiteley notes that the Hopi he talked to about Orayvi and Awat'ovi saw that the two events stemmed from similar causes (2002:150).

Burnt Corn Pueblo was never reoccupied, with only the apparent absence of primary roof beams to indicate possible salvage of the remains. Although survey of the surrounding acreage demonstrated that the countryside was used by pueblo farmers for at least another 200 years, the immediate vicinity of Burnt Corn remained empty (Snead 2004; 2008a). These circumstances are difficult to explain in material terms, both given patterns of systematic re-use of abandoned sites elsewhere in the region and the fact that even the heavily-used surroundings of Burnt Corn would have eventually regenerated. People found them attractive once, and in neutral conditions would eventually have found them so again.

Thus, any survivors of the destruction do not appear to have been in a position to maintain Burnt Corn as a place with living associations (Snead 2008b). In the absence of any alternative narrative, the meaning associated with the Burnt Corn landscape remained one of destruction. It is not difficult to imagine families of a later era sitting in a field house not far away, looking up at the ruins on the ridge, telling stories of witchcraft and violent death. The relationship of place and conflict at Burnt Corn was critical at the establishment of the community, its destruction, and during its long afterlife.

Conclusion

This consideration of the relationship between place and warfare in the Ancestral Pueblo world is intended to complicate debates about the nature of warfare in prehistory. First, it is evident that war is too narrow a term for what is seen on the ground in the Southwest. Perceiving the various manifestations of death and destruction in Southwestern cases as 'contexts for conflict' rather than as evidence for war in a reductionist sense allows us to rearrange an apparently diverse range of evidence into a larger framework. Thus, evidence for battles with numerous human casualties, such as that found at Castle Rock Pueblo (Kuckelman 2002) can be linked to Debra Martin's description of intra-personal violence in the nearby La Plata valley (1997) as well as to the destruction of places like Pot Creek and Burnt Corn Pueblo, where evidence for human remains associated with the event are scant.

If conflict is manifest at numerous scales and in different contexts, then the role of place can be seen as one overlooked variable among many. The academic lack of concern for place in traditional perceptions of violence reflects our own preoccupations, and our failure to grasp the idea that placemaking is a dynamic process has resulted in an impoverished interpretive approach. If the right to construct meaning is seen as one focus of conflict, then a broad range of events becomes much more comprehensible.

The Awat'ovi and Orayvi scenarios outlined for Burnt Corn are types of destruction-centred conflict that may have developed within the Pueblo cultural context. Although it has been argued that situating processes in this way may sidetrack the discussion of any 'root' causes (i.e. Lekson 2002:618), this is the only way ultimately to make sense of those deeper processes. It is difficult to imagine people intentionally destroying harvest and home in the face of winter, but that—with somewhat less intensity—is in fact what occurred at Orayvi itself.[5] Any 'witchcraft' element would have been epiphenomenal, implying that there were underlying stresses within the community, but that does not mean that it is irrelevant. In the Burnt Corn case, empirical questions remain, and while the preliminary nature of the investigation limits the ability to parse the details, additional scenarios can be imagined. Analyses of information from Burnt Corn continue and will provide new insights (Snead & Allen n.d.). As archaeologists working in the American Southwest edge toward a more historically and culturally-centred perspective on the Ancestral Pueblo past, it should not be surprising that this takes us into the much more tangled terrain that represents human lives as they were actually lived.

Both the Ancestral Pueblo case and the briefly-discussed Maya example hint at the broader implications of place in the consideration of conflict. Considerable archaeological evidence exists for similar processes at work in other examples, as researchers on areas as diverse as the Mississippian (i.e. Dye & King 2007; Milner 1999; Pauketat 2005) and the British Neolithic (i.e. Mercer 1988; Oswald & Barber 2001:129) have noted. Additional complexity is a good thing in anthropological discussions of warfare, and placing landscapes of meaning as resources alongside food, water, population and wealth is a considerable advance.

New light shed on perceptions of conflict by including ideas of place is additionally not restricted to remote contexts but may well illuminate our own experience. The ritualized ways that 21st century United States goes to war, in which one hundred million dollars is annually appropriated to retrieve the bodies of soldiers from distant and long-silent battlefields, would be quite familiar to the ancient Greeks (Alexander 2004; Lendon 1995:3). These attitudes and others may be profitably considered as part of a system of conflict without familiar places, in which only the place represented by the body can be secured as a 'site' for memory. Regardless, it is clear that, as in the specific

[5] The role of the federal authorities in events at Orayvi muddle the picture considerably. Many of the leaders of the expelled 'conservative' faction were quickly arrested, but governmental support also assisted in the establishment of the conservative community of Bacavi (Titiev 1988:87, 94).

case of the Southwest, war and place are integral to each other, and that studying this relationship will improve our grasp of the conflict process as a whole. In the words of a poet of the Mexica lords of Tenochtitlán (Matos Moctezuma 1995:102),

> On the edge of war, near the conflagration,
> you reveal yourself.

Bibliography

Adams, E C 2002 *Homol'ovi: An Ancient Hopi Settlement Cluster.* The University of Arizona Press: Tucson.

Agnew, J A 1989 'Devaluation of Place in Social Science', *in* Agnew, J A & Duncan, J S (eds.) *The Power of Place: Bringing Together Geographical and Sociological Imaginations.* Unwin Human: Boston. 9–29.

Alcock, S E 2002 *Archaeologies of the Greek Past: Landscape, Monuments, and Memories.* Cambridge University Press: Cambridge

Alexander, C 2004 'Across the River Styx', *The New Yorker,* Oct 25, 44–51.

Allen, M W 1994 *Warfare and Economic Power in Simple Chiefdoms: The Development of Fortified Villages and Polities in Mid-Hawke's Bay, New Zealand.* Ph.D. Dissertation, University of California, Los Angeles.

Ambrosino, J H, Ardren, T & Stanton, T W 2003 'The history of warfare at Yaxuná', *in* Brown, M K & Stanton, T W (eds.) *Ancient Mesoamerican Warfare.* Altamira Press: Walnut Creek, California. 109–23.

Anschuetz, K F 1998 *Not Waiting for the Rain: Integrated Systems of Water Management by Pre-Columbian Pueblo Farmers in North-Central New Mexico.* Ph.D. Dissertation, University of Michigan: Ann Arbor.

Arkush, E, and Stanish, C 2005 'Interpreting conflict in the ancient Andes: implications for the archaeology of warfare', *Current Anthrop* 46, 3–28.

Ashmore, W 2002 'Decisions and dispositions: socializing Spatial Archaeology', *Amer Anthrop* 104, 1172–83.

Basso, K 1996 *Wisdom Sits in Places.* The University of New Mexico Press: Albuquerque.

Bevan, R 2007 *The Destruction of Memory: Architecture at War.* Reaktion Books: London.

Billman, B, Lambert, P & Leonard, B 2000 'Cannibalism, warfare, and drought in the Mesa Verde region in the twelfth century AD,' *Amer Antiq* 65, 1–34.

Blades, B S 2003 'European military sites as ideological landscapes', *Hist Archaeol* 37, 46–54.

Bradley, R 1993 *Altering the Earth: the Origins of Monuments in Britain and Continental Europe.* Monograph Series 8, Society of Antiquaries of Scotland: Edinburgh.

—— 2000 *An Archaeology of Natural Places.* Routledge: London.

Brown, M K & Garber, J F 2003 'Evidence of conflict during the Middle Formative in the Maya Lowlands: a view from Blackman Eddy, Belize', *in* Brown, M K & Garber, J F (eds.) *Ancient Mesoamerican Warfare.* Altamira Press: Walnut Creek, California. 91–108.

Cameron, C 1990 'Pit structure abandonment in the Four Corners region of the American Southwest: Late Basketmaker III and Pueblo I Periods', *J Field Archaeol* 17, 27–37.

Carman, J 1999 'Bloody Meadows: the places of battle,' *in* Tarlow, S & West, S (eds.) *The Familiar Past? Archaeologies of Later Historic Britain.* Routledge: London. 233–45.

—— 2002 'Paradox in places: twentieth-century battlefield sites in long-term perspective', *in* Schofield, J, Johnson, W G & Beck, C M (eds.) *Matériel Culture: The Archaeology of Twentieth Century Conflict.* Routledge: London. 9–21.

Chapman, J 1994 'Destruction of a common heritage: the archaeology of war in Croatia, Bosnia, and Hercegovina,' *Antiq* 68, 120–26.

Chenault, M L & Motsinger, T M 2000 'Colonization, warfare, and regional competition: recent research into the Basketmaker III Period in the Mesa Verde region', *in* Reed, P (ed.) *Foundations of Anasazi Culture: The Basketmaker-Pueblo Transition.* The University of Utah Press: Salt Lake City. 45–65.
Creamer, W 1993 *The Architecture of Arroyo Hondo Pueblo, New Mexico.* The School of American Research Press: Santa Fe, New Mexico.
Crown, P A 1991 'Evaluating the construction sequence and population of Pot Creek Pueblo, northern New Mexico', *Amer Antiq* 56, 291–314.
Dahlin, B H 2000 'The barricade and abandonment of Chunchuchmil: implications for northern Maya warfare', *Latin Amer Antiq* 11, 283–98.
Darling, J A 1999 'Mass inhumation and the execution of witches in the American Southwest', *Amer Anthrop* 100, 732–52.
Demarest, A, Morgan, K, Wolley, C & Escobedo, H 2003 'The political acquisition of sacred geography: the Murciélagos Complex at Dos Pilas', *in* Christie, J J (eds.) *Maya Palaces and Elite Residences: An Interdisciplinary Approach.* The University of Texas Press: Austin. 120–53.
Demarest, A, O'Mansky, A M, C Wolley, Van Tuerenhout, D, Inomata, T, Palka J W & Escobedo, H 1997 'Classic Maya defensive systems and warfare in the Petexbatun region', *Ancient Mesoamerica* 8, 229–53.
De Marrais, E, Castillo, L J & Earle, T K 1996 'Ideology, materialization, and power strategies', *Current Anthrop* 37, 15–32.
Dumarest, N 1919 'Notes on Cochiti, New Mexico', *Mem Amer Anthrop Assoc* 6, 134–236.
Dye, D H & King, A 2007 'Desecrating the Sacred Ancestor temples: chiefly conflict and violence in the American Southeast,' *in* Chacon, R J & Mendoza, R G (eds.) *North American Indigenous Warfare and Ritual Violence.* The University of Arizona Press: Tucson. 160–81.
Earle, T K 1997 *How Chiefs Come to Power.* Stanford University Press: Palo Alto, California.
Ellis, F H 1979 'Laguna Pueblo', *in* Ortiz, A (ed.) *Handbook of North American Indians, Vol. 9, Southwest.* Smithsonian Institution Press: Washington, DC. 438–49.
Ember, C R & Ember, M 1997 'Violence in the ethnographic record: results of cross-cultural research on war and aggression,' *in* Martin, D L & Frayer, D W (eds.) *Troubled Times: Violence and Warfare in the Past.* Gordon and Breach: Amsterdam. 1–20.
Feld, S, & Basso, K H 1996 'Introduction', *in* Feld, S & Basso, K H (eds.) *Senses of Place.* The School of American Research Press: Santa Fe, New Mexico. 3–12.
Fewkes, J W 1893 'A-wa'-tobi: an archaeological verification of a Tusayan legend', *Amer Anthrop* 6, 363–75.
Ferguson, R B 1997 'Violence and war in prehistory', *in* Martin, D L & Frayer, D W (eds.) *Troubled Times: Violence and Warfare in the Past.* Gordon and Breach: Amsterdam.
Fowles, S M 2004 *The Making of Made People: The Prehistoric Evolution of Hierocracy Among the Northern Tiwa of New Mexico.* Ph.D. dissertation, Department of Anthropology, University of Michigan.
Friedel, D A 1998 'Sacred work: dedication and termination in Mesoamerica', *in* Mock S B (ed.) *The Sowing and the Dawning: Termination, Dedication, and Transformation in the Archaeological and Ethnographic Record of Mesoamerica.* The University of New Mexico Press: Albuquerque. 189–93.
Friedel, D A, Suhler, C K & Palma, R C 1998 'Termination ritual deposits at Yaxuna: detecting the historical in archaeological contexts', *in* Mock, S B (ed.) *The Sowing and the Dawning: Termination, Dedication, and Transformation in the Archaeological and Ethnographic Record of Mesoamerica.* The University of New Mexico Press: Albuquerque. 135–44.
Gilchrist, R 2003 'Introduction: towards a social archaeology of warfare', *World Archaeol* 35, 1–6.
Haas, J 1990 'Warfare and the evolution of tribal polities in the prehistoric Southwest', *in* Haas, J (ed.) *The Anthropology of War.* Cambridge University Press: Cambridge. 171–89.
Haas, J & Creamer, W 1993 *Stress and Warfare Among the Kayenta Anasazi of the Thirteenth Century AD.* Fieldiana Anthropology, n.s., no. 21.
Harrington, J P 1916 *The Ethnogeography of the Tewa Indians.* Annual report 29 1907–08, Bureau of American Ethnology, U.S. Government Printing Office: Washington, DC.

Hassig, R 1992 *War and Society in Ancient Mesoamerica.* The University of California Press: Berkeley.
Hegmon, M 2002 'Concepts of community in archaeological research', *in* Varien, M D & Wilshusen, R H (eds.) *Seeking the Centre Place: Archaeology and Ancient Communities in the Mesa Verde Region.* The University of Utah Press: Salt Lake City. 263–79.
Hill, P & Wileman, J 2002 *Landscapes of War: The Archaeology of Aggression and Defence.* Tempus: Stroud, Gloucestershire.
Inomata, T 1997 'The last day of a fortified Classic Maya centre: archaeological investigations at Aguateca, Guatemala', *Ancient Mesoamerica* 8, 337–51.
Keeley, L H 1996 *War Before Civilization.* Oxford University Press: New York.
Kohler, T A & Turner, K K 2006 'Raiding for women in the pre-Hispanic Southwest?', *Current Anthrop* 47, 1035–45.
Kolb, M J & Dixon, B 2002 'Landscapes of war: rules and conventions of conflict in Ancient Hawai'i (and elsewhere)', *Amer Antiq* 67, 514–34.
Kolb, M J & Snead, J E 1997 'It's a small world after all: comparative analyses of community organization in archaeology', *Amer Antiq* 62, 609–28.
Kuckelman, K A 2000 'The final days of Castle Rock Pueblo', *in* Kukelman, K A (ed.) *The Archaeology of Castle Rock Pueblo: A Thirteenth-Century Village in Southwest Colorado.* Electronic Document: http://www.crowcanyon.org/castlerock. Accessed February 16, 2005.
—— 2002 'Thirteenth-century warfare in the central Mesa Verde region', *in* Varien, M D & Wilshusen, R H (eds.) *Seeking the Centre Place: Archaeology and Ancient Communities in the Mesa Verde Region.* The University of Utah Press: Salt Lake City. 233–53.
Kuckelman, K A, Lightfoot, R R & Martin, D L 2002 'The bio-archaeology and taphonomy of violence at Castle Rock and Sand Canyon Pueblos, Southwestern Colorado,' *Amer Antiq* 67, 486–513.
Lambert, P M 2002 'The archaeology of war: a North American perspective', *J Archaeol Res* 10, 207–42.
LeBlanc, S A 1997 'Modeling warfare in Southwestern prehistory', *N Amer Archaeol* 18, 235–76.
—— 1999 *Prehistoric Warfare in the American Southwest.* University of Utah Press: Salt Lake City.
—— 2001 'Warfare and aggregation in the El Morro Valley, New Mexico', *in* Rice, G E & LeBlanc, S A (eds.) *Deadly Landscapes: Case Studies in Prehistoric Southwestern Warfare.* The University of Utah Press: Salt Lake City. 19–49.
—— 2003 *Constant Battles: The Myth of the Peaceful, Noble Savage.* St. Martin's Press: New York.
Lekson, S H 2002 'War in the Southwest, war in the world,' *Amer Antiq* 67, 607–24.
Lendon, J E 2005 *Soldiers & Ghosts: A History of Battle in Classical Antiquity.* Yale University Press: New Haven.
Levy, J E 1992 *Orayvi Revisited: Social Stratification in an AEgalitarian@ Society.* School of American Research Press: Santa Fe, New Mexico.
Lowell, J C 2007 'Women and men in warfare and migration: implications of gender imbalance in the Grasshopper region of Arizona', *Amer Antiq* 72, 95–124.
Lycett, M T 2002 'Transformations of place: occupational history and differential persistence in seventeenth-century New Mexico,' *in* Preucel, R (ed.) *Archaeologies of the Pueblo Revolt: Identity, Meaning, and Renewal in the Pueblo World.* The University of New Mexico Press: Albuquerque. 61–76.
Lynn, J A 2003 *Battle: A History of Combat and Culture.* Westview Press: Boulder, Colorado.
Malotki, E (ed.) 2002 *Hopi Tales of Destruction.* University of Nebraska Press: Lincoln.
Martin, D L 1997 'Violence against women in the La Plata River Valley (AD 1000–1300)', *in* Martin, D L & Frayer, D W (eds.) *Troubled Times: Violence and Warfare in the Past.* Gordon and Breach: Amsterdam.
Matos Moctezuma, E 1995 *Life and Death in the Templo Mayor.* University Press of Colorado: Niwot.
Mercer, R J 1988 'Hambledon Hill, Dorset, England', *in* Burgess, C, Topping, P & Maddison, M (eds.) *Enclosures and Defences in the Neolithic of Western Europe.* BAR International Series 403(I), British Archaeological Reports: Oxford. 89–106.
Meggitt, M 1977 *Blood is Their Argument: Warfare Among the Mae Enga Tribesmen of the New Guinea Highlands.* Mayfield Publishing Co., Palo Alto, California.

Milner, G R 1999 'Warfare in prehistoric and early Historic eastern North America', *J Archaeol Re* 7, 105–51.
Mock, S B 1998 'The defaced and the forgotten: decapitation and flaying/mutilation as a termination event at Colha, Belize', *in* Mock, S B (ed.) *The Sowing and the Dawning: Termination, Dedication, and Transformation in the Archaeological and Ethnographic Record of Mesoamerica*. The University of New Mexico Press: Albuquerque. 113–23.
Montgomery, R G, Smith, W & Brew, J O 1949 *Franciscan Awatovi: The Excavation and Conjectural Reconstruction of a 17th-Century Spanish Mission Establishment at a Hopi Indian Town in Northeastern Arizona*. Reports of the Awatovi Expedition, Peabody Museum. No. 3. Harvard: Cambridge
Munn, N D 1970 'The transformation of subjects into objects in Walbiri and Pitjantjatjara myth', *in* Berndt, R M (ed.) *Australian Aboriginal Anthropology: Modern Studies in the Social Anthropology of the Australian Aborigines*. University of Western Australia Press: Perth. 143–63.
Myers, F R 1986 *Pintupi Country, Pintupi Self: Sentiment, Place, and Politics Among Western Desert Aborigines*. Smithsonian Institution Press: Washington DC.
—— 2000 'Ways of placemaking', *in* Flint, K & Morphy, H (eds.) *Culture, Landscape, and the Environment: the Linacre Lectures 1997*. Oxford University Press: Oxford. 72–110.
Ortiz, A 1969 *The Tewa World: Space, Time, Being, and Becoming in a Pueblo Society*. University of Chicago Press: Chicago.
—— 1979 'San Juan Pueblo', *in* Ortiz, A (ed.) *Handbook of North American Indians, Vol. 9, Southwest*. Smithsonian Institution Press: Washington, DC. 278–95.
Oswald, A, Dyer, C & Barber, M (eds.) 2001 *The Creation of Monuments: Neolithic Causewayed Enclosures in the British Isles*. English Heritage: Swindon.
Otterbein, K F 1999 'A history of research on warfare in anthropology', *Amer Anthrop* 101, 794–805.
—— 2004 *How War Began*. Texas A & M University Press: College Station.
Pagliaro, J B, Garber, J F & Stanton, T W 2003 'Evaluating the archaeological signatures of Maya ritual and conflict,' *in* Brown , K & Stanton, T W (eds.) *Ancient Mesoamerican Warfare*. Altamira Press: Walnut Creek, California. 75–89.
Parker Pearson, M 2005 'Warfare, violence and slavery in later prehistory: an introduction', *in* Parker Pearson, M & Thorpe, I J N (eds.) *Warfare, Violence and Slavery in Prehistory*. BAR International Series 1374, British Archaeological Reports: Oxford. 19–33.
Parsons, E C 1929 *The Social Organization of the Tewa of New Mexico*. Memoirs of the American Anthropological Association 36. AAA: Menasha, Wisconsin.
—— 1994[1926] *Tewa Tales*. The University of Arizona Press: Tucson.
Pauketat, T R 2005 'Mounds, buildings, posts, palisades and compounds', *in* Pauketat, T (ed.) *The Archaeology of the East St. Louis Mound Centre, Part I: The Southside Excavations*. Illinois Transportation Archaeological Research Program 21. 113–92.
Plog, S 2003 'Social conflict, social structure and processes of culture change', *Amer Antiq* 68.
Pollard, T 2001 '"Place Ekowe in a state of defence": the archaeological investigation of the British fort at KwaMondi, Eshowe, Zululand', *in* Freeman, P W M & Pollard, A (eds.) *Fields of Conflict: Progress and Prospect in Battlefield Archaeology*. BAR International Series 958. British Archaeological Reports: Oxford.
—— 2002 'The mountain is their monument: an archaeological approach to the landscapes of the Anglo-Zulu War of 1879', *in* Doyle, P & Bennett, M R (eds.) *Fields of Battle: Terrain in Military History*. Kluwer Academic: Boston. 117–135.
Puleston, D E & Callender, D W, Jr 1967 'Defensive earthworks at Tikal', *Expedition* 9, 40–48.
Redmond, E 1994 *Tribal and Chiefly Warfare in South America*. Memoirs of the Museum of Anthropology of the University of Michigan, 28. University of Michigan Press: Ann Arbor.
Rice, G E & LeBlanc, S A (eds.) 2001 *Deadly Landscapes: Case Studies in Prehistoric Southwestern Warfare*. The University of Utah Press: Salt Lake City.
Rodman, M C 1992 'Empowering Place: multilocality and multivocality', *Amer Anthrop* 94, 640–56.
Sahlins, M 1992 *Anahulu: The Anthropology of History in the Kingdom of Hawaii, Vol. 1, Historical Ethnography*. The University of Chicago Press: Chicago.
Saunders, N J 2002 'Bodies of metal, shells of memory: 'trench art' and the Great War recycled', *in* Buchli, V (eds.) *The Material Culture Reader*. Oxford: Berg. 181–206.

Schaafsma, P 2000 *Warrior, Shield and Star: Imagery and Ideology of Pueblo Warfare.* Western Edge Press: Santa Fe, New Mexico.
Schama, S 1995 *Landscape and Memory.* Alfred A. Knopf: New York.
Snead, J E 2002 'Ancestral Pueblo trails and the cultural landscape of the Pajarito Plateau, New Mexico', *Antiquity* 76, 756–65.
—— 2004 'Ancestral Pueblo settlement dynamics: landscape, scale and context in the Burnt Corn community', *Kiva* 69, 243–69.
—— 2008a *Ancestral Landscapes of the Pueblo World.* The University of Arizona Press: Tucson.
—— 2008b 'History, place and social power in the Galisteo Basin, AD 1250–1325', *in* Varien, M & Potter, J (eds.) *The Social Construction of Communities in the Prehispanic Southwest.* Altamira Press: Lanham, Maryland. 255–70.
Snead, J E & Allen, M W (eds.) in prep *Conflict and Conflagration: Tano Origins in the Galisteo Basin, A.D. 1275–1375.* Anthropological Papers of the University of Arizona. MS under review.
Snead, J E, Creamer, W & van Zandt, T 2004 '"Ruins of our Forefathers": large sites and site clusters in the northern Rio Grande,' *in* Adams, E C & Duff, A I (eds.) *The Protohistoric Pueblo World, AD 1275–1600.* The University of Arizona Press: Tucson. 26–34.
Solometo, J 2006 'The dimensions of war: conflict and culture change in central Arizona,' *in* Arkush, E & Allen, M W (eds.) *Archaeological Perspectives on the Transformation of War.* University Press of Florida: Gainesville. 23–65.
Stewart, K C 1996 *A Space on the Side of the Road: Cultural Poetics in an 'Other' America.* Princeton University Press: Princeton, New Jersey.
Stoller, P 1980 'The negotiation of Songhay space: phenomenology in the Heart of Darkness', *Amer Ethnol* 7, 419–31.
Tarlow, S 1997 'The dread of something after death: violation and desecration on the Isle of Man in the tenth century', *in* Carman, J (ed.) *Material Harm: Archaeological Studies of War and Violence.* Cruithne Press: Glasgow. 133–42.
Titiev, M 1988 [1944] *Old Oraibi.* The University of New Mexico Press: Albuquerque.
Toren, C 1999 *Mind, Materiality, and History: Explorations in Fijian Ethnography.* Routledge: London.
Tuan, Y F 1979 *Landscapes of Fear.* University of Minnesota Press: Minneapolis.
Turner, C G II, & Morris, N T 1970 'A massacre at Hopi', *Amer Antiq* 35, 320–31.
Turner, C G II, & Turner, J A 1999 *Man Corn: Cannibalism and Violence in the Prehistoric American Southwest.* The University of Utah Press: Salt Lake City.
Walker, W H 1998 'Where are the witches of prehistory?', *J Archaeol Method & Theory* 5, 245–308.
Walker, W H & Lucero, L J 2000 'The depositional history of ritual and power', *in* Dobres, M-A & Robb, J E (eds.) *Agency in Archaeology.* Routledge: London. 130–47.
Webster, D L 1976 *Defensive Earthworks at Becan, Campeche, Mexico: Implications for Maya Warfare.* Middle American Research Institute, Publication 41. New Orleans.
—— 2000 'The not so peaceful civilization: a review of Maya war', *J World Prehist* 14, 65–119.
Webster, D L, Murtha, T M, Straight, K D, Silverstein, J, Martinez, H, Terry, R E & Burnett, R 2007 'The Great Tikal Earthwork revisited', *J Field Archaeol* 32, 41–64.
Wetherington, R K 1968 *Excavations at Pot Creek Pueblo.* Fort Burgwin Research Centre: Taos, New Mexico.
White, L 1935 *The Pueblo of Santo Domingo, New Mexico.* Memoirs of the American Anthropological Association No. 43. AAA: Menasha, Wisconsin.
—— 1942 *The Pueblo of Santa Ana, New Mexico.* Memoirs of the American Anthropological Association No. 60. AAA: Menasha, Wisconsin.
—— 1962 *The Pueblo of Sia, New Mexico.* Bureau of American Ethnology Bulletin 184, Washington, DC.
Whiteley, P 1988 *Deliberate Acts: Changing Hopi Culture Through the Oraibi Split.* The University of Arizona Press: Tucson.
—— 2002 'Re-imagining Awat'ovi', *in* Preucel, R (ed.) *Archaeologies of the Pueblo Revolt: Identity, Meaning, and Renewal in the Pueblo World.* The University of New Mexico Press: Albuquerque. 61–76.

Wilcox, D R & Haas, J 1994 'The scream of the butterfly: competition and conflict in the prehistoric Southwest', *in* Gummerman, G (ed.) *Themes in Southwest Prehistory*. School of American Research Press: Santa Fe, New Mexico. 211–38.
Wilcox, D R, Gregory, D A, Hill, J B & Funkhouser, G 2006 'The changing contexts of warfare in the North American Southwest, AD 1200–1700', *in* Wiseman, Regge, O'Laughlin, T C & Snow, C (eds.) *Southwest Interludes: Papers in Honor of Charlotte J. and Theodore R. Frisbie*. The Archaeological Society of New Mexico 32. Albuquerque. 203–32.
Wilcox, D R, Robertson, G Jr., & Wood, J S 2001 'Organized for war: the Perry Mesa settlement system and its central Arizona neighbors', *in* Rice, G E & LeBlanc, S (eds.) *Deadly Landscapes: Case Studies in Prehistoric Southwestern Warfare*. The University of Utah Press: Salt Lake City. 141–94.
Wilshusen, R H 1986 'The relationship between abandonment mode and ritual use in the Pueblo I Anasazi Protokiva', *J Field Archaeol* 13, 245–54.
Vencl, S 1984 'War and warfare in archaeology', *J Anthrop Archaeol* 3, 116–32.
Zuckerman, S 2007 'Anatomy of a destruction: crisis architecture, termination rituals and the fall of Canaanite Hazor', *J Med Archaeol* 20, 3–32.

THE ARCHAEOLOGY OF THE SIEGE OF LEITH, 1560

TONY POLLARD

ABSTRACT

This paper summarises the findings of two evaluations carried out in public spaces in the Leith area, both of which were specifically designed to establish the survival or otherwise of remains relating to the siege of Leith in 1560. Between 6 and 10 November 2006 a trial trenching evaluation was carried out within Pilrig Park to the south of the French citadel to 'ground truth' geophysical anomalies identified during a previous phase of work (Banks *et al.* 2006) and also to establish the character of topographic features on the ground. The main aim of the project was to establish the presence or absence of remains related to the siege fort known as Somerset's Mount which from a map drawn in 1560 is known to have been located in the vicinity. The evaluation identified the remains of a WWII air raid shelter, the remains of a building associated with Pilrig House demolished sometime in the early to mid 19th century, and a possible ditch associated with the fort, into which several archaeological features including the foundation slot of a small building or other structure and a probable blacksmith's forge had been cut.

The second part of this report concerns the evaluation at Leith Links, around 1 km to the north east of Pilrig Park and to east of the French citadel. A week long evaluation similar to that carried out at Pilrig took place in April 2007, the aim being to locate further evidence for siege works. Once again, attention focussed on geophysical anomalies resulting from the previous survey. The Links are traditionally associated with the siege through the presence of two mounds, which at least since the 19th century have been identified as the platforms for siege guns directed against the eastern face of the French citadel. An area between the two mounds, which are scheduled ancient monuments, was trial trenched along with an area further to the north. Only the latter produced physical remains which seem to relate to the 1560 map. These took the form of an earthen bank and possibly related ditches which run along the same alignment as a feature shown on the early map, though there is some question as to its function.

Introduction

The two projects reported here were the second and third phases of a programme of archaeological investigation geared toward the green spaces of Leith, in the first instance Pilrig Park and Leith Links (Figure 1; Pollard 2007). The programme was occasioned by the realisation that buried archaeological remains related to the siege of Leith, which took place in 1560, may survive in these localities. Overlaying the measured survey of the siegeworks drawn up in 1560 onto the modern street map indicates that various elements of

 DOI: 10.1163/157407808X382809

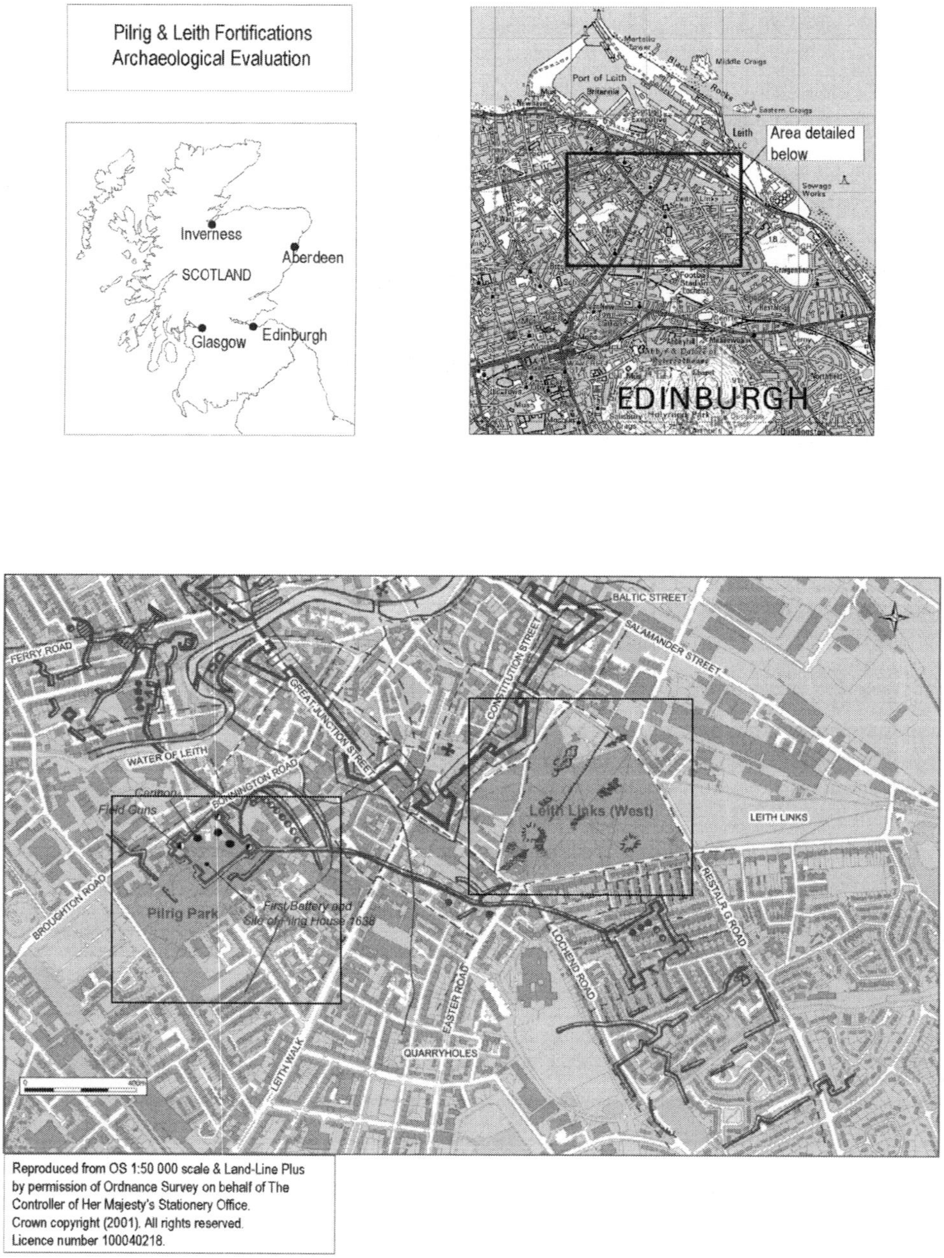

Fig. 1. Locations of areas of interest—Pilrig Park and Leith Links. Modern Ordnance Survey map overlaid with 1560 map.

the works, including an artillery fort, correspond to areas of open parkland, where remains may have survived below ground.

Geophysical survey (Banks *et al.* 1996) produced anomalies at both Leith Links and Pilrig Park, but those at Pilrig looked the most promising—this site corresponding to the location of Somerset's Mount. In addition to what was obviously a WWII air-raid shelter or trench system, the survey also revealed anomalies which may have related to the 16th century fort, which was an earthwork defence thrown up to protect batteries of siege guns. The detailed results, including contexts and pottery catalogue, from the work at Pilrig Park and on Leith Links can be found in the data structure report on both sites (Pollard 2007).

Site Location, Topography & Geology

The Pilrig Park site is located at NGR NT 2640 7575 to the south of the former French citadel of Leith, with the park formerly representing the estate and gardens associated with Pilrig House. The park was gifted to the Corporation of Edinburgh by the Balfour-Melville family in 1941, at which time they abandoned the house, which thereafter fell into disrepair, a later extension by William Burn being demolished in 1969 and the remainder of the house gutted by fire in 1971.

Leith Links (NGR NT 2724 7595) is the largest open green space in the Leith area and today accommodates playing pitches, bowling greens, children's play parks and other communal facilities. Both sites are located on a raised beach where the underlying drift geology consists of sandy soil, derived from previously mobile sand dunes, while the solid geology consists of sandstone.

Historical and Archaeological Background

The Siege of Leith

At the time of the siege in 1560 Leith had become almost an enclave of France, with 3,000 French troops brought into Scotland by the French widow of James V, Mary of Guise. Scotland at the time was divided along religious lines, with the Reformation making a strong impact on the previously dominant Catholic faith. The Protestants found a vociferous mouthpiece in the form of John Knox, while the Catholics sided with the dowager queen and her French allies. By 1560, however, the presence of the French was meeting with widespread objections and, with the Protestants on the ascendancy, moves were made to remove them.

In October 1559, after delivering an ultimatum, the newly empowered Lords of the Congregation put the town of Leith, first fortified by the French in 1548, under siege. Despite being bottled up in the fort and also on the island of Inchkeith (see Pollard, this volume), the French troops took the upper hand for some time and captured the siege guns on Carlton Hill. The result of this failure to take the town was an alliance between the Scots and the English; a clear sign as to how much the political situation had changed, largely through the catalyst of the Scottish Reformation, since the last English invasion which had climaxed with the dramatic Scottish defeat at Pinkie in September 1547. In April 1560, Elizabeth I sent north a fleet to blockade the Firth and an army, under Lord Grey de Wilton, to assist with the siege. The result was a complex series of siege works which entirely surrounded the town.

The siege lasted until 7 July, when the French garrison surrendered following the death of Mary of Guise in June. With the intransigent dowager queen removed from the scene, peace negotiations with the now hard-pressed garrison moved at an accelerated pace and resulted in the Treaty of Edinburgh. A stipulation of the treaty was that all French troops were to depart Scottish shores within 20 days and accordingly by 16 July, both the French and English armies had departed (Harris 1991).

In historical and archaeological terms the siege of Leith is of great importance. The fortifications of the town itself were based on the latest Italian design, with earth ramparts and artillery bastions. Likewise, the siege techniques utilised, with batteries connected by earthworks were based on recent European developments in siege warfare utilising cannon and small arms.

Leith is not the only major Scottish example of a 16th century siege, the other notable and near contemporaneous investment taking place not far from Edinburgh at the town of Haddington. Following the Scottish defeat at Pinkie in 1547, the town was fortified by the English under Grey de Wilton, who was later to command the English component of the besieging force at Leith. Haddington was the scene of the longest town siege in British history, with the English garrison keeping at bay a combined force of Scots and French for no less than 18 months before capitulating and retiring south of the border. Like the siege of Leith it was very much an international affair with the French bringing with them Italian and German mercenaries, while the English used Italian, Spanish and even Albanian troops to bolster the garrison. Not until the middle of the following century, with the onset of the Civil War would any sieges of similar scale take place. The archaeological potential of the Haddington siege has recently been highlighted (Cooper 2008) and it is hoped that a programme of investigation similar to that at Leith may be instigated at some point in the future.

The most important historical source for identifying the character, extent and location of the town defences and associated siegeworks is undoubtedly the Petworth map, named after its location in Petworth House, Sussex (Figure 2). This map appears to have been drawn up at the time of Leith's abandonment or immediately thereafter (Harris 1991); it includes what purports to be a measured plan of the various works superimposed on a three dimensional vista of the background landscape including Edinburgh on the horizon. In his 1991 paper on the map, Harris most usefully transposed modern street locations onto the measured portions of the map. As part of the present project this process was repeated by superimposing Harris's transcription of the Petworth projection onto an Ordnance Survey map of Leith (Figure 1).

Drawn at the end of the siege, the Petworth map shows the extensive siegeworks which had accumulated over the preceding 10 months, since the commencement of the investment in October 1559. The siegeworks may have been in part erected under the supervision of Robert Corneweyle, who was one of the leading exponents of siege warfare in England at the time. He was involved in the later slighting of defences at Dunbar in August 1560 and also translated and augmented the treatise of fortification by the Italian military engineer Giovanni Battista de' Zanchi (White 1967: 429).

According to annotations on the Petworth map (Harris, op. cit.) the earliest 'approach' made by the besiegers and reflected by impressive works took place in April 1560 to the south-east of the citadel, with a large artillery camp known as 'Pelham's Mount' located beneath Hawk Hill, just the east of Leith Links. Like the majority of other works, the site of this impressive structure was subsumed beneath the modern town. The second approach began at the end of April and saw the continuation of the trench system to the west and included a second camp (Figure 3), known as 'Somerset's Mount', in the vicinity of Pilrig House, which was built 78 years after the siege in the remnants of the fort. The third and final approach took the works over the Water of Leith in the vicinity of Old Bonnigton and resulted in the almost entire encirclement of the town. The bulging of the siege works to the south, which included the four-gun battery known as the Falcon, took in the entrenchment dug by the French to protect the mills along the eastern shore of the river. When this salient was eventually reduced, the area around Keddie Gardens was used to sink saps aimed at undermining the huge corner bastion known as the French Citadel Bastion on the western side of the river (Harris 1991: 366).

Archaeology

Although archaeological remains for the siege of Leith, in the form of town defences and siegeworks, have been denuded by over 400 years of urban

Fig. 2. The Petworth map of Leith and the Siege works in 1560, Edinburgh in background (thanks to West Sussex County Council).

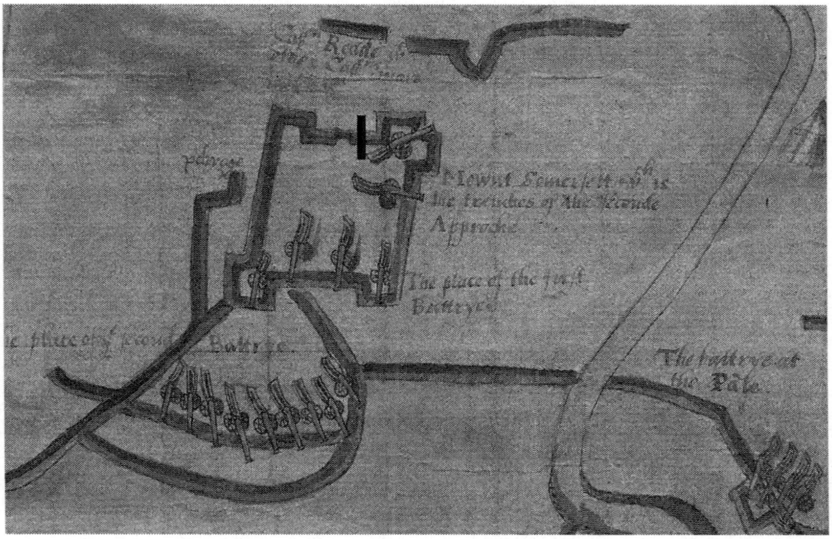

Fig. 3. Detail of Somerset's Mount—approximate location of Trench 2 shown as thick black line across rear rampart.

development, some traces have come to light in recent years and have been recorded by archaeologists working under planning control. Examples include a section of wall perhaps related to Ramsay's fort (Moore *et al.* 2002, 52) built between 1548 and 1549; an earthwork platform related to a gun battery (A-Kelly 2004, 56) was located at in Restalrig Terrace (NT 2747 7556 to NT 2762 7565), while a possible stone cannonball was recovered from Restalrig Churchyard (NT 2834 7446) and an iron example from Giles Street (Halstead 2004). Two mounds on Leith Links have long been interpreted as gun platforms and are protected as Scheduled Ancient Monuments; these are known as Lady Fife's Brae and Giant's Brae and have traditionally been associated with Pelham's battery and Somerset's battery respectively (see below).

Results

Pilrig Park

Figure 7 shows the location of the trenches in both areas in relation to the resistivity survey plot. Details of contexts and artefacts recovered are presented in the data structure report (Pollard 2007). Context numbers referring to cuts are shown in square brackets and those for fills in round.

Trench 1 (Figure 6)

This trench was located over the line of what appeared to be the remnant of a stone wall (1102). This feature ran north-west to south-east along the north eastern edge of the terrace which fronts Pilrig House. The position of the wall corresponds to a building shown on an 1817 map (Figure 5), which shows Pilrig House and the gardens in some detail. At its western end, the trench took in what appeared to be a half-moon shaped feature which was thought to represent a garden feature inside an enclosing wall (a similarly shaped feature appears on the 1817 map, where it is shown to be a path skirting the perimeter of the garden.). The trench extended to the north east for some 18 m, taking in the edge of the terrace and a portion of the lower ground beyond.

The wall survived to a height of approximately 0.5 m and was lime mortared. The western face still retained a thick covering of plaster, which is consistent with this being the interior side of the wall. To the east of the wall was a heavily disturbed area of slab paving (1104). To the west of the wall, the soil deposits were consistent with garden soils and related features; the curved topographic feature was visible as a gravel path, tying in well with the depiction of the area on the 1817 map. Beneath these garden features were the remains of a grubbed out wall (1013) consistent with the western wall of the building evidenced by the intact wall stump (1102). Support for the interpretation of the wall as being part of a building came in the form of fragments of red roof tile.

The archaeological deposits on the eastern side of the wall were more complex. One of the first features of interest to be revealed was a deposit of butchered animal bone and other domestic waste, which included fragments of wine bottles, pot sherds and pieces of heavily rusted iron, which included a door key. This midden deposit probably relates to the house and from the pottery and wine bottles appears to be late 18th/early 19th century in date.

This spread of midden material overlay an extensive band of mortar that contained some domestic rubbish, including pottery sherds, but not to the same extent as the midden deposit above it. Although it is tempting to relate the deposition of this material to the demolition of the building represented by the mortared wall, the presence of stone-free mortar in the deposit suggests that it was imported from elsewhere and used to provide some sort of surface or hard standing. At the eastern end of the trench, the mortar layer was subsumed within a series of road building phases. This road (Plate 1), some 6 metres wide, appears on the 1817 map as a major thoroughfare. The midden material overlying the road consists of artefactual material pre-dating the 1817 map, and it probably represents dumped material, possibly after the

Plate 1. North-west facing section through road deposits in Trench 1.

demolition of the building. The date of the road construction is not known, though it does not appear on the Roy map of the mid-18th century, which shows only an avenue leading to the front of the house.

Trench 2 (Figure 7 and Plate 2)

This trench was positioned across the western edge of the terrace located to the front of Pilrig House, and which appears on the 1817 map to delineate the main garden area related to the house. The trench lies just outside the area of geophysical survey but still on alignment with the linear anomaly shown running south-east to north-west on the plot. The trench was located across the slight bank defining the terrace edge and located immediately to the north of a hollow in the bank, which from the initial map work looked as though it may represent the entrance to the fort.

The initial trench was 14 m long, though this was extended to 18 m when it became apparent that archaeological features were present in the western end. The turf and topsoil overlay a deep mixture of garden soils (2002 & 2003) that contained several sherds of post-Medieval pottery, including a piece of German stoneware from the 17th century. Below the garden soils was a sand layer (2013), which could have been an undisturbed geological layer. As

Plate 2. View along Trench 2 from south-west. Linear feature in foreground, forge just beyond excavator.

it was uncertain whether the sand was entirely undisturbed, the western half of the trench was taken down in spits using the machine bucket, a process which revealed a complex stratigraphy in the section faces and exposed a number of discrete features within the trench.

Plate 3. Section through feature 2010 [trowel] in sand fill of ditch, taken from south-west.

Any suggestion that the sand represented undisturbed geology was dispelled when the machine bucket revealed an archaeological feature both cut into and buried within the sand (Plate 3). Partial excavation of the feature revealed a bowl-shaped cut with a possible step [2010]. The fill contained a white gritty ware jug handle and what appeared to be an iron point. It was at this point that it was realised that the trench was excavating the fill of a ditch, and further excavation continued with mechanical excavation, the aim being to locate the bottom of the ditch.

Removal of the sand and ditch fill revealed a very obvious darker sub-rectangular stain within the sand with a red sandy fill [2016]. There was a secondary feature cut into this deposit [2022], which contained a piece of modern glass, but it also displayed evidence of animal burrowing, which explains the presence of the glass in this location. Despite the compromised nature of the secondary feature [2022], it appeared to hold promise, especially as a sherd of 14th century white gritty ware came from the interface of the two features. The feature proved to be a rectangular cut filled with a high density of ash and cinder, with coal fragments, and heavily scorched sand. Stones in the feature (2018) may have been part of a flue, allowing the input of air into a trough containing the coal and clinker. The feature is undoubtedly related to the use of heat at high temperatures and the presence of the coal and clinker would suggest something like a blacksmith's forge or a small iron smelting site.

A second feature [2024], which again appeared to have been cut into the sandy base of the ditch, was exposed at the western end of the trench, at the same level as the forge feature. The feature appeared as linear band of dark silty sand with a stone protruding from it, the remainder of the sand deposit being almost entirely stone free. Two sherds of pottery were recovered from this deposit, a piece of Low Countries redware from a cooking pot, displaying an internal brown glaze and external sooting, and a sherd from a thin walled, green glazed jug. Both vessels date to the 16th century and are not at odds with activity taking place in or around 1560, and therefore possibly related to the fort and its occupation. The feature [2024] had a V-shaped profile at the north eastern end, but was curved at the other end. The fill included a fragment of probable cattle bone and an oyster shell. The feature appears to be a foundation slot for a wall or some sort of partition, but both ends of the feature disappeared beneath the section walls. Its stratigraphic position suggests it was at least broadly contemporary with the forge-like feature [2016].

Although these basal features may be contemporary with the fort, it is clear that there has been a lot of mixing and re-deposition of both soil horizons and artefacts. A 14th century piece of pottery was recovered from the interface of the forge and the rectangular pit, which also contained a fragment of modern bottle glass. Although this feature sat against the section face, there was no indication that it extended down through the profile from a higher level—which would obviously be expected if it were modern. It may therefore be safer to suggest that the bottle glass had found its way there via the animal burrows in the feature. The fragment of 14th century pot may have originated from this feature or the earlier forge, but does not prove that the forge itself is 14th century. Another example of this stratigraphic mixing was apparent in the bowl-shaped feature [2010], which produced a handle fragment from a white gritty ware jug, probably dating the 14th century and a fragment of possibly 16th century green glazed pottery.

It is clear that the site has been subject to a prolonged sequence of earthmoving, some possibly pre-dating the construction of the fort, while others are contemporary with it or its demolition. This was then followed by a prolonged period of horticultural activity when the ground became the garden of Pilrig House, with tillage continuing until WWII. A 16th century date is suggested for the linear feature [2024]; it is the only feature to have contained two pottery sherds from the same period (though these were on the surface of the fill and not within it). Dating the forge is not as straightforward, however, as the sherd of Medieval pottery may have originated from a later inter-cutting feature. Nonetheless, the stratigraphic relationship of these two features may indicate that they were contemporary with one another.

Trench 3

This trench was located to the south west of Trench 2 and again was positioned across a topographic feature in the form of a slight hummock or bank. This feature clearly lay outside the main terrace and did not seem to coincide with features on any of the maps or aerial photographs. Mechanical excavation revealed a deep garden soil, similar to that exposed in the previous trenches. The presence of gravel and grit in the upper part of the trench exposed the hummock to be nothing more than a footpath. A number of clay pipe fragments were found within the topsoil and are probably another indication that this ground has been heavily tilled, most recently as allotments during the Second World War.

Trench 4

This trench was positioned on the main terrace to the east of Trench 2, an area which may coincide with the interior of the fort. Nothing of interest was identified, and the overburden once again consisted of a deep homogonous deposit of garden soil with a high concentration of charcoal inclusions—probably from the use of domestic midden as fertilizer.

Plate 4. Concrete sections of collapsed air-raid shelter in trench 5.

Trench 5 (Plate 4)

This trench was positioned using the results of the magnetometer survey (Banks *et al.* 2006), which revealed a strong linear anomaly with a number of right angles to its shape; this suggested an air raid shelter or buried military trench system (this can also be seen on the resistivity survey in Figure 4).

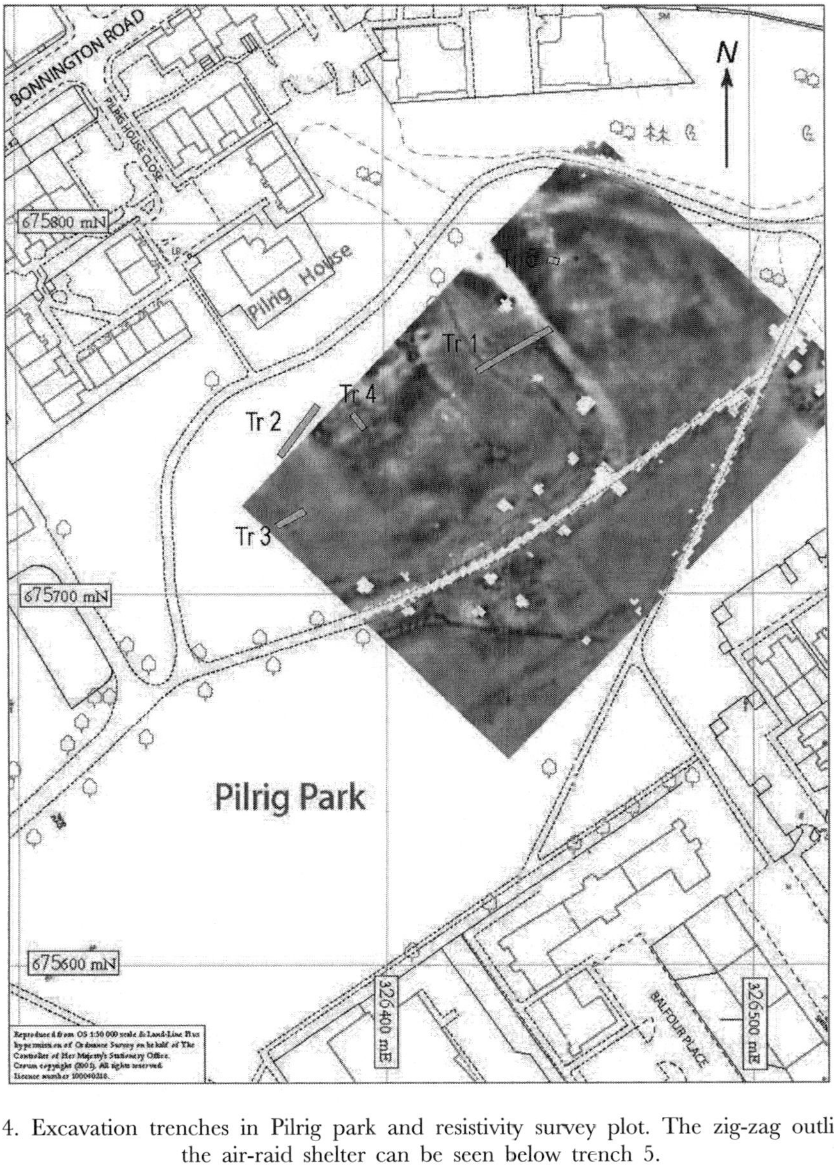

Fig. 4. Excavation trenches in Pilrig park and resistivity survey plot. The zig-zag outline of the air-raid shelter can be seen below trench 5.

Machine excavation down through a deep deposit of topsoil/garden soil terminated at a depth of just over 1 m on the exposure of concrete. What was at first thought to be an *in-situ* concrete access hatch was revealed to be a dislocated panel section from either the walls or the roof of the shelter. The panel was removed in order to examine further evidence for concrete elements

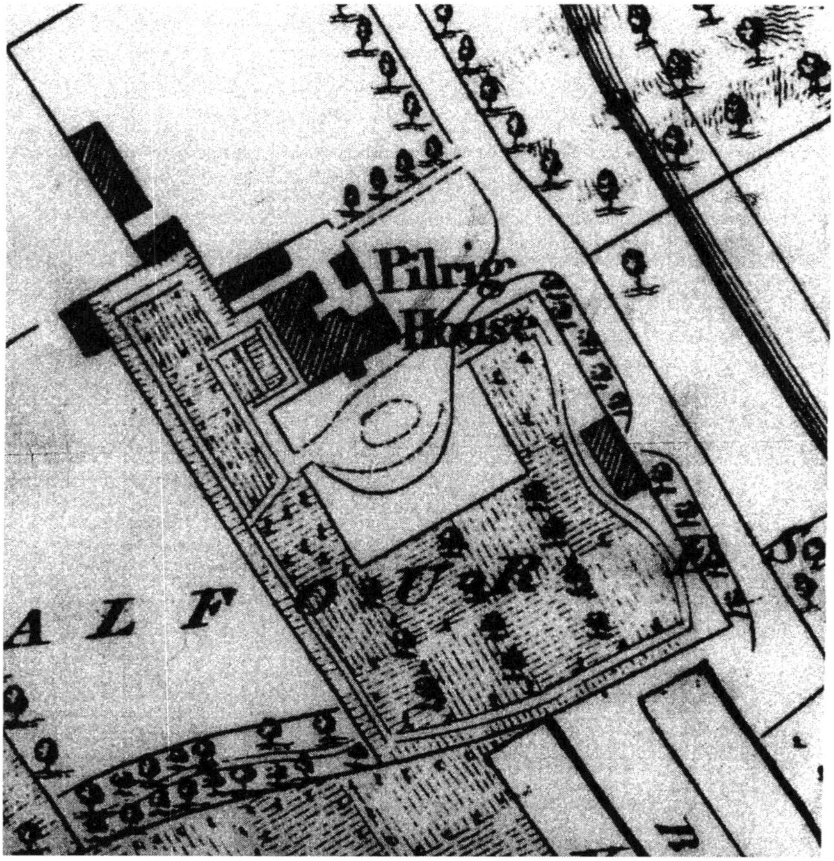

Fig. 5. 1817 map showing Pilrig house and gardens, building in trench 1 appears to right below house.

beneath it. Continued cleaning exposed three frames of concrete resembling goal posts lying like toppled dominoes one on top of the other. These were clearly the supports for a subterranean tunnel which had been demolished some time after the Second World War.

Although no evidence for a cut was detected in the trench sections, the shelter must have been constructed by first digging a trench and then slotting in the frames, probably using concrete panels to fill the voids between the frames and also to create the roof. Once constructed, the trench was then probably backfilled, at least to the point of covering the roof of the structure—though it is possible that the roof of the structure stood proud of the ground surface. What remains a mystery is the low height of the structure suggested by the length of the concrete uprights, which were not much more than a

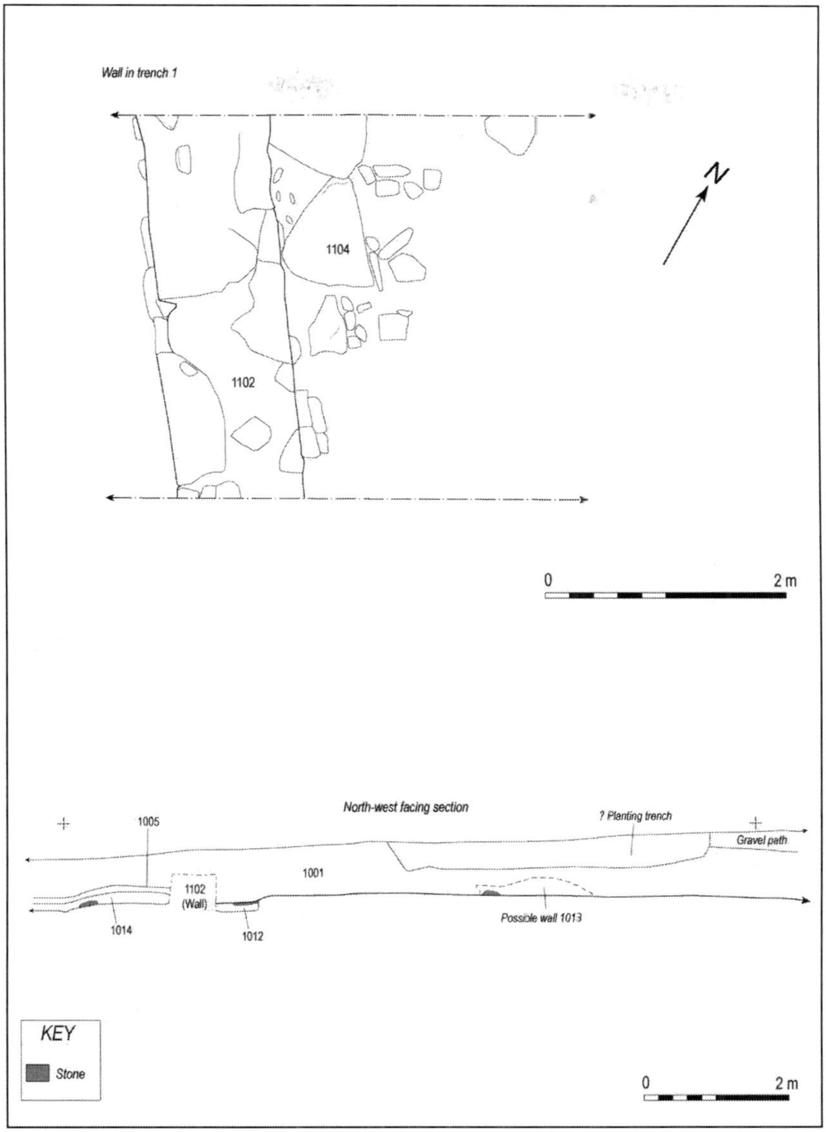

Fig. 6. Sections and features in Trench 1.

metre long. It is possible that other elements of the tunnel system were higher, but this would require further investigation. No parallels for this construction have been found so far, and further investigation of these remains is required to provide an understanding of the nature of the site. The outline of the shelter can be seen in the 1946 aerial photograph of the park but it is not possible to say whether this represents the intact shelter or was post-demolition—given

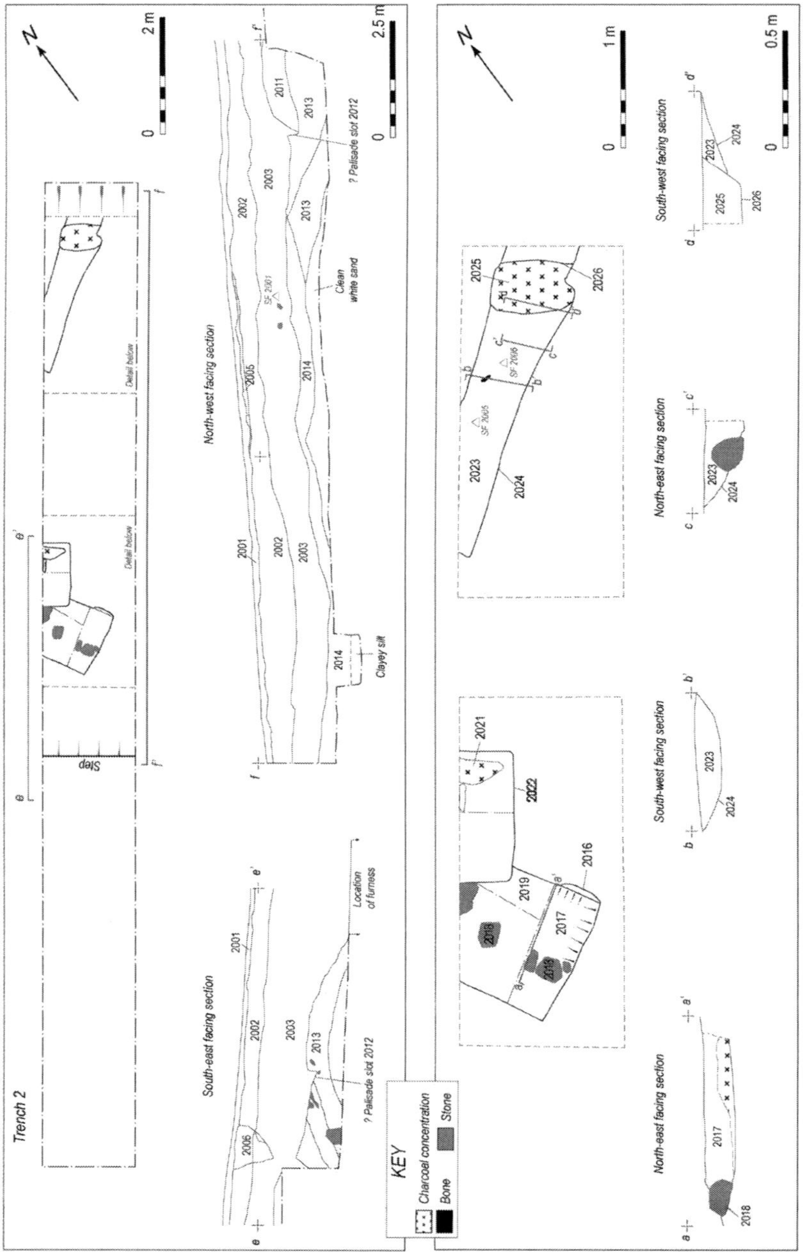

Fig. 7. Sections and features in Trench 2.

the immediate post-War date of the photograph, however, the former would seem the more likely.

Discussion of Pilrig Park Results

Summary of the Pilrig Fieldwork Results

The evaluation of the potential for archaeological remains relating to the 1560 fort and other periods of Leith's past at Pilrig Park was a very successful exercise. Three of the five trenches provided considerable evidence for human activity stretching over almost 400 years, from activity possibly related to the 1560 siege of Leith to the construction of an air-raid shelter between 1939 and 1940 and its later demolition. Sandwiched between these two distinct events was a prolonged period of domestic occupation related to Pilrig House and its associated gardens, with activity stretching from at least the 18th century up to perhaps the 20th.

The earliest features on the site, dated on the basis of pottery finds, were those probably related to the fort known as Somerset's Mount, which was built as an artillery emplacement by the English during the six month-long siege of Leith. The 14th century pottery sherds indicate earlier activity, but little more can be said about this on the basis of the current evidence. The location of the trench over what may prove to be the heavily denuded ditch on the western side of the fort was extremely fortuitous as it exposed two features, one of which was associated with 16th century pottery. This linear feature may represent the foundation slot for a shelter or hut of some sort. The other feature appears to be a blacksmith's forge, again sealed beneath the fill of the ditch. Its presence in the ditch makes sense, as it would surely not have been desirable to have a fire-related activity inside the fort, which given its function as an artillery defence would contain large quantities of gunpowder.

Evidence for the next obvious phase of human activity was provided by Trench 1, where the remains of a building associated with the garden of Pilrig House was identified. This building, which appears on the 1817 map of the area, was demolished some time thereafter, and is entirely absent from a map of 1870. The western wall was entirely removed, leaving only a shallow robber trench as evidence of its presence, while the lower courses of the eastern wall were retained, possibly as a form of garden feature to the rear of the flower beds. Material from the demolished building, including pan tiles from the roof were used in the upper make-up of a multi-phased roadway which passed from north-west to south-east close to the eastern side of the building. This material also included domestic waste dating back some considerable time prior to the destruction of the building, which included 17th or 18th century wine bottles and sherds of 18th and 19th century pottery.

The most recent activity of note comes from the smallest of the excavated trenches (Trench 5), which was positioned over a geophysical anomaly, which was thought to represent a defensive structure from WWII. This supposition was proved correct when concrete roof supports were found lying in the bottom of the trench, the probably semi-subterranean structure having been demolished sometime after 1945. It was a little surprising, however, that none of the locals questioned, even those of an age to remember the war, had any memory of there being a shelter in this location, though some of them did recall one to the west of Pilrig House (one visitor was good enough to bring along a photograph of a still upstanding brick blockhouse taken sometime in the early 1960s).

Interpretive Issues

The main interpretive issues relate to the features in Trench 2, where the problem of dating features on the basis of a mixed pottery assemblage has already been discussed (see Will, appendix in Pollard 2007). The other issue relates to the interpretation of the shallow ditch as part of the artillery fort constructed in 1560. On the basis of current evidence, this feature seems slighter than the deep defensive ditches one would normally associate with an earthwork fortification. However, a number of issues need to be considered here. One of these is the possibility that the ditch was not bottomed during the evaluation. Though every attempt was made to establish that the clean sand exposed in the bottom of the trench did represent the base of the ditch, through the digging of a sondage which exposed clean grey silt beneath clean sand (2014), it is possible that further machine excavation may have revealed this to be no more than another element of the fill. Another factor which needs to be taken into account is the probable deliberate slighting of the defences once the siege was over.

In order to prevent the various siegeworks from being used by any future aggressor, the Treaty of Edinburgh which brought an end to hostilities included a clause (item 6) which insisted that:

> That the walls of Leith should be thrown downe, and the fortifications demolished by viewe of the commissioners of the Queene of England, in such sort as they should see fit,

and the records further tell us that: 'the fortifications around Leith were beaten Downe' (Bruce 1840, 72). If the fort took the form of an earth bank or rampart, possibly topped by a timber palisade, fronted by a ditch—with material thrown up from the ditch creating the bank—then this process would be a much lesser undertaking than the much more substantial stone based walls of the citadel.

Consideration of the fort's character should also take into account the context of the fortification and the job it was required to do. The fort was built to house English siege guns, used in the reduction of the citadel walls and the bombardment of the interior. The defences would protect the guns from counter-battery fire, i.e. cannon firing at them from the citadel, and from raids by French troops making sallies from behind the citadel walls. Given that the direction of assault from both enemy artillery and infantry was likely to be against the face of the fort opposing the citadel—the north east, which ran directly parallel with the citadel wall, this would perhaps be expected to be the most substantial and impressively constructed portion of the fort, with the deepest ditch and the highest rampart. Correspondingly, the defences at the back of the fort may not have been as substantial as those at the front as they were not required to defend against incoming fire or hold up against direct enemy attack. The fact that the fort was fronted by a series of trenches would make a flanking manoeuvre, which brought the enemy to the rear of the fort, an unlikely occurrence. Indeed, as portrayed on the Petworth map, the fort is well to the rear of these defences as there is another dug-in gun battery located to its front. With this in mind, a very deep ditch to the back of the fort is perhaps unlikely. What survives is a wide, relatively shallow feature, with evidence for structures in its base, and a denuded bank behind it. Given that the bank was at some time pushed down and the soil from which it was formed used to create a garden, its vestigial character perhaps makes a little more sense.

The addition of a timber palisade may have further reduced the need for a substantial bank, and some evidence for this may take the form of possible post holes or construction slots cut (2012) into the face of the bank and visible in both the N- and S-facing sections (Figure 7). Equally possible, however, is that these 'V' shaped features represent spade cuts related to the throwing down of the bank. The above also assumes that the bottom of the ditch was reached during the excavation; this may not be the case, which would imply that the basal features (slot and forge) were constructed in the partial back fill of the ditch rather than its base.

Leith Links Evaluation Results

Area 1

Figure 8 shows the location of the trenches in both areas in relation to the resistivity survey plot. Details of contexts and artefacts recovered are presented in the data structure report (Pollard 2007).

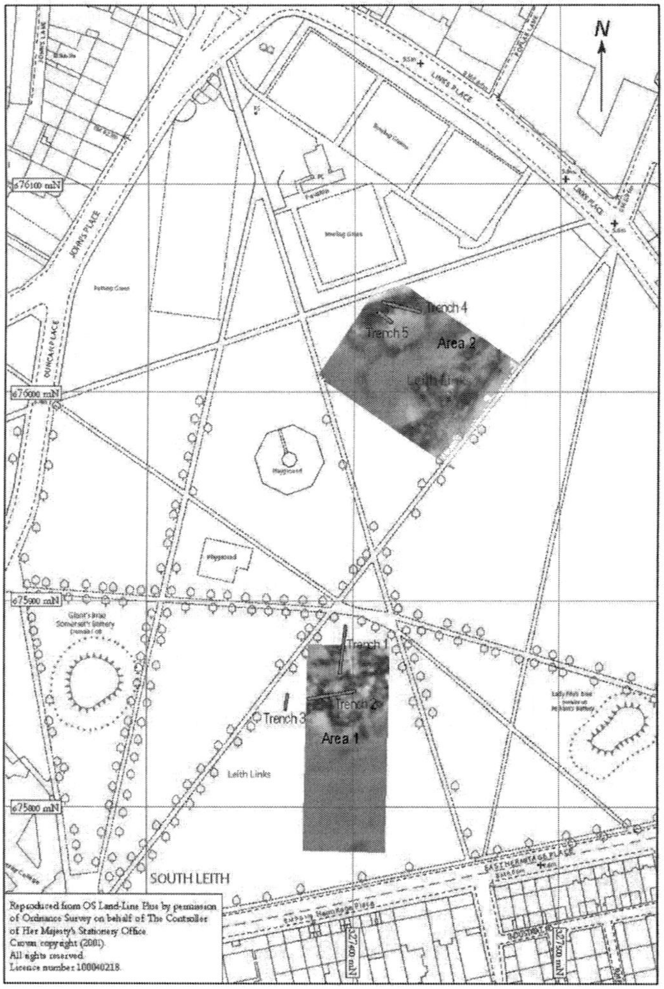

Fig. 8. Excavation trenches on Leith Links and resistivity survey plot.

Trench 1

This trench was 1.5 m wide and 24 m long on a north-south orientation. It was positioned to investigate a rectangular resistivity anomaly that was interpreted as a possible structure. Removal of the turf and topsoil exposed a number of archaeological features and further examination revealed a series of shallow, possibly truncated features that in one instance at least appeared to relate to a former flower bed. None of the features identified in the upper part of Trench 1 appeared to date earlier than the early 20th or later

19th centuries. The larger features may relate to earlier garden features in the park, while the smaller ephemeral features may relate to any number of activities to have taken place on the Links over the past century. It is perhaps notable that the Links were the location of a large First World War tented military hospital (Ken Ogilvy, pers comm), and a pair of what appear to be large tent pegs of angle iron, one of which was found in Trench 1 and the other in Trench 2, may relate to this period of the Links' long history.

To test whether archaeological features might exist beneath the sand at a greater depth, the mechanical excavator was used to cut a deep sondage in the southern end of the trench. The exposed spits and sections revealed deposits of wind-blown sand, with excavation ceasing at a depth of almost 2 m.

Trench 2

This trench, measuring 1.5 m by 24 m, was located to the south of Trench 1 and perpendicular to it, running E/W. It was located over a slight hump or eminence visible close to the footpath. Only one archaeological feature was identified, a small pit in the western end, packed with stones and pieces of masonry, including ashlar and brick. A further sondage was cut into the eastern end of the trench and again revealed deep wind-blown sand in keeping with the Links' origin as a series of sand dunes. No obvious explanation for the surface hump was apparent.

Area 2

While recording work continued in Area 1, a further trench (4) was opened some 150 m to the north, with a second trench (5) close by. As with Area 1, this location had been selected from the results of the resistivity survey. One of the most obvious results was a linear anomaly, which appeared to correspond to the line marked on the Petworth map (Figure 9), running in NE/SW and apparently aligned on Giant's Brae (Figure 1 & Figure 8). Although possibly an associated siegework, being portrayed using the same convention as the other entrenchments shown on the map, the feature is isolated from the other siege-related features on the map; it has been suggested that it represents a ditch surviving from an earlier campaign: possibly the temporary English incursion in May 1547, which preceded the Pinkie campaign in September of that year (Harris 1991, 368). However, such a construction would have been unnecessary in this lightning campaign, and it is perhaps more likely that it represents a defensive work thrown up by the Scots to defend Leith against the English invading force. An anonymous chronicler of the event described the closing stages of the assault on Leith thus:

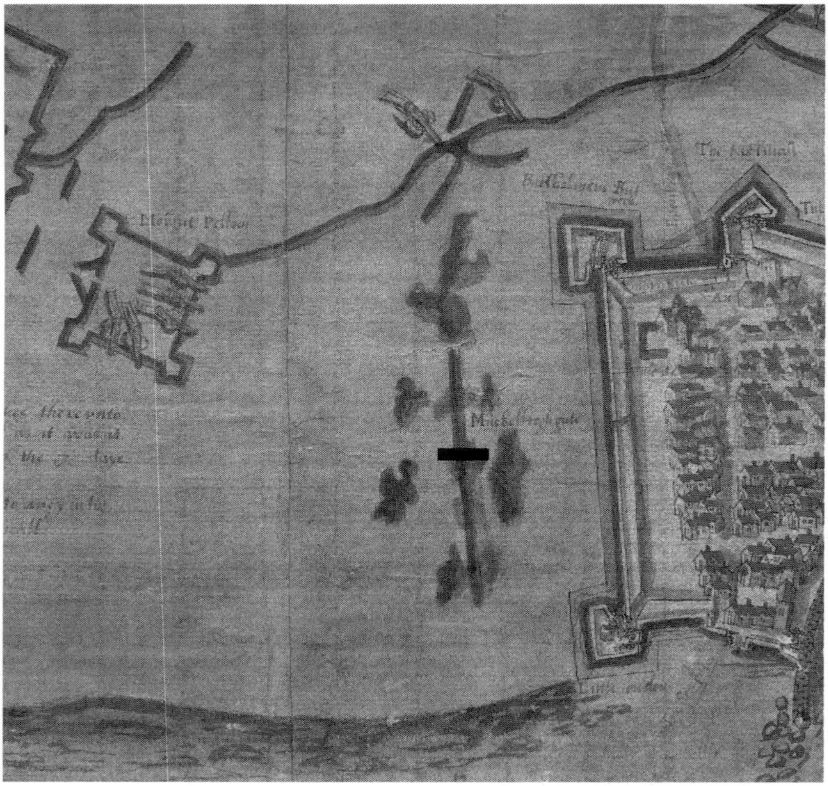

Fig. 9. Detail of Petworth map showing linear feature running across Leith Links. Approximate location of trench 4 shown as thick black line.

> And in this brunt, the victory being earnestly followed; the town of Leith was entered perforce and won with the loss only of two men of ours and hurt of three: where the Scots had cast great trenches and ditches purposely to have defended it. The same night, the army encamped in the said town of Leith; and by reason of the said ditches and trenches, we made there a strong camp (quoted in Pollard 1903: 40–41).

Alternatively, it may relate to an early attempt by the French to fortify the town in 1548, following the pattern at Haddington (J Cooper, pers comm). It was hoped that excavation may shed light on this feature, which quickly became the main focus for the Leith Links investigation.

Trench 4 (Figure 10)

The first of the two trenches opened in Area 2 was oriented just off E/W and was 20 m long. Removal of turf and topsoil revealed the same sandy soil as apparent in the previous trenches. As no archaeological features were

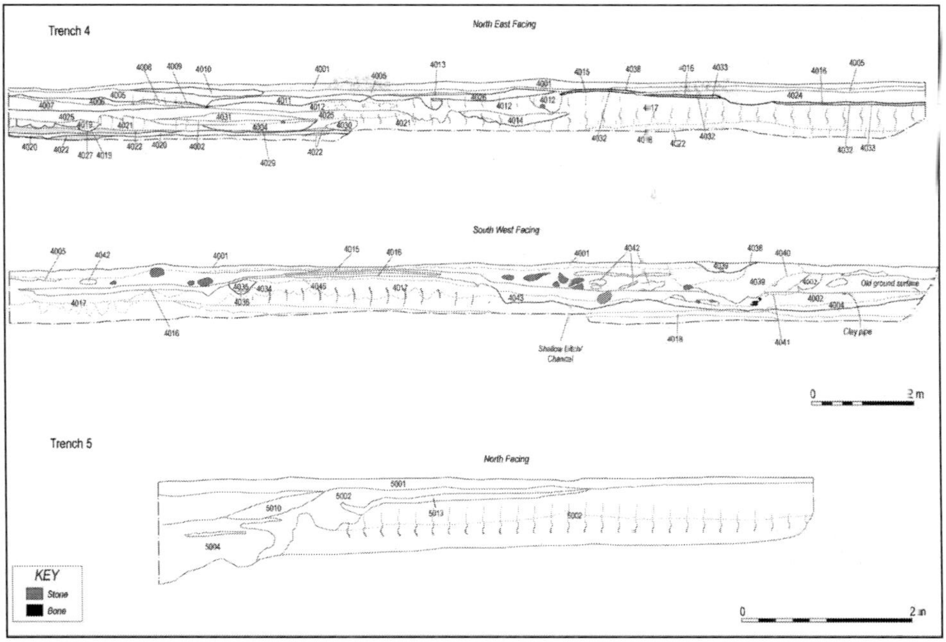

Fig. 10. Sections of trenches 4 and 5.

immediately apparent, the excavation was continued downward by machine, the intention being to record the stratigraphy by section rather than in plan.

Excavation ceased at a depth of around 1.5 m on a deposit of clean sand. The exposed sections revealed a complex sequence of events which included a feature commensurate with the linear feature suggested in the geophysics and shown on the Petworth map. Most of what follows relates to the SW-facing section, which provided the clearest evidence for the bank; the NE-facing section was much more disturbed by later activity. The full details of the stratigraphy are reported in the data structure report (Pollard 2007).

The main feature of significance was a deposit of what appeared to be natural wind-blown sand (4017: visible in both sections), with a series of undulations in its upper surface that appear to represent both cuts into the layer, in the form of shallow ditches or channels, and its subsequent mounding to create a cambered, bank-like feature. This feature was very obvious where it appeared in the SW-facing section, with edges dropping down on both sides to create a low bank some 6.5 m wide. However, the section may not have been cut at a right angle to the feature and the real width of the bank may be less than this. The NE-facing section displayed extensive later disturbance and, although the western edge of the bank was visible, it extended for only ca. 3.2 m before a series of later cuts and fills removed entirely the eastern portion of the bank.

The surface of bank (4017) contained a feature that suggests the back was a structural feature rather than the upcast from any of the linear features that can be seen in the section (eg putative ditches 4043 or 4004). The feature [4034] may represent a slot or posthole for a timber fence or palisade running along the west-facing edge of the bank. It may be no coincidence that this is the edge which faces the citadel from where enemy fire would be delivered. However, before any definitive statement is made on either the nature of the bank or any timber structure built into it, a much more substantial portion of the feature would require excavation.

Overlying the bank was a possible old turf line (4002), which continued off the bank in both directions along the section face. This sealed the feature cut into the western edge of the bank [4034] and the lower fills of two possible ditches (4004 and 4043) on the other side. The development of this surface would appear to post-date the active use of the bank and much of the filling on the ditches. On top of the bank, this layer was capped by a thin deposit of clay, which was itself covered by another, later turf line (4015).

The dumping of material into the ditches or channels (4004 & 4043) may represent an attempt to reclaim an area of generally wet ground indicated by what appear to be standing pools of water shown on the Petworth map. Today, Leith Links appears entirely removed from its original maritime environment. However, this separation of land and sea is a relatively recent phenomenon; an elderly local resident who lived through WWII remembers the floor of an air raid shelter behind the street not far to the north of the site (in the vicinity of Salamander Street) being inundated with water at every high tide.

Overlying these ditches/channels and the bank was a layer of re-deposited sand, within which were a series of dark organically rich deposits (4042) representing roughly cut sods of turf. The angles at which many of these turfs sit within in the sand suggest tip lines, indicating that they were deposited along with the sand.

John Ainslie's map of Edinburgh and Leith from 1804 shows a number of dune mounds scattered across the entire area, which is marked as 'a common for Playing at the golf.' The association with golf is probably the Links greatest claim to fame, being one of the earliest golf courses in Scotland. Golf was certainly being played on the Links by the mid-16th century, though it would have taken the hardiest of souls to have played a round during the siege. Many of the dune mounds are still in place on Johnston's plan of Edinburgh and Leith from 1851, though by this time the area is covered by a network of intersecting paths. This map shows the circular mound now known as Somerset's Mount on the eastern part of the Links as a distinct feature but does not go as far as to name it; this, along with no attempt to mark it out as a distinct feature on the earlier map, may suggest a quite late date for the tradition of associating the two present mounds with the siege (as also suggested by Harris 1991, 368)—though it does appear to have been in place by 1827 as the names are used in Campbell's *History of Leith.*

Neither of the maps shows any sign of wet ground in the vicinity of Trench 4 or in the wider part of the Links shown on the Petworth map to include what look to be pools (they have the same hatching convention as that used for Lochend Loch). This may indicate that the reclamation of wetland had already taken place by this time, though this does not appear to have been associated with the levelling out of dune mounds in this area. Two water-courses are shown on the 1851 map but these are further to the south. The southern terminus of one of these streams is marked as 'Lady Fyffe's well', which may provide the name origin for Lady Fife's Brae, which is close by (but is not marked on the map). The well also appears on the 1855 First Edition Ordnance Survey Map, though by this time the associated water course has disappeared and the mound is labelled as 'Lady Fife's Brae—remains of Pelham's Battery'. Also marked is 'Giant's Brae—Remains of Somerset's Battery'.

A photograph (sourced from SCRAN) showing roughly the same part of the Links as the location of Trench 4, with the still-standing 1878–9 Scottish Co-operative Wholesale Society Warehouse in the background, shows the uneven character of the ground at this time, with a series of undulations in the foreground. It is possible that bank (4017) in Trench 4 corresponds to one of these features, but it coincides with the feature on the Petworth map; it is also the only example to be seen in the trench, which might more convincingly suggest that these undulations were levelled out in the process of the deposition of the sand.

Trench 5 (Figure 10)

In order to expose a further section of the bank, a fifth trench was located to the south-west of Trench 4 on what was judged to be the line of the bank. Once again, however, the section faces revealed a picture of extensive modern disturbance, again especially apparent in the south-eastern portion of the trench. The eastern edge of the bank may be visible as a pronounced dip, where deposit 5002 dips down, but this may equally represent a later cut through bank deposits. What does seem possible is that the turf lines (5013) cover the top of the bank, which itself consists of possibly re-deposited sand (5002: equivalent to 4017 in Trench 4). The picture is far less clear in Trench

5 than it was in Trench 4, and if excavated in isolation, it is doubtful whether the observed deposits would have been interpreted as a bank.

Discussion

Summary of Leith Links Results

The excavation of evaluation trenches on Leith Links resulted in the identification of archaeological features, but the majority of these appear to be quite late in date (19th-20th century) and cannot be tied down to any particular event. This is especially true of those features in Trenches 1 and 2 (Area 1), where the quite ephemeral discrete features may relate to garden features or any one of the many events which have over the past two centuries taken place on the Links—including fairs, music festivals, military displays, circuses and possibly even a First World War tented hospital.

More substantial and complex archaeological deposits were identified in Trenches 4 and 5 (Area 2) and these may include the linear feature shown on the 1650 Petworth map (Figure 1). The feature, most clearly appearing in the SW-facing section of Trench 4, appears to have been constructed from sand and perhaps turf, excavated from a shallow ditch that runs along the eastern side of the feature. Interpretation was not assisted by a lack of dating material, with a complete absence of a pottery assemblage such as that found at Pilrig Park.

Interpretive Issues

Extensive site disturbance at a later period (19th and 20th centuries) has removed much evidence for the bank and on the basis of current evidence it is impossible to state confidently what the function of the bank was. It may be the feature shown on the 1560 map, but if so it need not necessarily represent a siegework; an earlier land division or raised trackway are two possible alternative suggestions. On the other hand, the presence of a feature [4034] cut into the western edge of the bank may suggest the presence of a fence or palisade that may be more in keeping with a siegework—though as previously noted, the possibility that it was a defensive work built by either the Scots in 1547 or the French in 1548 should also be considered. More excavation would be required at various points along the projected line of the feature, which given the presence of modern park features such as a children's play park, the bowling green and football pitches, would not be a straightforward operation.

Summing Up

Overall, the projects at both Pilrig Park and on Leith Links were a success in that they confirmed the presence of archaeological features first suggested by geophysical survey. The results also appear to confirm the survival of at least remnants of the 1560 siegeworks shown on the Petworth map in areas undisturbed by urban development, though even in the green spaces investigated, later landscape change has taken its toll. There can be little doubt that the work at Pilrig Park has been the most rewarding as far as the quality of the archaeology and the potential for future research is concerned. Whereas trial trenching on Leith Links did expose deposits that may represent a feature shown on the 1560 Petworth map, its interpretation is not straightforward, and this is not made any easier by the extensive levels of later disturbance evident in Trenches 4 and 5.

At Pilrig Park, the results surpassed expectations, with relatively complex archaeological deposits relating not only to the 1560 siege but also to later activity surviving at various points across the site. The identification of two substantial archaeological features, the possible forge and construction slot, in what appears to be the ditch of the artillery fort bodes well for the prospects of further work on the site. Given that one of the remits of the current project was to assess the potential for a community-based archaeological project based on one or both locations there seems little doubt that Pilrig Park could accommodate such a project, whereas Leith Links probably would not, although the site certainly has archaeological potential which should be taken into account in any future planning scenario.

Acknowledgements

I would like to thank John Lawson of Edinburgh City Council Archaeology Service for all his efforts to ensure that these projects took place. Funding for the project was provided by City of Edinburgh Council and the Leith Open Spaces Project.

Bibliography

A-Kelly, C 2004 'Restalrig Terrace and Restalrig Churchyard', *Discov & Excav Scotland* 5, 56.

Banks, I, Pollard, T & Poller, T 2006 *Leith Open Spaces Project (Leith Siege Works) Geophysics*. GUARD Data Structure Report 2200.

Bruce, J (ed.) 1840 *Annals of the First Four Years of the Reign of Queen Elizabeth by Sir John Hayward; edited from a manuscript in the Harlein Collection by John Bruce*. Printed for the Camden Society by J.B Nicols & Son, London.

Cooper, J 2008 *Whitecoats and Rascals: In Search of Fortifications and Siege Works from the Siege of Haddington 1548–1549*. Unpublished MLitt dissertation, University of Glasgow.

Halstead, S 2004 'Blast from Past', in *Edinburgh Evening News*. 5 August 2004.
Harris, S 1991 'The fortifications and siege of Leith: a further study of the map of the siege in 1560', *Proc Soc Antiq Scot* 121, 359–68.
Moore, H, Wilson, G & Franklin, J 2002 '8a and 8b Tower Street, Leith', *Discov & Excav Scotland* 3, 52.
Pollard, A F (ed) 1903 *The Late Expedition into Scotland by an anonymous author found in 'Tudor Tracts'*. Westminster, Constable and Co.
Pollard, T 2007 *Pilrig Park & Leith Links Evaluation Report.* GUARD Data Structure Report 2424.
White, L 1967 'Jacopo Anconio as an Engineer', *Amer Hist Rev* 72/2, 425–44.

THE ARCHAEOLOGY OF THE SIEGE OF FORT WILLIAM, 1746

TONY POLLARD

Abstract

In August and September 2007, the Centre for Battlefield Archaeology and Glasgow University Archaeological Research Division (GUARD) conducted a programme of archaeological investigation of the remains of the old fort at Fort William and part of the Parade in the town of Fort William on the west coast of Scotland. The fieldwork involved geophysical survey at the fort and the Parade, followed by trial excavation of anomalies. Trial trenches at the Parade exposed several rich midden deposits and material providing evidence for the burning of the town of Maryburgh, as suggested in contemporary accounts in 1746. The results at the fort were not so positive, as most traces of the garrison were removed in the 19th and 20th centuries through its use as a railway yard; however, a trench outside the fort suggests survival of midden deposits pre-dating this period of destruction. This part-Heritage Lottery assisted project was a Highland 2007 initiative supported by Lochaber Community Fund and Highland Council, and included active participation on the part of the local community, including school groups and metal detectorists.

Introduction

The Fort William and Inverlochy Archaeological Project is a community-based programme carried out by the Centre for Battlefield Archaeology at Glasgow University and GUARD (Glasgow University Archaeological Research Division). The primary aim of the project, which was first proposed during a conversation between Dr Tony Pollard, Dr Michael Foxley and John Hutchison at the Highland Council Quality Awards in 2005, was to carry out a project focussing on the town of Fort William and involving members of the local community. In 2007, the project became a reality and took place as one of the many events within Highland Year of Culture. Sponsorship and grant funding for the project was generously provided by Highland Council, Lochaber Community Fund 2007 and the Heritage Lottery Fund. The fieldwork reported here was carried out over two weeks between 10 and 21 September.

The main focus for the project was Fort William's military past, but more generally it sought to examine archaeological evidence for conflict in the Highlands, particularly during the volatile 17th and 18th centuries. The town (Figure 1) grew up as a direct consequence of this conflict, originating in the 17th century as a satellite settlement to the fort named after William III, the usurper of James VII & II for whom the Jacobites are named. One of the

 DOI: 10.1163/157407808X382818

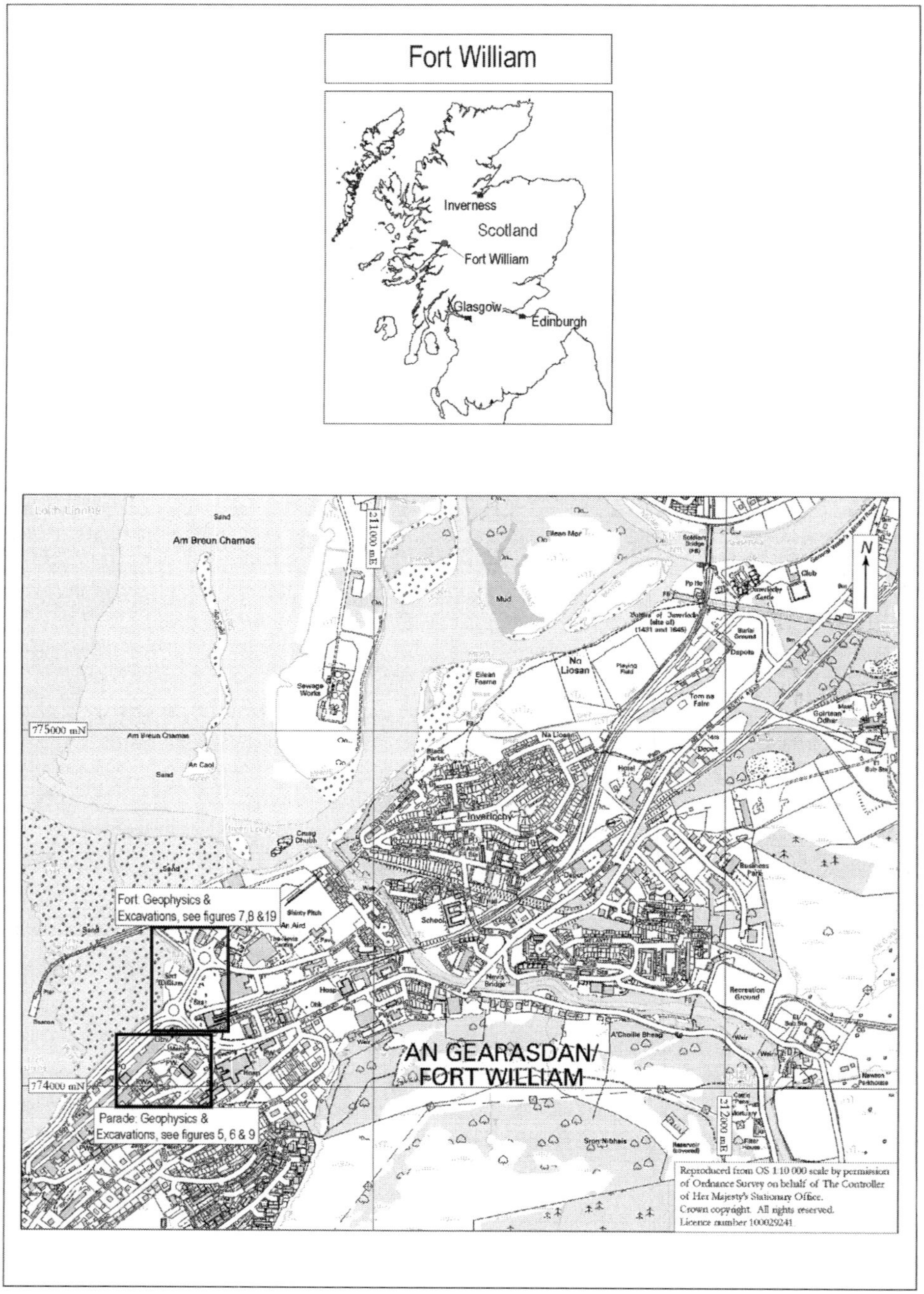

Fig. 1. Site location—Parade and Fort

archaeological attractions of the locality is this mix of military and civilian activity, with the fort hosting what was effectively a hybrid police force and army of occupation within the Highlands. Despite increased interest in the archaeology of post-Medieval rural settlement, particularly in the Highlands, over the past 20 years there has been little attempt to study the archaeology of urban development in this same context. The close relationship of town and fort is emphasised through reference to early maps of the town, which due to its strategic importance must be one of the most thoroughly mapped Highland locations of the 18th century. A number of these maps, of which that reproduced as Figure 3, drawn around 1736, stands as one of the best examples, show the High Street leading directly to the fort entrance. The map also shows an open square, marked as the Parade, around which buildings are grouped. This open area in part still exists today as a public space with war memorials, park benches and a putting green, and is still known as the Parade.

In 1746, the threat of a Jacobite siege prompted the destruction of much of the town by the garrison in order to deny cover to the enemy at so close a distance to the fort's defences. Later maps show that the area around the Parade was not redeveloped until well into the 19th century and even then, areas which had once been occupied by buildings, such as the southern side of the High Street adjacent to the Parade, were never redeveloped. This is very clear today where the post-war shopping arcade opens onto the road, across the other side of which is the Parade. The potential for building remains surviving on the south side of the street was an important motivation for the project work on the Parade (see Figure 1 for this area and for photo see Plate 1). The location of the early town is further emphasised in the entry for Kilmallie parish from the *Old Statistical Account of Scotland*, which states:

> Maryburgh or Gordonsburgh, is the only village of note in the parish and is situated on the seashore, south side of Locheile, within a few yards [to] the south-west of Fort William. Anciently, the place where it stands was called Auchintore-beg. The village was then built on the ground where the esplanade (Parade) is now (Fraser in OSA 1791–99: 138).

Although the fort was largely demolished in the 20th century, a process which began in the 19th century with the arrival of the railway, a small portion does survive on the waterfront, where remnants of the outer wall bound an open space occupied by picnic benches. The area corresponding to the rest of the fort is now covered by roads and the supermarket car park. Reference to the detailed plans of the fort, most dating from the 18th century, show that a number of buildings were present in the small area which today remains undeveloped and it was hoped that some trace of these structures may survive beneath the grass. However, 20th century maps, including the Ordnance

Plate 1. Looking to the west across the Parade. Trench 2 on the right and 3 on the left

Survey from 1904, show that the fort interior was drastically modified by the railway, with the surviving portion of the interior used as an engine yard, complete with sheds and a turntable. A further indication of the extent of this disturbance was gleaned from photographs from the 1960s which show the fully functioning yard. Despite these various phases of railway-related development, it was hoped that some remnant of the original fort may survive and perhaps provide evidence for its function as a fortification and as a garrison in which troops lived.

It was clear at the outset of the project that both the town and the fort had the potential for the survival of archaeological remains relating to both, dating to at least as far back as the first half of the 18th century, and possibly earlier (Figure 3 is the 1736 map which shows areas of potential survival). If this were the case, then it was hoped that an examination of the civilian and military settlements might allow some observations to be made regarding the relationship between the civilian population on the one side and the military garrison on the other. A key element of the project was therefore the evaluation of this potential, first through geophysical survey and then through limited trial trenching.

In addition to the examination of the Parade and the fort, a third component of the project was geared toward a period of conflict pre-dating the construction of the fort in 1654 (the results of this latter element of the project are not reported here—see Pollard & Lelong 2007).

Site Location, Topography and Geology

The surviving portion of the fort at Fort William (NGR NN 104 742) sits close to the shore of Loch Linnhe and is bounded on its northern side by the culverted River Nevis, which at this point flows into the loch. To the south of the site is a supermarket, car park and the railway station (much of the fort was demolished in the late 19th century to make way for a railway yard). The surviving portion of the fort is bounded by battered stone walls, which display some evidence for modification and repair. A sally port (small gate) gives out onto the banks of the river from the northern wall. The interior is an open grassed area accommodating picnic tables, a footpath and a monolithic display panel for the Great Glen walker's route.

The Parade is generally regarded as the centre of the modern town of Fort William and is something akin to a village green crossed with a town square. The area is traversed by footpaths and accommodates park benches, flower beds and several memorials, including the town's war memorial (Plate 1). The site was once the Parade ground for the fort, hence its name, and is bounded to the north-west by the High Street. Today the Parade is located some 150 m to the south of the surviving portion of the fort.

Historical and Archaeological Background

Fort William

The present town of Fort William takes its name from the fort first built in 1654 by General Monck in the wake of Cromwell's invasion and occupation of Scotland, though the 'William' element does not go back that far. During its early years, the fort was simply known as the Inverlochy Garrison or Inverlochie, and indeed the Gaelic name for the town today is An Gearasdan or 'the Garrison'. Little is known of the nature of any contemporary settlement in the vicinity of the modern town, and it is possible that the use of the Inverlochy placename by Monck indicates that this was the nearest settlement (MacCulloch 1939). Pont's map from 1583 (Figure 2) shows Inverlochy castle—built in the 13th century and someway outside the modern town—but nothing by way of settlement at the mouth of the River Nevis. It does, however, show a settlement some distance to the south-west, which is marked as 'Achaintour'. This place name still exists today as Auchintore and refers to the land holdings on the loch shore to the immediate south-west of the

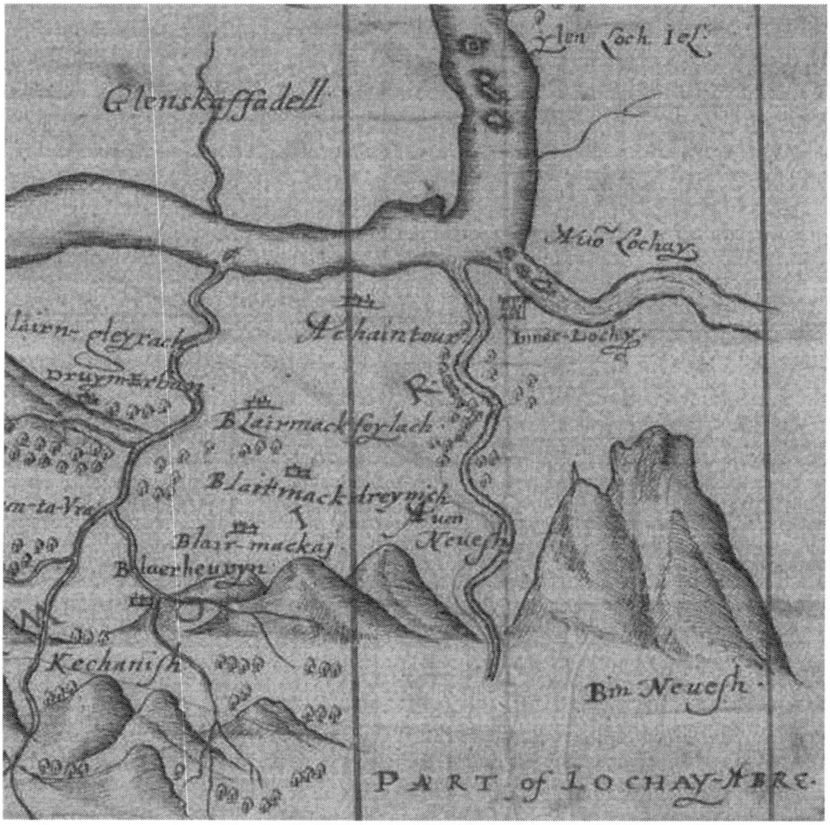

Fig. 2. Timothy Pont's 1583 map (courtesy of the Trustees of the National Library of Scotland)

modern town, where much of it today accommodates houses, hotels and B&Bs alongside the coast road (the *Statistical Account* entry already quoted refers to the town sitting within 'Auchintore-beg').

However, while the first Jacobite rising of 1689–90 was still to be suppressed, the government commander, Major-General Hugh Mackay, was ordered to rebuild Monck's timber and earth fort, which had been at least partially slighted following the departure of the garrison with the Restoration in 1660. There had been calls for the fort's rebuilding before then, when levels of lawlessness in the West Highlands were bad enough to prompt some clan chiefs to join in this plea, but this was outweighed by those who would regard any fort as a symbol of oppression (Simpson 1996: 58). No such considerations of sensitivity were to get in the way with the arrival of the Jacobite threat.

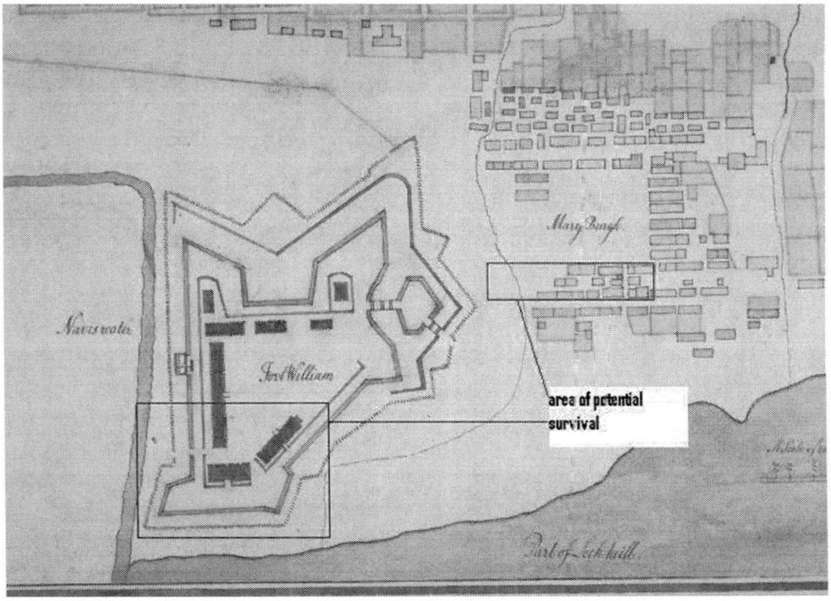

Fig. 3. 1736 showing areas of potential survival (courtesy of the Trustees of the National Library of Scotland)

In 1690, it took just 11 days for MacKay's men to throw up something that could be described as a fort or, as one man put it, a 'trinch' (Hopkins 1998; 238) on top of the remains of Monck's construction, though it was probably some time before the timber palisades were fully replaced by sturdy stone walls. In keeping with the times, the site was called Fort William after William III, who was installed as king during the 'Glorious Revolution' of 1688, and the settlement which grew up around the fort was known as Maryburgh, after William's wife.

The earliest manifestation of Maryburgh—the part destroyed in 1746 (see below)—was located to the south-west of a burn which ran down slope not far from the front gates of the fort. This feature appears to have separated the fort from the town and may have been recognised as an official demarcation marker (see burn which runs through left hand side of Parade 'area of survival' shown on Figure 3 and uppermost burn on Figure 4).

That the fort influenced and indeed encouraged the growth of the town is clear from, among other things, a legal record from 1736 that states, with reference to Colonel John Hill, created Governor of the rebuilt fort by the king in November 1690:

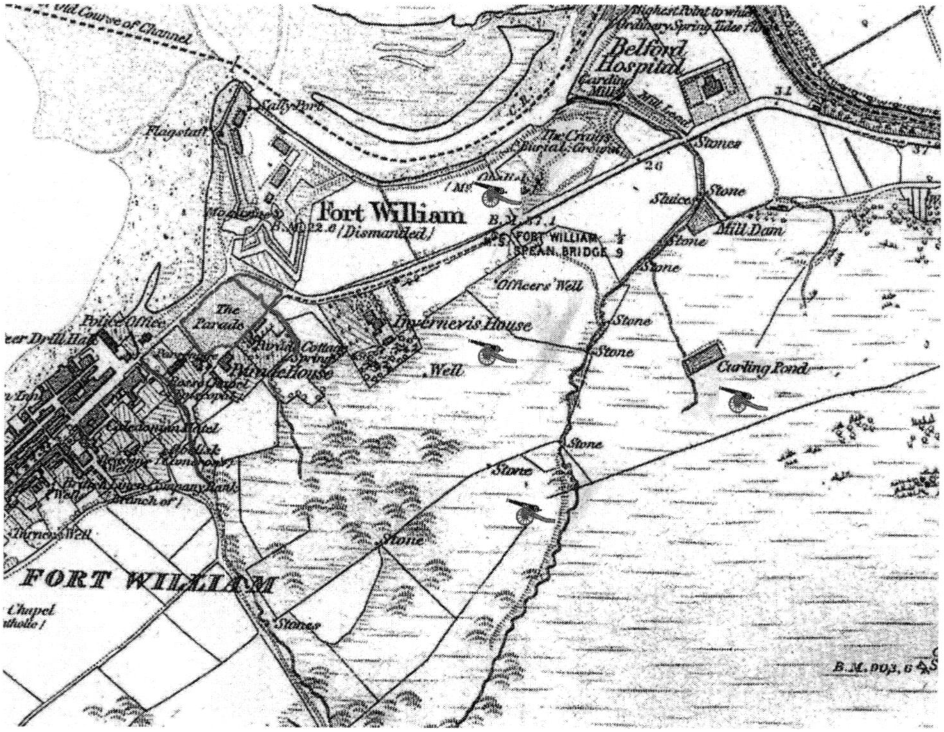

Fig. 4. 1876 Ordnance Survey map—small cannon symbols denote Jacobite batteries

> ... both he and his successors in office, having given considerable encouragement to the merchants and tradesmen to come and reside there, and several merchants and trading persons well affected to His Majesty purchased houses and took up their residence in the said Burgh of Barony called Maryburgh (quoted from transcript by Iain Rose).

A Burgh of Barony was a town which had certain trading privileges, including the right to hold markets and trade overseas, which were controlled by the tenant-in-chief. In this case, however, the king and queen disregarded the usual protocols and also the actual landowner, the Duke of Gordon, and awarded title to the Governor of the fort. This situation was to cause unrest, including that from 1736 (Rose 2007). The town was for a while during the latter half of the 18th century known as Gordonsburgh, after the Duke, and for a while after 1836 as Duncansburgh, after the superior of the town at the time (MacCulloch 1939). Only after these crises of identity did the town become known as Fort William, this time apparently after the Duke of Cumberland rather than William III (though debate over the name has continued—see below).

The fort would go on to be garrisoned by the government throughout all of the Jacobite uprisings during the first half of the 18th century. Its most infamous role came early on, when in 1692, the fort provided the spring board for the government-sanctioned massacre of the MacDonalds of Glencoe. The final order for the massacre was issued from the fort by Lieutenant-Colonel Hamilton, second-in-command to the Governor, Colonel Hill, in February 1692 (Hopkins 1992: 335), and the intention was for 400 troops from the fort to play an active role in the affair. However, thanks to a fierce snowstorm, the troops did not arrive on the scene until after the dreadful deed had been committed (MacCulloch 1939); their departure was also delayed by fear of being observed by the local population and word getting back to the intended victims before their arrival (Hopkins, *op cit*: 336).

The fort was further modified under Wade in the 1720s, when it became the westerly outpost of the chain of three forts extending through the Great Glen from Inverness in the east. The only occasion on which the fort, which the Duke of Cumberland regarded as the 'only fort in the Highlands of any consequence,' came under attack was in early 1746. We are fortunate to have a detailed series of letters from various parties involved on the government side, in addition to Captain Scott's journal, which when viewed in total provide a fairly thorough if one-sided account of the events which led up to the siege and the period of the investment itself. That these events were also of great interest to the public at the time is also demonstrated by the accounts of the siege published in the *Scots Magazine* in March and April 1746, the first of these appearing while the siege was still underway (these are reported to be based on an officer's accounts and differ to Scott's).

Background to the Siege of 1746

The Battle of Falkirk, on 17 January 1746, was in principle a Jacobite victory but in truth marked a fatal downturn in Jacobite fortunes, followed as it was by their return northward. Despite the best efforts of Loudon, who at the time had around 2,000 hastily-raised government troops in Inverness, the Jacobites forced Loudon to retire to the north, and leaving Fort George in the town in the hands of 200 men (one company of Guises's Regiment and two of Loudon's Highlanders). The ensuing siege barely merited the term, with the garrison surrendering after just two days, during which time they had fired hardly a shot.

Having taken Inverness, the Jacobites next turned their attentions on Fort Augustus, at the western end of Loch Ness. The fort was unsuited to defence against artillery, its poor design being commented on by many, including

Cumberland himself (Kingsford 1922: 370). The Jacobites, benefiting from the guidance of a French engineer, established three gun batteries and a mortar battery around the fort and began their attack on 22 February. Their first success was the destruction of the storehouse, which contained powder and shells, with a bastion of the old barrack also reduced by cannon fire. The next day, there was another explosion when 3,000 cartridges and a barrel of powder went skyward. The garrison surrendered on 1 March and provided the Jacobites with a windfall of supplies and ordnance, the latter consisting of 16 four-pounders, two six-pounders, six coehorn mortars and plentiful ammunition. Wade's line of Highland forts was quickly rolling up.

The last intact link in the chain was Fort William, undoubtedly the most important of the three forts—giving access to the sea and from there a direct route to the west coast and the lowlands. The garrison had been hemmed in for some time, but had yet to feel the pressure of a full blown siege. Recognising this fact, Cumberland, who by 27 February was in Aberdeen, appointed Captain Caroline Frederick Scott of Guise's as the new garrison commander. He had useful engineering experience (Kingsford 1922, 373), and he effectively replaced the aged Governor Campbell and Captain Miller, neither of whom much regarded the other.

Having for months been fairly isolated in what was regarded as enemy territory, the garrison in late February 1746 consisted of no more than three companies of Guise's (6th Foot) Regiment, with 140 men reported as fit for duty by their then commander, Captain James Miller, in a letter to Major-General Campbell in Inverary. The regiment had returned from the West Indies after the failed expedition of 1741–42, during which time its numbers had been reduced largely by disease to 100 actives (Kingsford 1922). They had been in Guantanamo Bay in Cuba, which is today infamous as the site of an American prison for terrorist suspects; for a time, it was known as Cumberland's Bay after its capture by the British in 1741 (Gott 2004: 40). The regiment was brought back up to strength with new recruits and at the outset of the '45 had been assigned to garrison duties in the north of Scotland, including Fort William. Other garrisons were: Fort Augustus—three companies, Fort George—two companies, Ruthven—one company, Bernera—one company and Duart Castle—a part company. Much earlier in the campaign, on 15 August 1745, the fort was denied reinforcements in the form of two companies of the 1st Foot when they were intercepted by a Jacobite force at Highbridge, just 10 km away, and surrendered after what was the first land action of the '45. Miller's letter also notes a town guard consisting of about 60 residents of Maryburgh which, although disbanded three weeks earlier by the Governor, Alexander Campbell, were, according to Miller, still prepared to assist in the defence of the fort. In order to reinforce this modest garrison, Major-General Campbell advised Miller that three officers and 50 men from Guise's Regiment had been despatched from Kilchurn Castle via Dunstaffnage along with three companies of Johnson's regiment, sent from Edinburgh on the orders of the Duke of Cumberland. Campbell also sent along a company of Argyll militia to join the enhanced garrison.

This exchange of letters between the Governor and the Major-General also resulted in the fort being supported throughout the siege by a pair of armed sloops, which were to add the fire of their guns to those of the fort—the latter consisting of eight twelve-pounders, 12 six-pounders, two thirteen-inch mortars and 10 coehorns (Kingsford 1922: 373). The *Serpent* was already anchored off the fort where she remained, to be joined later by the *Baltimore*. Also sent north was an engineer called Russell, who on his arrival was to find the fort in pretty poor shape. Captain Scott arrived at the fort on 14 March, after a delay caused by Jacobite activity in the narrows around Corran Ferry, some 15 km to the south-west of the fort. No doubt after conferring with Russell—who afterward returned to Inverary—and inspecting the defences, he set the garrison to work making repairs and improvements, which included the heightening of the parapet in the most vulnerable places.

Meanwhile, the Jacobites had been busy bringing forward their guns, including those captured after the fall of Fort Augustus. According to the *Scots Magazine*, the Jacobite guns began to arrive in the vicinity of the fort on 7 and 8 March. Since late February, the fort had been

> . . . blockaded by the rebels, who they say are 1500, including the French piquets. Brig. Stapleton commands the siege. Lochiel commands the highlanders, consisting chiefly of his own clan, the Macdonalds of Keppoch and Glenco (*sic*), and the Stewarts of Appin (*Scots Magazine*, March 1746).

The Jacobites were fired on by cannon from the fort, apparently at this point in an attempt to provide the garrison gunners with some much-needed training (Fergusson 1951: 145). Although it is popularly assumed that sieges afford the besieger a little more comfort than those cooped up inside the walls, the Jacobites did not find life easy during the siege, with food and fodder in short supply along with sufficient horses to draw the guns into position (Fergusson, *op cit*: 144).

In order to prepare fully for the coming siege, the Governor of the fort ordered the town of Maryburgh to be burned, in order to deny the Jacobites shelter among the buildings, possibly as much from the elements as from his guns. The proximity of the settlement to the fort had long been a bone of contention between the military and the civilian population. It was an issue raised during a court case brought in 1736 by the town's inhabitants against the Governor (then Major-General George Wade) and his deputy Campbell, against whom most of the charges of unfair dealing and extortion were levelled (Rose 2007). According to a letter written in the late 1720s by Captain Burt, one of Wade's officers:

> The houses were neither to be built with stone nor brick, and are to this day composed of timber, boards and turf. This was ordained to the end that they might the more suddenly be burnt, or otherwise destroyed, by the order of the Governor, to prevent any lodgement of an enemy that might annoy the fort, in case of rebellion or invasion (MacCulloch 1939: 28).

On 22 February, Governor Campbell wrote: 'On my part, I have order'd all the gardens, and part of the town of Maryburgh to be destroy'd, as they may not harbour our enemys' (Fergusson 1951: 108). A council of war was held at the fort three days later, during which the Governor decided that it was:

> . . . absolutely necessary to reduce the town of Maryburgh to ashes which result I put into execution after giving notice to the inhabitants to remove their effects into the garrison. But, notwithstanding this precaution, many well affected townspeople are ruined (Fergusson, *op cit*: 168).

No less than 40 people remained in the fort for protection, some of these presumably being members of the previously dissolved town militia who were still prepared to take up arms against the Jacobites. The event was also reported in the *Glasgow Journal* of 31 March, 1746, which stated:

> Fort William. That place Governor Campbell has bravely defended; and to prevent the rebels sheltering themselves near the fort has caused [to] burn the town of Maryburgh (MacCulloch 1939: 28).

Not every building in Maryburgh was put to the torch, though, as Captain Scott's journal entry for 31 March states:

> At one point in the morning the rebel's set fire to the Governor's brew-house, out of the walls in Maryburgh, and under the light of which they fired very smartly at our working men and at our Fort in general, both with round and grape shot, old nails, iron etc., which lasted a couple of hours until the brew house burnt down (Kingsford 1922: 377).

Granted, the brew house was at the most south-westerly extent of the town, but there would still appear to have been one rule for the general population and their houses and another for the Governor and his brew house.

The levelling of the town was not the only act of destruction carried out by the garrison of the fort, nor was it the first. Before the Jacobite attack on the fort, troops from the garrison had harried the local rural population to dissuade them from joining the Jacobites. These attacks included cattle raids—which continued throughout the siege as the garrison sought to supplement its food supplies—and the burning of houses and farm buildings owned by those who were suspected of having Jacobite sympathies. These punitive actions were part of a wider programme of destruction and intimidation, carried out across the western Highlands at this time. Among the most notorious of these was the 'burning of Morvern' which, on the orders of Major-General Campbell, saw troops from Mingary Castle board the sloop aptly named the *Terror* and set off along the coast of Morvern. On 10 March, they disembarked to burn the farms of all those believed to be away fighting for the Jacobites or sympathetic to the cause (Fergusson 1951: 118–19). Indeed, it is possible that these raids made the siege inevitable, as Lochiel realised that while its garrison was allowed to wreak havoc he could not rely on the commitment of the Camerons or the MacDonalds in operations located away from their threatened homes (Kingsford 1922: 372).

There was, however, more to these actions than a straightforward conflict between Hanoverian and Jacobite. It was also a very bitter and deeply engrained civil war between Whig and Jacobite clans, with the Campbells of Argyll arrayed against those such as the Camerons, the MacDonalds and MacLeans of Morvern. Such actions on the part of government forces and the Campbells in particular naturally fostered resentment and a thirst for revenge, and on 20 March at Glennevis House, home of Alexander Cameron of Glennevis, a letter was signed by Lochiel and Keppoch in which they called upon Charles Edward Stuart to sanction reprisals against the Campbells and expressed their hope to 'hang a Campbell for every house that shall hereafter be burnt by them'. This animosity was nothing new, and it was clearly a motivating force during the battle of Inverlochy in 1645.

On 20 March, the Jacobites began the siege in earnest when they opened fire from their newly erected batteries. The besieging force numbered in excess of 1,000 Highlanders and around 200 French troops (including Scots or Irish in regular French service).

The garrison, which benefited from regular re-supply by sea and on 23 March took delivery of more men, held out for a further two weeks and in doing so was to remain the only one of the three Great Glen forts not to fall into Jacobite hands. An exact figure for garrison numbers during the siege is hard to come by but it appears to have been in excess of 400. The siege came to an end on the night of 2–3 April, when the Jacobites launched what shells they had left at the fort before abandoning most of their cannon and mortars and retiring toward Inverness. The final battle would be fought near Inverness on 16 April, on Culloden Moor.

During the siege, the garrison lost six killed and 24 wounded, three of the latter when they tried to defuse a mortar shell. Although the walls were never breached by artillery fire, damage to the fort interior was considerable, largely thanks to the use of the mortars with exploding shells; what were described at the time as the old barrack buildings were almost entirely demolished. An account from 29 March gives some impression of the lengths the Jacobites went to reduce the fort:

> This morning, by break of day, they unmasked a new battery at the Craigs, of 3 brass four pounders, within 100 yards of the walls, and cannonaded us from that and the other 3 batteries. As they carried a furnace along with them, they threw in a great many hot bullets, and some bearded pieces of iron a foot long, and inch thick, which they designed should stick in our timber work, and set us on fire. They fired grape and partridge shot, and plied us hard from all hands with small arms; but have done us very little damage (*Scots Magazine*, March 1746).

One defence against these hot shells falling on the roofs of the barracks was to heap earth in the attic spaces.

Skirmishing outside the fort was a regular occurrence as, for one thing, the fort lacked a well and so parties from the fort needed to collect water on an almost daily basis; the cattle raids have already been mentioned. Perhaps the most notable action was a sally made by 150 men of the garrison against the batteries at the Craigs and the Governor's Garden on the last day of March, which resulted in the capture from the Jacobites of three four-pound guns, two mortars and a bullet-heating furnace and bellows, all of which were taken into the fort.

After the Siege

The town seems to have recovered relatively quickly after the siege, and a survey map drawn up in 1753 for the landowner Alexander, Duke of Gordon, who was still in dispute over compensation related to the Burgh, shows 161 houses and other buildings positioned either side of the High Street. This is slightly at odds with a report by a visitor in 1787 that the town's population was only around 100 people (MacCulloch 1939: 31). It is notable that all of these buildings were positioned to the south-west of a burn that on earlier maps (e.g. those of 1710, 1736 and 1740) had marked the westward limit of the town (Figure 4: the lower of the two burns shown on extract of 1876 OS map); according to those same maps, therefore, these buildings were all newly constructed after the siege. Of the earlier town, to the north-east of the burn, there is no trace, nor was there any attempt to rebuild on the land previously occupied by the destroyed town. The area now known as the Parade is shown as an open space and marked 'The Esplanade' in 1753; the only feature on it is a pillar, which is the market cross related to the earlier settlement and shown on previous maps, including one dated to 1740. Leaving this area barren in the wake of the '45 would certainly have prevented the town's destruction once again should another rising take place. That a military interest in this ground continued into the 19th century is demonstrated by an 1818 map on which the south-westward burn referred to above is marked as the 'limit of the Ordnance Lands'. By this time, however, some development had begun to encroach on to the land to the east of the burn, with an Episcopal chapel and a small number of other buildings fringing the open space marked as the 'Parade'.

This period in the place's history also seems to be reflected in a colour drawing of the town and fort which today hangs in the West Highland Museum (Plate 2). This rendition shows the town and fort beyond, but with a considerable open space between the two (the ruins of Inverlochy castle can be seen in the background to the right). The drawing appears to date from the 1750s, at a time after which the town had been rebuilt. The single building close to the fort would appear to be the garrison forge which is shown on the 1753 map. What is clear from this drawing, perhaps even more so than the map, is the extent to which any trace of the destroyed town, in the form

Plate 2. Looking north east across Maryburgh and the fort. Note the open space between town and fort and original gate (now at Craigs cemetery). Drawing from c.1750s (courtesy of the West Highland Museum)

of vestigial foundations or other remains, had been removed by this time. Any recyclable materials would undoubtedly have been in demand during the programme of rebuilding. What the drawing does appear to show are houses with stone walls, rather than turf and wattle-and-daub; this shift is possibly due to the removal of the town from the fort's proximity, which alleviated any risk of the town providing cover for an attacking enemy should trouble break out once again.

Further development does not seem to have occurred around the Parade until the late 19th century. The Ordnance Survey map of 1876 (Figure 4) still shows no buildings standing to either side of the High Street where it borders the Parade and the bulk of the town is still positioned to the west side of the western boundary burn (lower of the two burns). This left the fort, which is shown on the map but marked as 'Dismantled', still standing in not-so-splendid isolation.

The fort became less important in the aftermath of the '45, when the new Fort George at Ardersier, near Culloden, became the most important defended garrison in the Highlands. After serving as a base of operations for anti-smuggling patrols, and later being garrisoned by small numbers of men of the Staffordshire Volunteers, the fort was finally sold into private hands in 1864. Following its final decommissioning, the fort was used as a place of residence, with gardens established in the ditches. In 1889, however, it was sold to the West Highland Railway Company and many of the remaining buildings were demolished to make way for engine sheds. Aside from the remains by the shore, the only other remnant of the fort is the stone arch of the inner gateway which, since 1896, has marked the entrance to the Craigs cemetery, almost exactly on the same spot as one of the Jacobite siege batteries (Plate 3).

The cemetery itself is directly associated with the fort's history, being the last resting place for some of the soldiers serving in the garrison; it is marked as 'the new burial place' on a 1740 map. Traditionally, the graves to the west side of the cemetery are military and those to the east civilian. Most of the stones marking the military graves have long since disappeared and only the grass-covered grave mounds are left. Among these anonymous graves is the last resting place of one-time soldier and fencing master Donald MacBane (MacCulloch 1939: 37), who as one of Mackay's men was credited in his own memoirs with jumping across 'Soldier's Leap' after the Battle of Killiecrankie in 1689 (Macbane 1728).

Today, most of the area occupied by the fort sits beneath a supermarket and associated car park. The only upstanding remains are the ramparts around the north-east corner, which include a demi-bastion and sally port giving access to the river side (Plate 4). The area inside these upstanding elements is devoid of any surface trace and is used as a picnic area. A watching brief

Plate 3. Gate from fort now at Craigs cemetery

carried out during the erection of a display board revealed nothing but rubble reported to be associated with the railway yard (Farrell 2002). The upstanding ramparts and a small border around them are protected as a Scheduled Ancient Monument.

Unlike the fort, the associated town has thrived in the modern era and is today a premier holiday destination for tourists wishing to climb Ben

Plate 4. Looking to east across fort ramparts showing Fort Trench 3. Note sally port in wall and supermarket in background

Nevis or to explore the spectacular scenery of the area. The growth of the town as a busy hub for tourism can be traced back to the arrival of the West Highland Railway in the early 1890s, an event which was to have a seriously detrimental impact on the survival of structures associated with the fort.

Results Of Fieldwork

The location of excavation trenches was influenced by the results of the geophysical survey—the plots from the magnetometer surveys are included as Figures 5 and 6. A more complete report on that work, along with more detail on the archaeological contexts summarised below, can be found in the data structure report (Pollard & Lelong 2007). Trench locations are shown in Figures.

The Parade (Figure 7)

Parade Trench 1

This trench measured 3 m by 3 m and was opened in the western part of the Parade, in an area where geophysical survey recorded several small anomalies. The topsoil was removed, revealing a linear arrangement of three

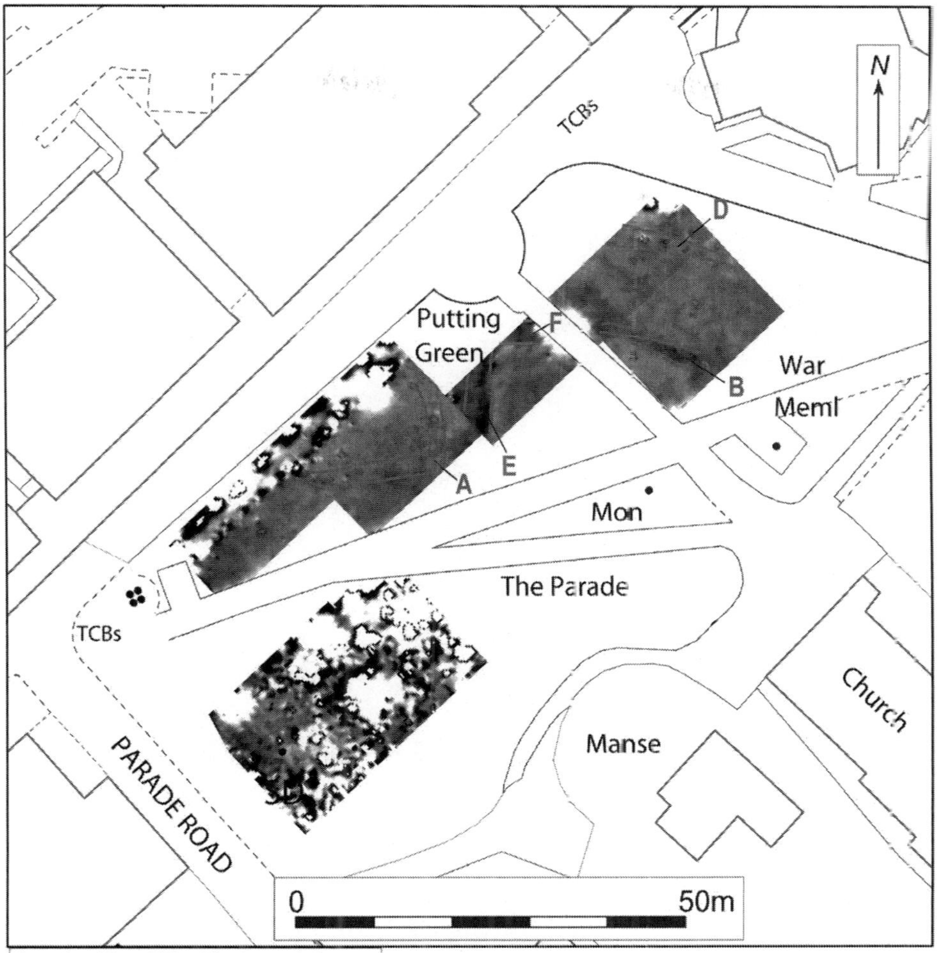

Fig. 5. Magnetometer survey of the Parade showing suggested shape of anomalies

large concrete slabs (103) lying end to end and running SE to NW across the trench (Figure 8). The slabs were interpreted as the remains of the floor of a large Nissen hut which had stood in this part of the Parade since before World War II (it appears on the 1938 map), housing the Garrison Theatre, and subsequently served as a school canteen and a venue for youth clubs (information from local informants and contemporary photographs). The gritty matrix surrounding the slabs may have derived from the destruction and removal of the surrounding floor.

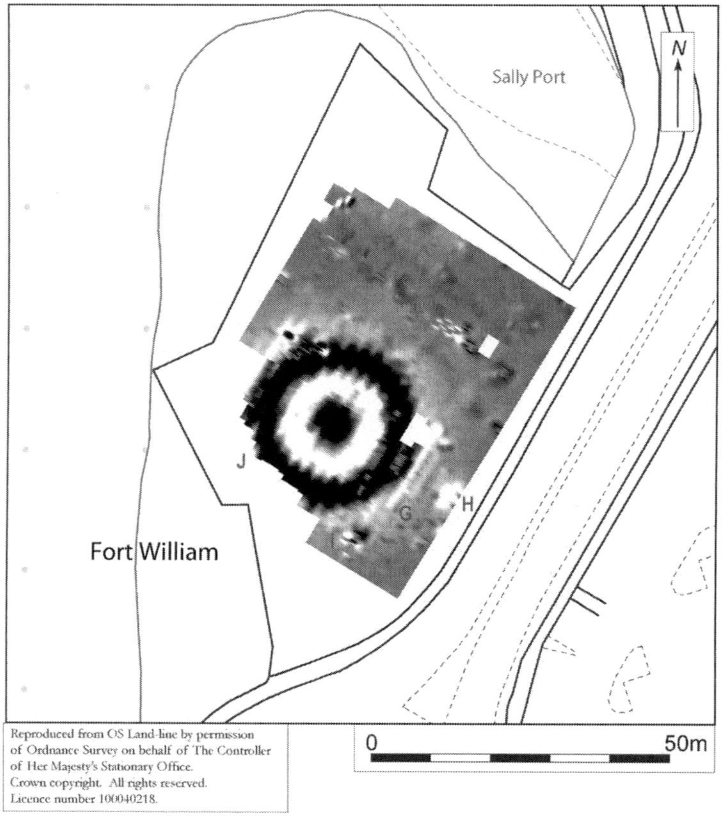

Fig. 6. Magnetometer survey of the Fort showing railway turntable

The concrete slabs sealed a series of soil deposits, the earliest of which were the bases of plough furrows overlying undisturbed geological soil. A sondage excavated through this deposit to a depth of 0.12 m established the presence below it of another sterile layer, perhaps a raised beach deposit. Excavation halted at this point.

Parade Trench 2 (Plate 1)

This trench originally measured 4 m ESE/WSW by 2 m, and was opened over a linear geophysical anomaly (B) that was initially interpreted as a possible structure, though its similarity in location to the burn shown on the maps was noted (see Figure 4 and 5). The trench was enlarged with an extension measuring 1.5 m ESE/WSW by 1 m at its northern corner when the depth of deposits made the existing trench sections unsafe. Figure 9 and Plate 5 show the trench section, while Figure 10 shows the earlier features and deposits in plan.

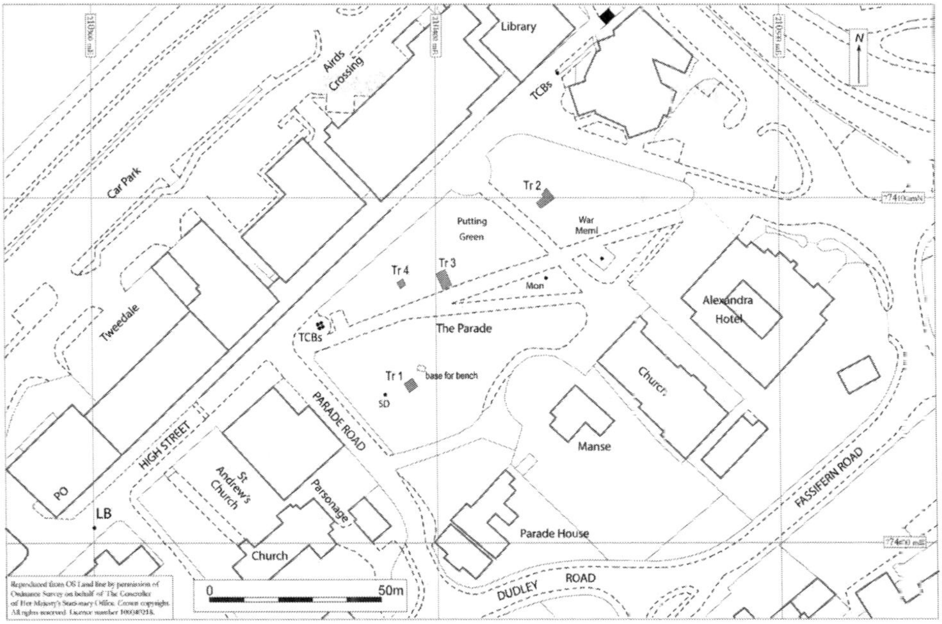

Fig. 7. Trench locations on the Parade

The modern turf and topsoil overlay deposits that contained abundant sherds of 19th and 20th century pottery and glass and other relatively modern artefacts. They both appeared to comprise made-ground, relating to modern landscaping of the Parade. Below this, in the north of the trench was a roughly metalled surface (PT204), although not a particularly concentrated or well-defined one. The soil deposit relating to this metalled surface produced fragments of possibly burned brick, along with sherds of 18th to early 19th century wine bottles; abundant, probably early 19th century china; some yellow and brown slipware sherds and pieces of stoneware and brown-glazed red earthenware, some of these being indicative of 18th century activity.

Below these deposits lay what was interpreted as a former water course. The base and edge of this putative burn course lay below and beyond the northern and southern limits of excavation, so its character could not be conclusively established. However, 18th and 19th century maps clearly show a burn running across the Parade in the approximate location of the trench (see Figure 3—runs through left of area of survival and is the uppermost burn in Figure 4), and this appears to be the most plausible explanation.

Within the water course was a linear stone-built feature running approximately east/west across the centre of the trench (Figures 9 and 10). Removal of the deposits to either side of it (see below) showed that this was a substantial

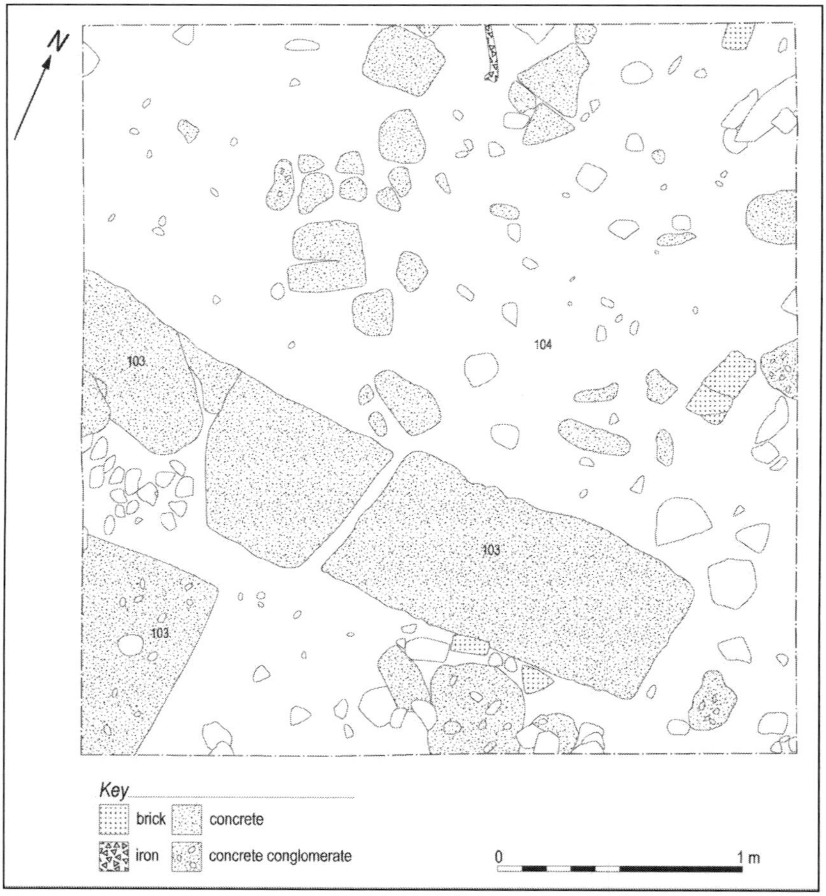

Fig. 8. Plan of Parade Trench 1

wall [PT213]: it ran for 2 m across the full width of the trench and stood up to 0.6 m high and 0.6 m wide. It was not clear whether the wall was originally of drystone construction: a matrix of loose grey silty clay lay between and around the stones, and this may have been deposited to bed and bond the components of the wall. It contained sherds of 18th century pottery (tin-glazed ware, brown-glazed red earthenware, cream ware) and wine bottle fragments; in addition, one of the very few pipe bowl (rather than stem) fragments from Trench 2 came from this deposit, and is of a distinctly 18th century type.

The wall was abutted on either side by deposits filling the upper part of the putative burn course, and it had been built on the lower fills. A spread of gravel up to 0.2 m deep on either side of the wall contained sherds of

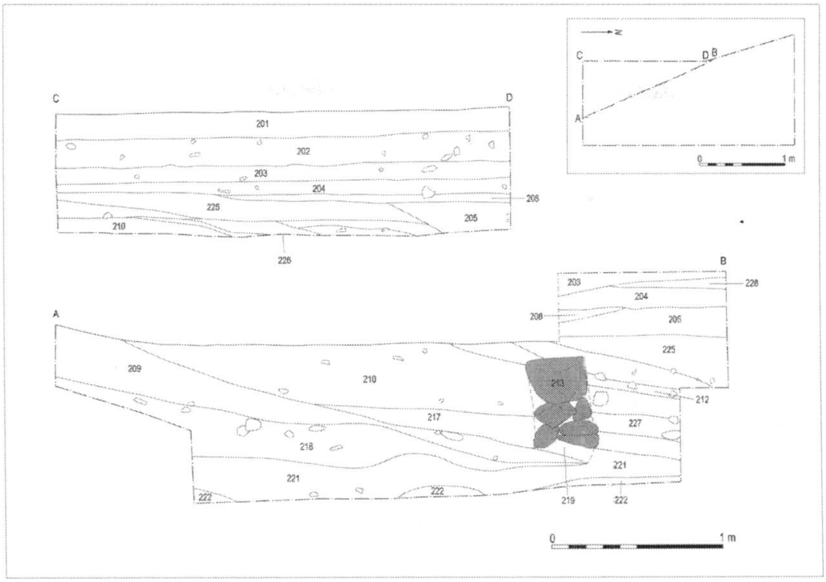

Fig. 9. East facing section of Parade Trench 2

Plate 5. South-east facing sections in Parade Trench 2, note partially removed wall on right

Fig. 10. Plan of features in Parade Trench 2

stoneware, salt glaze, slipware, the ubiquitous brown-glazed red earthenware and a fragment of decorated china, the last most probably 19th century in date.

A concentration of stones extending westward from the south side of the trench was interpreted as the remnants of another wall with clay bonding, although the stones were small and displayed little structure in their pattern of deposition. They rested on the surface of a midden-rich deposit (PT210), which lay 0.32 m thick against the wall and extended for 2.4 m to the south. It was heavily stained with flecks and larger pieces of charcoal and burnt peat and burnt animal bone, and also contained abundant fragments of 18th century wine bottle, pottery and clay pipe stems and some window glass and fragments of roofing slates. Although some of the pottery is undoubtedly 19th century in date, there was one piece of earlier, painted tin-glaze pottery which had been burned. A fragment of a wine glass stem with a base knob closely matches examples from the 1730s and 40s, and there was also the neck of a medicine bottle from the first half of the 18th century. The base of this midden-rich fill merged with a lower deposit (PT217) equally rich in artefacts. It also contained fragments of glass, including the stem of a trumpet-shaped wine glass of early to mid-18th-century date, concentrated at the surface of the layer. Most notable, though, were some quite large sherds from what may have been a vase or jar, made from white earthenware with blue painted decoration. This may be early 18th or even 17th century in date.

Beneath the two midden-rich deposits was a silt deposit containing sherds of pottery and glass of 18th to 19th century date. It was interpreted as having been naturally deposited, probably by the action of water, but while occupation was going on in the immediate vicinity. There was a similar layer of gravel that appeared to be water-borne in origin, but it also contained 18th and possibly 19th century artefacts, including salt glaze and slipware (though possibly cane ware).

Parade Trench 3

Parade Trench 3 was opened to test the character of a linear geophysical anomaly (E) to the north of the main E/W footpath crossing the green (see Figure 5). It originally measured 4 m N/S by 2 m wide, but was extended to measure 5 m by 3 m. Figure 11 shows the main features in plan, and Figure 12 shows them in section.

When the modern layers were removed, a linear feature of sandstone fragments (PT303) was exposed running NW/SE across the trench. It was interpreted as metalling for a road or track, which had been dumped along with sand quarried from the same source and topsoil to provide a firmly packed

Fig. 11. Plan of features in Parade Trench 3

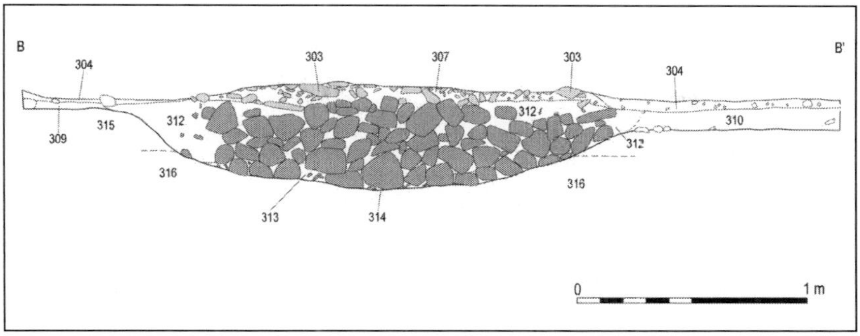

Fig. 12. Section through road in Parade Trench 3

surface. The lower fabric of the road consisted mainly of larger stones with occasional fragments of handmade brick and slate. The soil around and between the stones contained occasional flecks of charcoal, small pieces of coal and a few fragments of clay pipe, 19th century pottery and heat-affected glass. It was set into a cut measuring 0.4 m deep; the excavation of such a deep trench to bed the road suggests that good drainage was a particular concern for the builders.

Below the level of the road lay a silt deposit containing fragments of brick, pieces of coal and charcoal, along with 18th to 19th century pottery and glass. On the western side of the road, toward the north, it merged with a deposit of silt (PT305), that contained a high proportion of burnt material: frequent lenses of fine bright orange-pink silt (probably deriving from peat ash or burnt daub) along with pieces of burnt glass, sherds of 18th and 19th century pottery, iron objects, a copper alloy coin and fragments of 18th century clay pipe (some of them burnt). They appeared to represent re-deposited heat-affected material, such as demolition debris from burnt structures or hearth waste, rather than material that had burnt *in situ*.

Parade Trench 4

Parade Trench 4 measured 2 m by 2 m, and was opened in an area to the west of Parade Trench 3 to establish the presence or absence of features relating to Maryburgh in that part of the green.

The modern topsoil sealed a spread of silt and gravel that contained frequent fragments of coal and charcoal and occasional lenses of heat-affected sediment (Figure 13). Sherds of 18th to 19th century pottery, glass and clay pipe were found throughout (all five pipe bowls from the trench were of 18th century type). This deposit was interpreted as the result of levelling and landscaping in the 19th century. Beneath this was another, almost identical

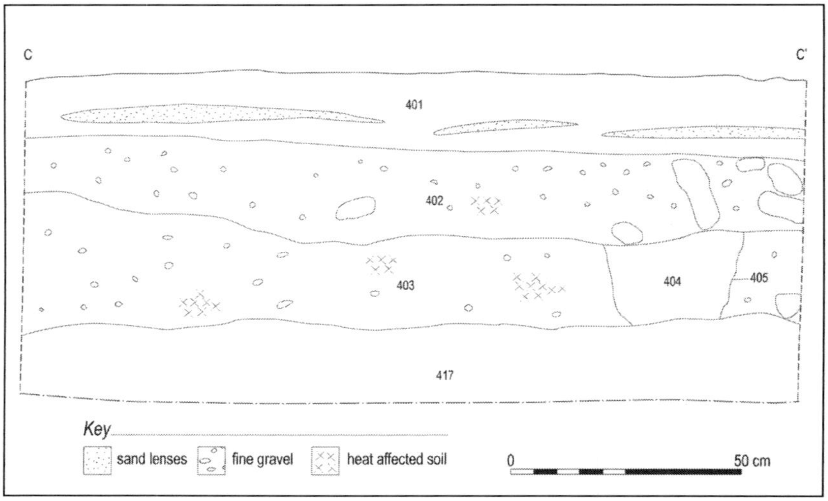

Fig. 13. South-west facing section through deposits in Parade Trench 4

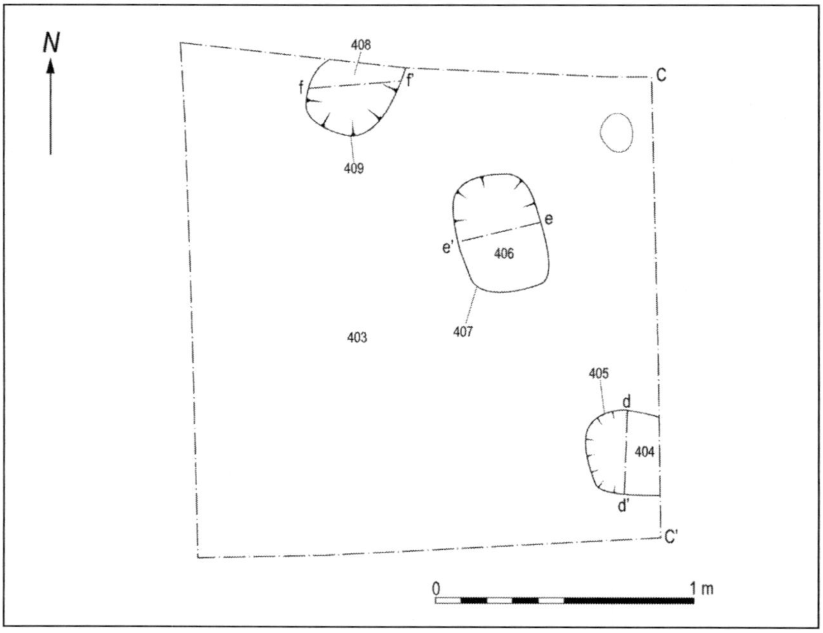

Fig. 14. Plan of upper features in Parade Trench 4

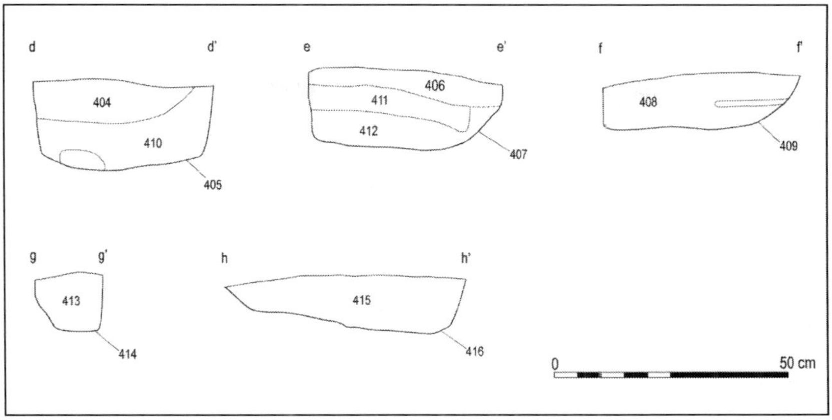

Fig. 15. Sections through upper and lower features in Parade Trench 4

layer, which appeared to be another levelling deposit (possibly relating to the same general phase of landscaping).

Cut into this deposit were three features, which lay in a line running south-east to north-west across the trench (Figures 14 and 15). The south-eastern-most [405] and the central feature [407] were rectangular with rounded corners, while the north-western feature [409] was sub circular in plan. The consistent size, depth and profiles of the features indicate that they formed a coherent suite, and may have served as post-holes. Their relatively clean, loose fills and the lack of packing material suggest that any posts were removed and the holes were backfilled when the putative structure they supported was dismantled.

The lower levelling deposit into which the possible postholes were cut sealed a layer containing occasional fragments of coal and charcoal (PT417). Two features were found cut into this layer (Figure 16). One, partially exposed and running into the north and west baulks, appeared to be a large oval feature [416; fig 15, h-h']. It contained occasional fragments of coal but was otherwise apparently sterile. To the south of this was another possible feature [PT414; fig 18, g-g']. No firm conclusion can be drawn on these latter features, but their position at the bottom of the profile beneath the levelling deposits may represent activity related to the original settlement of Maryburgh.

The Fort (Figure 17)

The geophysical survey of the fort was dominated by a very large circular anomaly in the magnetic data, which was interpreted as a railway turntable.

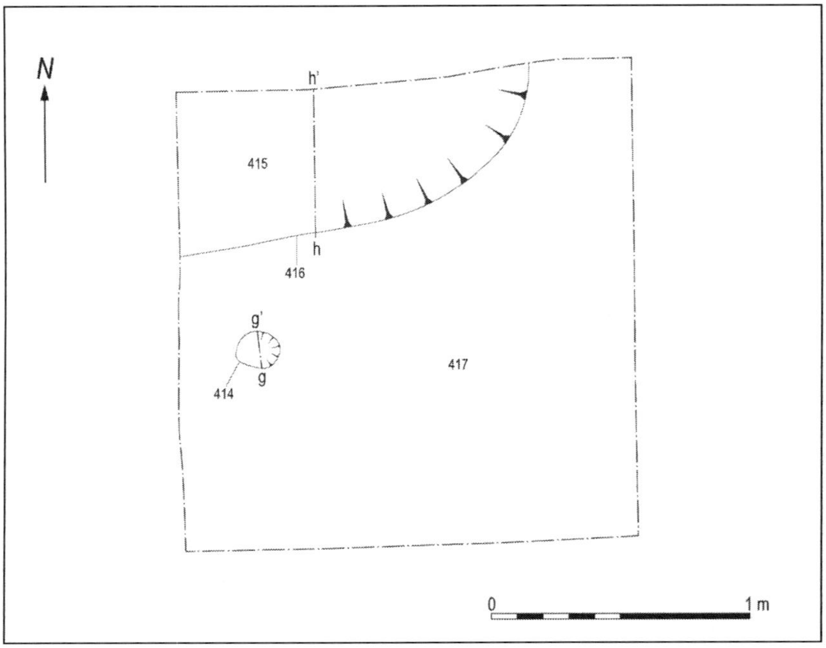

Fig. 16. Plan of lower features in Parade Trench 4

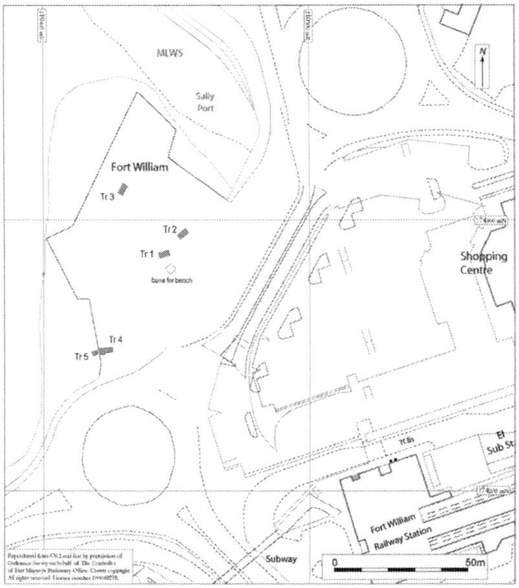

Fig. 17. Location of excavation trenches in Fort

There was little that was distinct in the resistivity data, other than some linear and circular anomalies that did not seem to relate to the buildings of the 18th century fort.

Fort Trench 1

This trench measured 4 m by 2 m and was located to the north of the monolith marking the Great Glen Way, which stands within the surviving portion of the fort. The location was influenced by a rather vague geophysical anomaly which suggested some sort of structure in this location (Figure 6: ?E and F). Removal of turf and topsoil exposed a spread of tarmac, which sealed a deposit of semi-rounded sandstone blocks and bricks in a gritty matrix soaked with oil. Excavation ceased after a depth of around 0.5 m, as the bricks and rubble appeared to continue down for a considerable distance. They may have sat in an inspection trench associated with an engine shed known to have been located in this area in the twentieth century. The bricks are likely to have originated from the demolition of the shed.

Fort Trench 2

Trench 2 also measured 4 m by 2 m and was located several metres to the west of Trench 1, close to a picnic bench. The purpose of this trench was to expose the edge of the railway turntable so obviously displayed as a circular anomaly in the magnetometer survey. Although clearly not related to the fort, the turntable was thought to be an interesting enough feature to merit some investigation. Removal of the turf and topsoil, however, revealed nothing more than a deep deposit of gritty shale containing a high proportion of brick fragments and other stone. Also contained within this deposit were large angular fragments of sandstone. A dense deposit of bricks was partially exposed in one corner of the slot cut down into the eastern end of the trench. Excavation ceased at a depth of around 0.70 m without encountering the base of the deposit. It seems likely that the trench missed the edge of the turntable pit and coincided with nothing more than the demolition debris used to backfill the pit during the programme of levelling which followed the demolition of the railway yard facilities.

Fort Trench 3 (Plate 4)

Trench 3 was located toward the north-western corner of the fort, as close to the scheduled area as was thought practicable without incurring any risk of impinging upon it. Although little was apparent on the geophysical plots in this area, the location did correspond to a building shown on the early 18th century maps.

Measuring 4 by 2 m, Trench 3 proved to be another frustrating exercise in the removal of demolition deposits and made ground. An irregular concrete slab beneath the topsoil was at first mistaken for a paved stone floor, which for a short while appeared to bode well for the survival of older features. However, once its true character was revealed, it became obvious that this trench also contained nothing but re-deposited debris relating to the demolished railway yard. The slab was confined to the western portion of the trench, with gravel similar to that in Trench 2 to the east of the slab. Removal of this gravel, which contained fragments of brick and was oil stained, exposed what appeared to be natural beach gravel at a depth of around 0.65 m below the modern ground surface. It therefore appeared that in this location, at least, whatever structural elements once existed had been scoured out to the level of the undisturbed geological deposits.

Fort Trench 4

As three trenches within the fort interior had drawn a total blank as far as surviving elements of the fort were concerned, it was decided to excavate a fourth trench as close to the wall as possible, in a location where vestigial pockets of archaeology might survive away from the more intensively utilised interior. Much of the fort wall is protected as a scheduled ancient monument, but one stretch, on the western side of the fort, remains unscheduled, and so the trench was positioned against this feature.

The trench measured 2 m by 4 m, but only the portion closest to wall was taken down deeper than the base of the topsoil. Any suggestion that this area may have avoided later disturbance was almost immediately dispelled when a brick-lined sewer inspection hatch was exposed close to the wall in the western end of the trench.

No meaningful archaeological horizons were encountered in the pair of small sondage pits positioned against the wall. The presence of crisp packets and modern ceramics from this soil profile clearly demonstrates that once again the deposits encountered relate to a much later period in the fort's existence.

Fort Trench 5 (Figure 18)

The evaluation of the fort's interior demonstrated that the railway yard had destroyed the archaeology of the interior of the fort. A final attempt to reveal the archaeology of the fort was directed toward the fort's exterior. It was hoped a trench opened against the base of the wall at the back of the beach might provide some insight into the fort's construction, and also expose midden material that was perhaps dumped over the wall of the fort during its

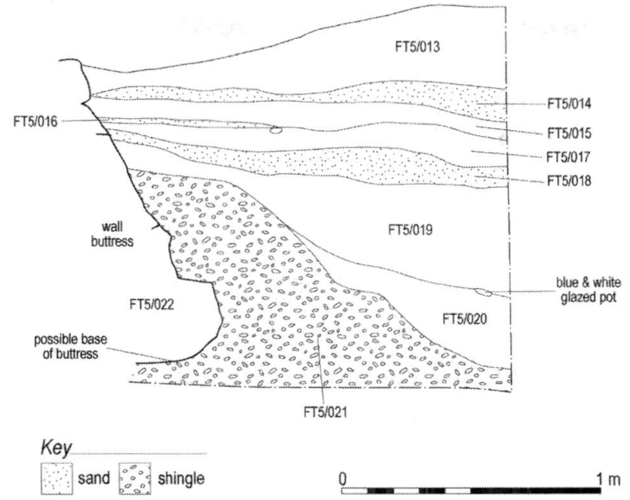

Fig. 18. North facing section through Fort Trench 5

occupation. As only a limited portion of the wall and adjacent beach remains unscheduled, the trench was located almost directly opposite Trench 4. Clearing an area for excavation involved the removal of considerable amounts of flotsam from the beach and modern rubbish. Some cutting back of vegetation was also required, as scrubby trees and bushes have colonised the rear of the beach in the shelter of the fort wall and adjacent sea wall.

A sondage or test pit measuring around 1.5 m by 1.5 m was positioned against the base of the wall (Figure 17). Beneath the topsoil was a soil rich in modern detritus, which overlay clean sand that in turn sealed a midden deposit with abundant sherds of bottle glass and ceramics that were largely 19th and 20th century in date. Perhaps the most noteworthy object from this context was a small ceramic lion with a boy perched on its back, which is a very unusual piece. Below this, and separated by a layer of sand was another midden deposit, which contained a tortoise shell hair comb, three perforated bone pins of a decidedly prehistoric character, a ceramic ink well, sherds of transfer print china, a possible brown ceramic tea pot base and butchered animal bone from cows and sheep/pigs. This layer also contained two dark green/blue wine bottle necks of an 18th or possibly early 19th century type. One of the only artefacts with a clearly military association was a brass composite button bearing the insignia of the Inverness-shire Rifle Volunteers, first raised in Inverness in 1859, with a second company raised in Fort William in 1860. The last company to be raised was in Roy Bridge in 1869.

Despite the presence of possible 18th century wine bottle fragments in the foregoing midden deposit, this did not appear to indicate a stratigraphic chronological transition, as beneath it a further layer of clean sand covered another midden deposit, dominated by 19th century material. Artefacts here included the steel blades from two ice skates (from different pairs). These most probably relate to the curling pond on the slope of Cow Hill, which appears on the Ordnance Survey map of 1876 (along with the military button they suggest deposition some time in the second half of the 19th century).

The underlying beach shingle was partially concreted due to lime wash from the wall, and so excavation ceased not far below its upper surface. The shingle, however, appeared to sit beneath the lower part of the wall, which was cambered outward to form a buttress. Older midden deposits and a continuation of the wall footings may exist beneath the basal deposit of beach gravel, but exploration would have required more time and a larger trench.

Interestingly, the railway turntable shown on the 1904 1:10,560 map is not the one identified during the geophysical survey. That turntable is too far to the south and had disappeared by the time of the 1938 1:10,560 map. The one identified by geophysical survey was the example shown in the 1960s photographs of the railway yard; it was constructed sometime between the Second World War and the 1960s.

Discussion

Summary of the Fieldwork Results

The Parade

The earliest feature encountered on the Parade was the burn course in Trench 2 (there now seems little doubt that this is a burn and the one shown on the various maps). It contained successive layers of both midden-rich material and water-borne silts and gravels, which would indicate that at times water flowed along it and at other times domestic rubbish was dumped into it. Most of the excavated material appears to have been dumped mainly after the construction of a wall that ran along the burn's alignment, near its base. This may have been built to revet the sides of the partially infilled burn.

The nature and date of the artefacts found in the burn course suggest that they probably derived from the settlement of Maryburgh. However, the burn was still extant in 1876, at least enough to merit inclusion on an Ordnance

Survey map (Figure 4); therefore, it is unlikely that enough material was dumped during the occupation of the original settlement of Maryburgh to infill entirely the course of the burn. This is also indicated by the presence of later, nineteenth-century material in the upper deposits. The condition of much of the material, which is essentially fresh and unrolled in appearance, does not suggest that the earlier material was washed from upstream or re-deposited after some considerable time lying around elsewhere. This conclusion is supported by the stratigraphy, which demonstrates phasing in the sequence of deposition rather than indicating a single deposition of earlier and later material moved from elsewhere. It should also be noted that the burn deposits were not fully excavated because of timetabling and health and safety issues, and the deposits appear to continue to even lower levels.

The spread of scorched material in Trench 3 may also relate to this early phase of settlement. The abundant lenses of burnt sediment and wood and heat-affected glass could have originated in the torched buildings of the town, which were later levelled across the area of the Parade. Also notable in Trenches 3 and 4 are the relatively high concentrations of wine bottle fragments which have been discoloured and distorted through exposure to high temperatures. Taken in association with the other evidence for burning, it would seem reasonable to suggest that this points to the burning of buildings. Although a few fire-distorted bottle fragments were recovered from the midden deposits in Trench 2, these were in much lower concentrations, which may suggest that Trenches 3 and 4 were located in closer proximity to the sites of burned buildings.

The concrete slabs representing the Nissen hut in Trench 1 attest to the much more recent military and civilian use of the Parade during wartime and its conversion to wholly civilian use in the aftermath, during the mid-20th century. The plough furrows sealed beneath soil deposits beneath the concrete slabs may well date to the 18th century and relate to garden plots shown on several of the contemporary maps.

Despite its quite impressive dimensions and well-made character, the road in Trench 3 was initially interpreted as nothing more than a footpath crossing the Parade, largely on the basis of a photograph taken around 1910. However, study of the 1904 OS map, which includes the path, suggests a relationship between this feature and a road, which prior to the demolition of the fort would have led directly into the main entrance. Granted, anyone travelling along from the fort along this route would have to cross the High Street to access the Parade, but the fact that the route leads directly to the Governor's house in the south-west corner of the Parade, would suggest a relationship. Given the absence of the path on the 1870s maps, this route would appear to have been constructed very late in the fort's history and in the light of this the forgoing should perhaps remain hypothetical rather than a statement of fact.

Trenches 2, 3 and 4 resulted in the recovery of a rich assemblage of material culture. These artefacts included numerous sherds of pottery dating from the 20th century back to the 17th century. For the purposes of this report, only a cursory examination of the pottery has been carried out, but it has been enough to suggest that the people of Maryburgh had access to a rich and varied material culture, which may differ from that of more rural settlements, a number of which have been excavated over recent years (e.g. Fairhurst 1968; Fairhurst & Petrie 1964; Lelong & Wood 2000; Atkinson, in prep). In addition to pottery, sherds of wine bottles were also recovered, with a number of styles evidenced from the form of bases and necks. As previously noted, a large proportion of these bottle fragments had been distorted through exposure to high temperatures, and it has been suggested that this may relate to the destruction of the town in March 1746, as described in the contemporary accounts.

Although artefactual evidence for the 18th century settlement of Maryburgh was plentiful, some fire-damaged when the town was put to the torch, along with secondary evidence for structures in the form of brick fragments, burnt daub, fragments of window glass and charcoal etc, very little evidence was identified for surviving features *in situ*, such as rubbish pits, hearths or postholes. The cultural material recovered, although related to Maryburgh, is possibly nothing more than demolition debris spread over the Parade to create the level surface visible on photographs taken in the late 19th century and still evident today. The postholes identified in Trench 4, cut into the destruction deposits, probably relate to the later use of the Parade. This may indicate that all remains of buildings were removed from the site, or indeed that the actual site of the buildings was not on the surviving portion of the Parade itself, but just outside it—perhaps even corresponding to the present location of the High Street. However, the presence of the rather ephemeral features cut into the natural in the base of Trench 4 (Figure 18) provides a tantalising suggestion of structural survival in this vicinity—the relationship, if any, between these features and the geophysical anomaly (Fig 6, A) in this area has yet to be established.

The foregoing cautious appraisal notwithstanding, the results from the Parade have demonstrated high archaeological potential for the locality, and further work would certainly be merited. The former bed of the burn alone, which over time has been used as a receptacle for rubbish, would be worth re-visiting, as the midden deposits identified in Trench 2 were not fully excavated during the 2007 season of excavation. Further excavation in the vicinity of

Trenches 3 and 4 may also result in the identification of structural remains and buried features beneath the deposits of made-ground, which included large quantities of debris from the Maryburgh settlement and its destruction in 1746.

The Fort

The trial excavation of the fort's interior provided no evidence for the survival of archaeological features related to the fort prior to the arrival of the railway in the 19th century. Even traces of buildings which were for a long time part of the railway yard, such as those located along the lochside wall, appear to have been entirely removed. This absence should perhaps come as no great surprise given the heavy, industrial character of the railway activities which took place in the yard. These were related to large engine sheds and a turntable set within a large circular pit. What is interesting to consider is that this process may relate to a 'cleansing' of the site, which local people may have viewed as an unwanted reminder of unhappy times. It has certainly been suggested (Hopkins 1988: 493) that pressure from local people was at least in part responsible for the removal of much of the fort by the railway company in the 50 years after 1890. The difficult nature of this past is also evident in periodic efforts to change the name of the town, again to remove the association with troubled times (MacCulloch 1939: 362).

It is possible that small pockets of fort survival may exist within the interior, but these are likely to be limited to old ground surfaces sealed beneath the earth banks which form part of the surviving defences along the lochside wall and within the demi-bastion in the northern corner. These areas are rightly protected as part of the Scheduled Ancient Monument, but may merit some investigation in further stages of the project.

Excavation outside the fort, against the stone wall at the head of the beach has suggested that midden deposits related to the fort's use as a garrison may survive here. The area with highest potential may be the ground adjacent to the sally port, which would have been close to where materials would have been brought into the fort from boats moored in the River Nevis. Today, this area is occupied by a series of grass-covered mounds lying against the base of the wall. Again, these sit within the part of the site protected by scheduling but should be considered as possible targets for excavation in any future archaeological work on the site. The recovery of ceramics and other midden material originating in the fort would provide a useful means of comparing life in the garrison to that of the civilian population of Maryburgh already suggested by the rich deposits encountered on the Parade.

The residents of Maryburgh appear to have benefited from imported goods, the port town also being the point of departure for various exported trade goods, including salted fish, wool, sheep, horses and black cattle. According to the *Old Statistical Account* entry for the parish, by 1791 wool was being shipped to Liverpool and other English towns and fish were destined for foreign ports such as Bilbao in Spain and Ostend via Aberdeen. The fish sent to Spain found a ready market in a strongly Catholic country and in return the town benefited from the import of wines and spirits (Rose, pers comm). According to the OSA, by the 1790s the list of imports included: 'meal, flour, butter, cheese, whisky, foreign spirits, salt timber, tar and all kinds of mercantile goods' (Fraser in OSA 1791–99: 133).

The fort and town had a varied relationship as far as provision of goods was concerned. The town may have originated as a sutler's station (trading post) to provide the garrison with goods, but by the 1730s it was the fort, or at least its Governor and commander, that was controlling trade. The court case of 1736 mentioned above was brought against the fort authorities, in whom the authority of the Barony was invested; it was claimed that they had placed unfair controls on the sale of goods, preventing traders in the town from running markets without paying a fee and selling goods to the inhabitants at inflated prices.

Interpretive Issues

The fieldwork at Fort William has produced a wealth of information about a locality which had previously been largely ignored as far as archaeology is concerned. Limited trial trenching of the Parade produced not only a rich assemblage of material culture, but also evidence for the burning of the town through the presence of charcoal-rich deposits which included concentrations of burnt daub. Although the daub is in keeping with the idea of buildings made from impermanent materials, the recovery of hand-made brick fragments, roofing slates and window glass from several contexts in the main Parade trenches would suggest that, even before 1746, the buildings may have included more permanent elements than those stipulated by the Governor. As yet, though, it is unclear whether these deposits merely represent demolition material which was spread over the area during land renewal or whether they more closely relate to the positions of structures destroyed by fire. The high concentrations of material and the generally unabraded condition of much of the material would point to structures very close by, and the features identified in the base of Trench 4 may offer a further indication of this. It is possible that the buildings shown on the various early maps were located outside the limits of the Parade, but further work would be required to establish this beyond doubt.

It initially appeared that the interior of the fort was entirely bereft of archaeological deposits dating back any earlier than the late 19th century. However, since the completion of the project, trenching works related to the laying of new services in the supermarket car park, to the north of the surviving ramparts, exposed what appear to be the foundation courses of stone walls related to the defences as they would have existed in 1746 (Abernethy 2008). These remains, which were not subject to archaeological recording, but photographed by the quick-thinking works foreman, sit at a depth of around 1 m below the present ground surface and provide some indication of limited survival in some places. In the vicinity of the surviving surface remains, the potential for earlier deposits would appear to be confined to the areas sealed beneath the earthen banks of the ramparts and in the areas outside the fort, where midden deposits may be heaped against the walls.

Conclusion

The project has highlighted the good potential of archaeological deposits relating to the early history of the town of Fort William to survive within the modern town's precincts. This factor should obviously be taken into consideration in any future development within the town, which should at least be accompanied by an archaeological watching brief. It is hoped that both areas will be subject to further investigation in future years as a continuation of this ground breaking project, with the intention of building on this community-based work to uncover the history and development of the town of Fort William. Much still survives to reveal the details of life in 18th and 19th century Fort William, and future work may well go beyond the archaeology of the fort and siege. The current work has given a small picture of Fort William's development, and provides the basis for future work on the Parade, the parts of the fort outside the upstanding remains, and other features such as the location of the Jacobite artillery batteries. It has shown how the archaeological investigation of military events can benefit more traditional areas of archaeological knowledge, examining parts of the archaeological record that have frequently been ignored.

Acknowledgements

The project was made possible by generous grant funding from the Heritage Lottery Fund, Highland Council, Highland Council Archaeology Service and the Lochaber 2007 Community Fund. Dr Michael Foxley was instrumental in making the project happen and also provided the use of his former surgery as accommodation for the dig team. Dorothy Ferguson of Highland Council played a key role in the long term organisation of the project and did much to facilitate its success. Dorothy Maxwell, head of Highland Council's Archaeology Service, facilitated grant funding and provided invaluable support in-kind.

Ian Abernethy, Andy Hickie and Iain Rose provided invaluable historical information, gave freely of their local knowledge and were enthusiastic supporters of the project, as was Mairi Mooney, curator of the West Highland Museum. Ian Deveney of Battlescar did a splendid job of organising the battle re-enactment, which took place half way through the project and was enjoyed by several hundred people, despite terrible weather. This event which would not have been possible without further funding support from Highland Council and Historic Scotland.

The geophysical survey was carried out by Dr Iain Banks. Dr Olivia Lelong supervised the excavations at the Parade and provided trench reports which provide the basis for part of this report. The professional excavation team consisted of: Andrew Baines, Natasha Ferguson and Paul Murtagh, assisted by students: Sam Colclough and William Sutherland. Steve Thomson added his much appreciated considerable excavation experience to the core team. Kirsty Cameron of Highland Council worked alongside Natasha Ferguson as education officer, and their work was complemented by Shirley Watson. Many thanks to all the local volunteers who took part in various aspects of the project, including Robert Cairns and Bridget Willoughby, who provided sterling service throughout on the fort excavation (Bridget also provided photographs and maps from the collections of the town library). Also: Ritchie Cummings, Richard Bourne, Lorraine Phillips, Carol Snelgrove, Graeme Livingstone, Fiona Ball, Alexander Walker, Colin MacLeod, Ivor Erskine, Hector Mackenzie-Rogers, Sandy Mackay, John Mackay, Frank Drummond, Iain and Jan (apologies to anyone who has inadvertently been left off this list). Thanks also to all the teachers and pupils who visited the project and took part in the various activities.

Bibliography

Abernethy, I 2008 Untitled newspaper report, *Lochaber News*, 12 April 2008.

Fergusson, J 1951 *Argyll in the Forty-Five*. Faber & Faber: London.

Fraser, A 1791–99 'Parish of Kilmalie', *The Statistical Account of Scotland* 1791–1799. EP Publishing Ltd (1981).

Gott, R 2004 *Cuba: A New History*. Yale University Press: New Haven & London.

Fairhurst, H 1968 'Rosal: a deserted township in Strath Naver, Sutherland', *Proc Soc Antiq Scot* 100, 135–69.

Fairhurst, H & Petrie, G 1964 'Scottish clachans II: Lix and Rosal', *Scot Geog Mag* 80, 150–63.

Farrell, S 2002 *Report on a Watching Brief at Fort William*. Unpublished report.

Hopkins, P 1998 *Glencoe and the End of the Highland War*. John Donald: Edinburgh.

Kingsford, C L 1922 'The Highland forts in the Forty-Five', *Eng Hist Rev* 37, 361–82.

Lelong, O & Wood, J 2000 'A township through time: excavation and survey at the deserted settlement of Easter Riatts, Badenoch, 1995–99', *in* Atkinson, J, Banks, I & MacGregor, G (eds), *Townships to Farmsteads: rural settlement studies in Scotland, England and Wales*. BAR British Series 293, Archaeopress: Oxford. 40–49.

MacBane, D 1728 *The Expert Sword-man's Companion; or the true art of self-defence; with an account of the authors life, and his transactions during the wars with France; to which is annexed, The art of gunnerie*. Glasgow.

MacCulloch, D B 1939 *Romantic Lochaber, Arisaig and Morar*. (revised 1999 edition). Lines Publishing.
Pollard, T & Lelong, O 2007 *Archaeological Investigations at Fort William*. GUARD data structure report 2348.
Rose, I (nd) *What Happened at the Siege of Fort William*. Privately published.
Rose, I 2007 'The Fort William court case 1736', *Scottish Cultural Studies, Lochaber: Clansmen to Clearances*. University of Aberdeen Extramural course pack.
Simpson, P 1996 *The Independent Highland Companies*. John Donald Publishers: Edinburgh.
Stephenson, D 1980 *Highland Warrior: Alasdair MacColla and the Civil Wars*. John Donald: Edinburgh.
Wedgewood, C V 1952 *Montrose*. (1995 reprint), Sutton Publishing.

BETWEEN MEMORY AND MATERIALITY: AN ARCHAEOLOGICAL APPROACH TO STUDYING THE NAZI CONCENTRATION CAMPS

ADRIAN T MYERS

Abstract

By its very nature, historical narrative that is rooted exclusively in textual sources is destined to be more linear, more univocal, and less equipped to deal with the problematic. On the other hand, due to its unique abilities and approaches, historical archaeology thrives on the tensions inherent to any attempt to understand past and present experience. In this article I negotiate between two approaches to studying the concentration camps of the Third Reich—one canonical the other experimental. It is suggested that when studying the camps, we are faced with a series of tensions: between past and present, between remembering and forgetting, and between live human actors and the material record. This article explores two research paradigms: first, the traditional text-centric historical approach, and second, an approach that might be called 'historical archaeological'. I embrace the inherent tensions between the two approaches, and put forward some innovative ways for coming to terms with these places of internment.

> In such places there is a terrible presence of absence—not the dead bodies of pre-twentieth century conflicts, but human beings vaporised into nothingness by technology, a community of 'the missing' in our midst (Saunders 2004: 1)

> If anything, this is an archaeology of the future, if we take such an oxymoron seriously (Buchli & Lucas 2001: 9)

Introduction

Two illustrations from contemporary Germany provide a fitting entrée for a discussion as to how we might approach the history and archaeology of one of the defining experiences of the 20th century, that of the concentration camps of the Third Reich. In August 2006, a controversy erupted in Germany that quickly gained worldwide attention. Nobel Prize-winning author Günter Grass, an outspoken critic of the way Germany has dealt with its Nazi past, admitted that he had been a member of the elite *Waffen-SS*, the combat arm of the *Schutzstaffel.* In the days that followed, an intense and emotion-driven debate played out in the press. Literary, historical, and political heavyweights such as John Irving, Joachim C Fest, and Lech Wałęsa publicly asserted their views, from praise for his present honesty to condemnation for his past lies and hypocrisy. In one piece entitled *Snake in the Grass,* critic Christopher Hitchens (2006) first likened Grass to 'a high horse, always tethered

 DOI: 10.1163/157407808X382827

conveniently nearby' and then opined that he may have even 'uncork[ed] the hideous revelation to enhance the sale of his latest memoirs'. Everyone had an opinion, and no one with a podium at hand could resist airing it.

The second illustration is provided by a graffiti enthusiast who spotted and photographed a stencil on a wall on *Oranienburger Strasse* in Berlin (Duncan Cumming, pers comm.). The simple, monochrome piece depicted waif-like concentration camp prisoners, one standing, the others laying, in their wood bunks (Figure 1); a shadowy recreation of one of the most famous photographs of the Nazi Judeocide. The photograph (Figure 2) was taken in April 1945 in Buchenwald by liberating American troops, its fame surely due in part to the fact that Elie Wiesel, another Nobel Prize-winner, is visible in the photo. In the *Oranienburger Strasse* stencil, Wiesel's placid visage is hauntingly plain.

Each of these two illustrations evokes themes with repercussions both influential and potentially insidious. What is intriguing about the recent dispute over Grass is not the moral character of an elderly man and his relationship with his country's past *per se*. Important as this may be, more fascinating is the fact of the debate itself, that it even occurred in the first place. It is clear from the incident that Germans, and others around, the world still care passionately about events of over 60 years ago. And what of the stencil graffiti; what are the meanings and repercussions of its existence on a wall in Berlin? I would posit that to some Berliners, this subversive street art, in its dreadful and stark simplicity, speaks to them more clearly about the Holocaust than any textbook ever will.

These recent events illustrate not only the critical relevance of a not-so-distant Nazi era—the Second World War was recently described by historical archaeologists as 'arguably the most significant event of world history' (Schofield & Johnson 2006: 111)—but more importantly, they demonstrate both the continuity and the 'series of tensions' between past and present, between 'remembering and forgetting', and between live human actors and the material record (Johnson 1999; Buchli & Lucas 2001). The intent of this article is to compare and negotiate between two approaches to studying the camps, one canonical and the other experimental. It is to be hoped that the tensions between the two may begin to be resolved through this process.

The paper will explore and debate two research paradigms: first, the traditional text-centric historical approach, and second, an approach that might be called 'historical archaeological'. The historical archaeological approach treats texts as just one manifestation of material culture among many. It also draws on previously unconsidered, or little considered, avenues for dealing with the recent and contentious 'contemporary past' of the Nazi era (Buchli & Lucas 2001). As such, the historical archaeological approach may or may

Fig. 1. Berlin stencil (Courtesy of Mr. Duncan Cumming)

Fig. 2. Buchenwald at liberation (work of the US government in the public domain, courtesy of the National Archives and Records Administration)

not include excavations in the traditional sense of the word. Working with, and even embracing, the inherent tensions between the two approaches, should reinvigorate attempts to better understand both the world of the concentration camps as they were once-lived and the world today where, in another sense than the past, they clearly still live.

The Context and Materiality of Text

As Hicks has suggested, conventional historical studies have been exposed as

> . . . reliant upon a purely arbitrary selection of one source of evidence ('texts', or documents stripped of their materiality), disregarding the superabundance of other material sources of evidence (Hicks 2003: 316)

While weaknesses inherent to conventional historical studies have long been discussed among historical archaeologists, some conventional archaeological approaches still need to be challenged as well. Certain archaeologists still treat texts as somehow apart from the subaltern people *they* study. They make certain use of texts, but

> in ignoring the engagement between texts and the 'people without history', they deny themselves the possibility of fully understanding the mechanisms through which the later were exploited (Moreland 2001: 96).

Unquestionably, it is no longer possible to study only texts. However, neither can material culture and text be studied independently, as though different lines of evidence:

> For if it is the case that material culture should be seen as a product of human creativity, as an active intervention in the social production of reality, then it must follow that this applies to *all* human creations—including written sources (Moreland 2001: 83; emphasis in original).

Following Johnson's (1996) call to treat texts as artefacts, it binds the researcher to the challenge of dealing with the 'context and materiality' of those written sources (Moreland 2001). The primary texts that emerge out of the concentration camp experience are highly problematic, and it is only with an approach that deals with these texts' context and materiality that we might breathe fresh air into what has become a stale historical discussion.

Presence of Absence at Sites of Genocide

Buchli & Lucas state that

> the elimination of the body by murder and its secret burial always leaves its trace, if only in the gap left by its absence, an absence as physical as any presence (2001: 122)

Their insight seems especially apropos with regard to murder on a mass scale. Buchli & Lucas refer to the presence of absence of a single human, the gap left by a single murder. Consider then what size gap, and how strong a presence of absence, could be expected when there has not been only one murder, but hundreds of thousands of murders. Not surprising is the sense of emptiness that many visitors to Holocaust sites experience.

If an overwhelming absence is present at the sites of concentration and extermination, then it follows that this absence is also present in the primary textual record that has grown out of the camp experience, the body of work labelled Holocaust literature. It is this condition of overwhelming absence that exposes the one fundamental and inherent bias shared by every memoirist of the concentration camp experience: the fact that the author survived. This bias has remained largely unchallenged.

It is well documented that the social organization of camp life was dominated by a pernicious social hierarchy. Every prisoner fell into a rigid category ranging from the highly powerful ethnic German professional criminals and 'politicals' to the piteous and usually powerless Jews. This social hierarchy maintained the disparity between classes of prisoners that formed the framework for a hegemonic system dominated by a core of elite prisoners (see Glicksman 1953; Gutman 1984; Sofksy 1999). Both survivors and historians often credit luck with strongly affecting the outcome of who survived and who did not. However, survival was also contingent on the prisoner's position in this hierarchy, which determined access to food and trade goods, and their resulting socio-economic power. In the blunt words of one survivor, in the camps 'whoever has grub, has power' (Borowski 1976: 31).

In the context of the concentration camp experience, the subaltern, the people without history, are those that did not survive. There are vast numbers of people who perished without ever writing anything of their experience. The logical response to this observation is that those who did survive the experience and who took the opportunity to write their memoirs are a kind of elite, comparable to the elite described in larger paradigms of historical archaeology. In a disconcerting similarity, the class system not only existed in the lived past of the camps, but has been carried through and perpetuated by the literary record. After the war, survivor Ella Lingens-Reiner (1948: 50) admitted that those who were among the camp elite are 'the only ones who can still give a comprehensive report on the camps'. It was largely the elite who survived, meaning that the emphases and biases in the written record have been largely formed by that group. Hence, the history of the camps (both its formation by survivors and historians and its consumption by the public) has relied on documentary and oral evidence drawn from an inherently 'flawed' sample.

If the canon of historical research on the concentration camps is deeply rooted in this particular sample, then it is a body of work that has overlooked a large cross-section of its past actors. However, if historical archaeology is specially suited to bringing to the fore populations forgotten or overlooked, by making the 'familiar unfamiliar' (Buchli & Lucas 2001), it may provide the appropriate framework needed to put these forgotten past actors back into the lived past. Concentration camps and the material culture therein must be seen as sites and objects made, used, and experienced by not only the people who survived to tell about them, but also by those who did not survive.

The story of the concentration camps of the Third Reich is overwhelming, in spatial distances and distribution, in the sheer number of actors and their differing personal experiences, and in difficulty in comprehension. A comprehensive comparison of the textual and archaeological ways that the camps can be studied is, of course, impossible here. Rather, the goal is to explore certain key examples of how this new approach compares to the dominant textual approach. Looking in depth at a select few representative areas should illuminate some innovative ways for coming to terms with this overwhelming absent-presence of the concentration camps.

Victim and Perpetrator: The Space Between

The more challenging writings on life in the camps attempt critical readings of Holocaust memoirs to try to tease out the intricacies of the internment experience. Such writings confront a commonly told version of the camp experience, one that does not allow for the fallibility of those murdered by the Nazis. Revered Holocaust historian Raul Hilberg (1993: ix) discusses the 'perpetrators', 'bystanders', and 'victims', three groups 'distinct from one another': 'Each saw what happened from its own, special perspective and each harbored a separate set of attitudes and reactions'. Hilberg sees the three categories as totally unambiguous:

> In this text, perpetrators, victims, and bystanders will appear separately. The twenty-four chapters, each dealing with a segment of one of the three groups, are written as modules. They are intended to be self-contained and may be read in any order (1993: xii)

Unfortunately, this neat moral division is not a viable interpretation of the camp experience, for such an approach reduces highly complex social relationships into a series of too simplistic moral polarities. Despite the fact that it would be more palatable to believe that the 'perpetrators' were all sadists and the 'victims' either died as martyrs or survived morally unblemished as heroes, this evidence demonstrates that the reality of the camps was never quite that simple.

A few key Holocaust memoirists remind us that in the concentration camps there was often no clear-cut division between the perpetrators and the victims. Memoirists such as Tadeusz Borowski (1976) and Primo Levi (1986; 1988) describe how they often found themselves in complex and morally ambiguous situations where the roles of the perpetrators and the victims were distorted or overlapping. Combining these exceptionally frank memoirs of survivors with careful readings of other memoirs and documents, sociologist Wolfgang Sofsky managed to produce a more nuanced version of life in the camps. Sofsky (1999) emphasized the influential social hierarchies and black markets that dominated the prisoners' daily lives to highlight the fact that not all prisoners were equal.

It is apparent from this more recent scholarship that careful work with textual sources can provide keen insight into the camp experience. But what of an approach informed by historical archaeology—might we add to the interconnected stories of social hierarchies and black marketing by thinking about the camps in an archaeological way? While the entire body of work on hierarchies and black marketing draws exclusively on a textual evidentiary base, the two themes are clearly intertwined with the traditionally archaeological conceptions of spatiality and material culture.

The Spatiality of the Camp

The complex system of power relations in the camps was established and reified by both real and conceptualised spatial boundaries. From the electrified and very tangible barbed-wire fencing (Figure 3) which separated the prisoners from the civilian world, to the sometimes unmarked divisions within an individual bunkhouse that delineated the personal area of the infamous *Kapos*, boundaries and conceptions of boundaries played large in hierarchical systems and power relations. The black marketing of the camps was of course fundamentally rooted in materiality. While services (human labour) were also part of the systems of trade, series of exchanges were never far removed from material culture. The ultimate goal of each trader was to increase his chances of survival by increasing his caloric intake; thus, smuggled and stolen goods of every description were traded for consumables in trade networks involving prisoners, guards, and civilians. If discussions of social hierarchies and black marketing are intertwined with those of spatiality and material culture, then it is clear that historical archaeology has something to contribute.

Fig. 3. Auschwitz-I fence (author)

Detailed archaeological survey of the above-ground remains of the concentration camps—beginning at landscape scale, and then down to the interior layout of individual bunkhouses—could provide new information about the nature of, and the relationship between, spatiality and power. In her exploration of the potential for archaeological work at the Long Kesh/Maze prison site, McAtackney states that

> a reflexive archaeological investigation of the Maze site has the ability to tell the stories of the lowly, the disenfranchised and the subversive through their negotiations with this institution of the dominant.

Archaeology could be used to

> examine the negotiation of the prisoners and the prison officers with the material culture that surrounded them, both structural and movable, through examination of the buildings and artefacts connected to the site (2005b: 23).

A partial test of how power relations might have affected the built environment could compare the original documentary plans for the construction of the camp with how it was actually built and possibly adapted over time:

> we can ascertain how the buildings were originally conceived, and what alterations by the prison authorities and subversions by the prisoners occurred (McAtackney 2005a: 14).

The early stages of survey and recording of the concentration camps would benefit from recent work by Schofield *et al.* (2006), who have developed a preliminary methodology for the recording of modern English army camps.

The Materiality of the Camp

Inside the concentration camps, despite the most extreme conditions, and despite the landscape of death and deprivation, interaction between humans and material goods was continuous (Myers 2007). Combining data obtained from landscape and building survey with data obtained through representative, targeted subsurface testing will reveal not only something of the spatial distribution of artefacts, but also how this distribution relates to larger hypotheses about spatiality and power relations. Such a study of the context of excavated artefacts would reveal fascinating, problematic, and possibly subversive, evidence about resistance and collaboration, the different classes of prisoners, and their economic interaction (see also Casella 2000).

Following Cochran & Beaudry's comment that

> understanding and interpreting material culture has become more important than simply identifying and classifying excavated objects (2006: 191)

an approach to artefact analysis is needed that focuses on the potential of small finds, and indeed, 'the small stories' that follow. Ronald Hirte's *Buchenwald Found Objects* project has perhaps inadvertently demonstrated the potential to apply the small finds approach to the concentration camps. Hirte (nd) excavated war-era Buchenwald middens, 'resulting in a collection of several thousand found objects, primarily simple articles of everyday life in the camps':

> The majority of them were made or improvised by the inmates themselves from scraps of various materials; many of them changed hands more than once. They include makeshift toiletries and medical articles, cutlery and dishes often bearing initials, inmate numbers and engravings, factory and identification tags, jewellery, game pieces and religious objects.

There is great potential in a biographical approach to interpreting the personal artefacts of such an assemblage. Not only will this approach 'provide intimate portraits of individual lives and of the construction of personal and social identity' (Cochran & Beaudry 2006: 192), it may also contribute to wider questions about black marketing and the socio-economics of the camps.

The Subtlety of Resistance

Another theme apt for comparison is that of resistance. Unlike the previous themes of social hierarchies and black marketing, the notion of resistance in the camps has been intensively covered by historians. The writing of a history of resistance developed partly in response to the early conception that the victims of the Nazis (and especially the Jews) went to their deaths like sheep to the slaughter. Survivors, theorists, and historians empowered the prisoners by beginning to look at their active resistance to the Nazis. In *Fighting Auschwitz: The Resistance Movement in the Concentration Camp*, memoirist Józef Garliński made it clear that the camp had a widespread and structured resistance movement. The most famous act of resistance occurred in October 1944, when a group of prisoners working at the crematoria complex at Birkenau successfully blew up one of the crematoria buildings. Although the explosion was a success, every participant was apprehended and executed.

Another resistance theme covered by memoirists and historians is that of escape. Though extremely rare relative to the total number incarcerated, the few key escape stories prove inspiring to readers of Holocaust literature. One celebrated instance is the successful escape from Auschwitz of Rudolf Vrba and Alfréd Wetzler, who in April 1944 managed to flee the camp in a bid to apprise the Allies of the ongoing genocide. Vrba's escape and its aftermath are covered in his powerful memoir, *I Cannot Forgive*, and was the subject of recent scholarly attention by Ruth Linn of Haifa University (Vrba 1997; Linn 2004). A resurgence of interest in Vrba was evidenced by the widespread, worldwide, media coverage of his death in March 2006.

While memoir and historical writing on resistance have most often focused on discernable events and specific acts of resistance in the camps, resistance can be more subtle concept. Under the 'extremity' of the concentration camp (as described by Des Pres 1976), simply staying alive was a form of resistance. In a very real sense, any minute act that bettered the prisoner's situation, that provided benefits physical or psychological, must be considered as an act of resistance. Thus, if the aim is to deal not only with the big events of resistance, such as the blowing up of a crematorium, or an escape from Auschwitz, then a historical archaeological approach may be particularly suitable. While resistance, and thus perhaps agency could be investigated in a multitude of ways at the camps—and is related to the above discussion of personal artefacts—the present research is limited here to two potentially fruitful avenues: concentration camp graffiti and the research potential of the camp privies.

Graffiti in the Camp

In the summer of 2002, while at Birkenau, I took a picture of a row of bunks in a wood block house (Figure 4). Only recently did I look at the picture again; I saw hundreds of markings covering the wall in the picture. What

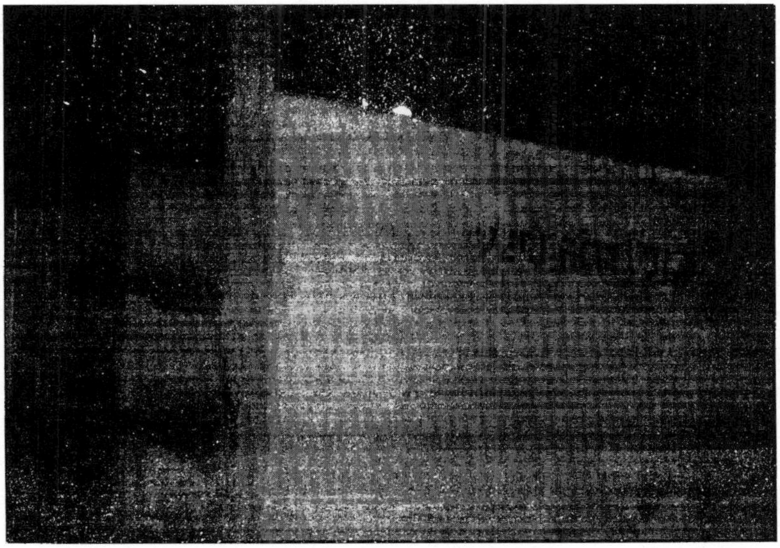

Fig. 4. Auschwitz-II birkenau bunks (author)

I had barely noticed when I had taken the picture is now much more interesting to me than the original subject of the photograph. While the extent and nature of markings on the walls of standing buildings at the concentration camps is unknown, some of it is obviously still extant. Cocroft *et al.*, discussing graffiti in the modern context of English military bases, state:

> People have always decorated their surroundings. Whether on walls in prehistoric caves, Roman villas or medieval churches, paintings are motivated and inspired by forces as diverse as the images. Murals, graffiti and casual doodles connect directly with a moment in time and with past residents, be these ancient Egyptian artists, Roman soldiers or recent service personnel (2006: 44).

Graffiti in the concentration camps could be used to study a range of themes, such as Nazi oppression (through a close look at the official painted murals and slogans); however, the avenue seems especially suited to an investigation of resistance. As Cocroft *et al.* suggest: 'Spontaneous graffiti are . . . effective at communicating a message of protest or subverting a hated structure' (2006: 47).

The study of graffiti at concentration camps can not be treated as a study of graffiti produced between 1933 and 1945. The history of the camps did not end at liberation, and the creation of new graffiti certainly did not end either. While the study of pre-1945 graffiti will reveal life during that critical era, post 1945 graffiti will reveal the changing reception of, and reactions to, the camps since the end of the war. Not only can art 'create a dialogue between the past and the present' (Cocroft & Schofield 2003: 44), but it can also contribute to a larger goal of the archaeology of the recent and contemporary past, that of 'serving as a critique on the world we ourselves have created' (Schofield 2006: 2). Recent developments in the study of graffiti by historical archaeologists are encouraging. With innovative work in both military and civilian contexts pushing the boundaries of both method and theory, a precedent has been set for the development of similarly critical work at the concentration camps of the Third Reich (see for example, Buchinger & Metzler 2006; Cocroft & Schofield 2003; Cocroft & Wilson 2006; Cocroft *et al.* 2006; Cole 2006).

Privies in the Camp

In the daily life of the camp, the privies were of central importance, as excrement played a primary role in the life of the common prisoner. The combination of diet and disease was such that the majority suffered from potentially lethal diarrhoea for the duration of their incarceration. Those who were able to wait lined up for the cruelly inadequate privies (in both number and cleanliness). Those who could not wait, or could not get up from their bunks, defecated where they stood or lay. Thus, survivor and theorist Terrence Des Pres (1976), in his seminal work *The Survivor: An Anatomy of Life in the Death Camps* appropriately devotes a chapter to his concept of 'the excremental assault'. Accepting Wheeler's (2000: 12) description of the privy as an 'opportunistic midden', it seems very likely that the camp privies would have been used for the disposal of the material culture of resistance. In the highly controlled environment of the camps where bunks were inspected daily, the privies were likely used as the final repository for illicit items when the margin of safety had become too thin. While there are accounts of prisoners cleaning out the privies, and other accounts of murder by drowning in the privies, it is nearly inconceivable that any authority in the camps would have gone near the fetid liquid in the privy shaft.

Any privy excavation at a concentration camp requires a special set of considerations. Survivor testimony consistently confirms that everything had value to the inmates; any bit of string, piece of paper, lump of grease, was secreted for future use or held for its trade value. It is unlikely that privies were used to deposit common refuse. In fact, it is unlikely that the prisoners produced much, if any, refuse at all. It is far more likely therefore that camp-era privy deposits consist primarily of two classes of materials (other than human waste): items lost accidentally, and illicit items deliberately deposited. A final consideration is the possibility of a deposit stemming from an abandonment event.

While the happenings of the closing weeks of the war differ vastly from camp to camp, we can nevertheless make certain generalisations. In a relatively consistent pattern, the camps were abandoned by the Nazis days or hours ahead of the approaching allies, and to varying degrees, and with varying success, the former camp rulers attempted to destroy the evidence of their crimes. At Birkenau, the crematoria were set with explosive charges and destroyed, and many of the wood block houses were burned. Thus, it is possible that the Nazi administration used the privies as 'opportunistic' evidence dumps too. Any distinct privy abandonment deposit might provide a fascinating window into the final hours of the Nazi era of the camp.

Conclusion

The concentration camps cannot be seen as a phenomenon of the 1930s and 1940s. The history and legacy of the camps is far to complex and far too intertwined with the very fabric of the 20th and 21st centuries to relegate such sites to a time now past. As Wilkie (2001: 11) suggests, as we 'delve into the archaeology of the early twentieth century, we will find the past and present more difficult to extricate from one another'. While some historians continue to aim for a higher standard of critical textual interpretation, by its very nature narrative that is rooted exclusively in textual sources is destined to be more linear, more univocal, and less equipped to deal with the problematic. On the other hand, due to its unique abilities and approaches, historical archaeology thrives on the tensions inherent to any attempt to understand past and present experience. Historical archaeology is specially suited to challenge that which is taken for granted, to deal with conflicting interpretations, 'contradiction rather than consistency' (Hall 1999: 193), and to subvert dominant methods and interpretations.

The series of tensions between past and present, between remembering and forgetting, between live human actors and the material record, and between the recent lived past and the textual record of the recent lived past have spawned a new tension. This new tension is between a text-centric approach and a more holistic, historical archaeological approach—the canonical versus the experimental. As the necessarily limited examples in this article demonstrate, the story of the concentration camps is multi-layered, multi-vocal, and messy. If we are to continue to try to understand the concentration camp experience and to probe the relevance of that experience to the present day, then a new perspective that is grounded in recent developments in method and theory in historical archaeology provides a way forward. Such an approach, rather than relying on the singular 'excavation' in the traditional sense of the word, might include a series of excavations: into the soil, the texts, the imagery, the landscape, and the memory. Such an approach might negotiate between the canonical and the experimental.

The Nazi Holocaust—with little debate the moral nadir of the 20th century—is part of our collective heritage, a 'negative heritage' perhaps (Meskell 2002), but our heritage nevertheless.

> As time distances the personal contact and the number of visitors with personal sensitivities to be respected diminishes, we move towards an era when the concentration camps will be sites of education, warning and remembrance, but no longer places where the heritage hurts quite so much (Beech 2002: 205).

Continuing to deal with the events of the Holocaust, the sites of the Holocaust, and the repercussions of the Holocaust that are noticeable daily as we advance into this new century remains our responsibility. Historical archaeologists, on the cutting edge of the theory and practice of questioning our world, are uniquely equipped to lead the way.

Acknowledgements

Great thanks go to Christopher Friedrichs, David Robinson, and Paul Myers. Thanks are also due to the editors and referees of this journal. Responsibility for the interpretation presented is the author's alone.

Bibliography

Beech, J 2002 'The differing development paths of Second World War Concentration Camps and the possibility of an application of a principle of equifinality', *in* Schofield, J *et al.* (eds) *Matériel Culture: The Archaeology of Twentieth Century Conflict.* Routledge: London. 199–207.

Borowski, T 1976 *This Way for the Gas, Ladies and Gentlemen.* Penguin: New York.

Briggs, C 2000 'Literacy, reading and writing in the Medieval West', *Journal of Medieval History* 26, 397–420.

Buchinger, M-L & Metzler, M 2006 'The Soviet murals in Forst Zinna near Jüterborg (Germany), a cycle of paintings in the barracks of the 57th Construction Battalion', *in* Schofield, J *et al.* (eds) *Re-Mapping the Field: New Approaches in Conflict Archaeology.* Westkreuz-Verlag: Berlin. 28–34.

Buchli, V & Lucas, G (eds) 2001 *Archaeologies of the Contemporary Past.* Routledge: London.

Casella, E 2000 '"Doing Trade": A sexual economy of nineteenth-century Australian female convict prisons', *World Archaeology* 32(2), 209–21.

Cochran, M & Beaudry, M 2006 'Material Culture Studies and Historical Archaeology', *in* Hicks, D & Beaudry, M (eds) *The Cambridge Companion to Historical Archaeology*, 191–204. Cambridge University Press: Cambridge.

Cocroft, W & Schofield J 2003 'Images of the Cold War: combat art', *Conservation Bulletin* 44, 43–44.

Cocroft, W & Wilson, L 2006 'Archaeology and art at Spadeadam Rocket Establishment (Cumbria)', *in* Schofield, J *et al.* (eds) *Re-Mapping the Field: New Approaches in Conflict Archaeology.* Westkreuz-Verlag: Berlin. 15–21.

Cocroft, W, Devlin, D, Schofield, J & Thomas, R J C 2006 'Art of war', *British Archaeology* 86, 44–47.

Cole, S 2006 'Images of War: the photographic recording of wall art', *in* Schofield, J *et al.* (eds) *Re-Mapping the Field: New Approaches in Conflict Archaeology*. Westkreuz-Verlag: Berlin. 39–42.

Des Pres, T 1976 *The Survivor: An Anatomy of Life in the Death Camps*. Oxford University Press: Oxford.

Garliński, J 1975 *Fighting Auschwitz: The Resistance Movement in the Concentration Camp*. Julian Friedmann: London.

Glicksman, W 1953 'Social differentiation in the German concentration camps', *in* Pinson, K (ed) *YIVO Annual of Jewish Social Science*, 123–50. Yiddish Scientific Institute: New York.

Greif, G 2005 *We Wept Without Tears: Testimonies of the Jewish Sonderkommando From Auschwitz*. Yale University Press: New Haven.

Gutman, Y 1984 "Social stratification in the concentration camps", *in* Gutman, Y & Saf, A (eds) *The Nazi Concentration Camps. Proceedings of the Fourth Yad Vashem International Historical Conference—January 1980*, 143–176. Yad Vashem: Jerusalem.

Hall, M 1999 'Subaltern voices? Finding the spaces between things and words', *in* Funari, P *et al.* (eds) *Historical Archaeology: Back from the Edge*. Routledge: London. 193–203.

Hicks, D 2003 'Archaeology unfolding: diversity and the loss of isolation', *Oxford J Archaeol*, 22 (2003), 315–29.

Hilberg, R 1993 *Perpetrators Victims Bystanders: The Jewish Catastrophe 1933–1945*. HarperPerennial: New York.

Hirte, R nd 'Found objects', *The Buchenwald and Mittelbau-Dora Memorials Foundation* (accessed 27/11/06) <http://www.buchenwald.de>

Hitchens, C 2006 'Snake in the grass', *Slate.com* 22/08/06 (accessed 20/11/06) <http://www.slate.com/id/2148094/>

Johnson, M 1999 'Rethinking historical archaeology', *in* Funari, P *et al.* (eds), *Historical Archaeology: Back From the Edge*. Routledge: London. 23–36.

Levi, P 1986 *If This is a Man: Remembering Auschwitz*. Summit: New York.

—— 1988 *The Drowned and the Saved*. Summit: New York.

Lingens-Reiner, E 1948 *Prisoners of Fear*. Victor Gollancz London.

Linn, R 2004 *Escaping Auschwitz: a culture of forgetting*. New York: Cornell University Press: Ithaca.

McAtackney, L 2005a 'Long Kesh/Maze: an archaeological opportunity', *Brit Archaeol*, 84 (2005), 11–15.

—— 2005b 'What can archaeology tell us about the Maze site?', *Archaeol Ireland*, (2005), 22–24.

Meskell, L 2002 'Negative heritage and past mastering in archaeology', *Anthrop Quarterly*, 75 (2002), 557–74.

Moreland, J 2001 *Archaeology and Text*. Duckworth: London.

Myers, A 2007 'Portable material culture and death factory Auschwitz', *Papers from the Institute of Archaeology*, 19 (2007), 57–69.

Saunders, N (ed) 2004 *Matters of Conflict: material culture, memory and the First World War*. Routledge: London.

Schofield, J 2006 *Constructing Place: when artists and archaeologists meet*. Diffusion E-Book: www.diffusion.org.uk.

Schofield, J & Johnson, W 2006 'Archaeology, Heritage and the recent and contemporary past', *in* Hicks, D & Beaudry, M (eds) *The Cambridge Companion to Historical Archaeology*. Cambridge University Press: Cambridge. 104–22.

Schofield, J, Evans, D, Foot, W & Going, C 2006 'Thematic characterisation: recording England's army camps, 1858–2000', *in* Schofield, J, *et al.* (eds) *Re-Mapping the Field: New Approaches in Conflict Archaeology*. Westkreuz-Verlag: Berlin. 53–63.

Sofsky, W 1999 *The Order of Terror: The Concentration Camp*. Princeton University Press: New Jersey.

Vrba, R & Bestic, A 1997 *I Cannot Forgive*. Regent College: Vancouver.

Wheeler, K 2000 'Theoretical and methodological considerations for excavating privies', *Historical Archaeology*, 34 (2000), 3–19.

Wilkie, L 2001 'Black sharecroppers and white frat boys: living communities and the appropriation of their archaeological pasts', *in* Buchli, V & Lucas, G (eds) *Archaeologies of the Contemporary Past*. Routledge: London. 108–18.

BOOK REVIEW

The Deadly Politics of Giving: Exchange and Violence at Ajacan, Roanoke, and Jamestown by Seth Mallios (2006, Tuscaloosa, University of Alabama Press, ISBN: 9780817353360, 150pp)

In February 1571, an Algonquian Indian christened 'Don Luis' by the Jesuits who had converted him, led a group of missionaries from Spain into the heartland of his native tribe, seemingly eager to help the priests convert more of his fellows. Joined by a few other Algonquians, Don Luis claimed that he wished to help the Jesuits build a new church to help in their proselytising mission. After gathering up the priests' iron tools, the neophyte swiftly decapitated the chief Jesuit, Father Segura, with a hatchet while his comrades massacred the others.

In July 1585 Lord Grenville led the crew of the *Tiger* into the Carolinas, at Roanoke, during one of the first English attempts to colonise the Americas. Grenville led his men into the Secotan town of Aquascococke to make contact with the natives, but the only event recorded in the ship's journal was the theft by the natives of a silver cup. After giving them three days to return the cup, which they failed to do, Grenville led his men back to the village and burned it to the ground.

In May 1607, two weeks after landing at the site of what would become Jamestown, the first permanent English settlement in North America, the English colonists received a visit from local Paspahegh tribesmen, who presented them with the carcass of a deer and a promise that the colonists could take as much land as they desired. During the visit, in an echo of the event at Aquascococke 22 years earlier, one of the natives stole a hatchet. One of the colonists intervened and the men soon came to blows, with the Englishmen drawing their weapons. Fortunately, the situation was soon calmed down and no blood was spilt. This was one of the rare occasions where a confrontation of this nature between European settlers and the indigenous natives did not descend into violence and bloodshed. There would be many more such incidences to come.

These three early European settlements in North America—Ajacan, Roanoke and Jamestown—are the core case studies of Mallios' book. To European eyes, the actions of the native inhabitants of the areas they were trying to colonise could seem bafflingly opaque. Some tribes would greet the colonists with elaborate feasts and the presentation of gifts one moment, and then respond with sullen disinterest or outright violence the next. Mallios makes a good case here that such seemingly aberrant behaviour has often been explained away under the rubric of "cultural differences", without any real attempt to explain or elucidate what these cultural differences may be. He believes that a study of *economic* differences could illuminate more than it obscures, and that such clashes as did occur between settlers and natives resulted either from mutually exclusive economic systems operating in tangent, or (in the case of the Spanish) from a proselytising tradition that saw spiritual salvation as the ultimate commodity, where the natives would have desired something more tangible in recompense for slights or offences.

For the majority of Algonquian tribes in what are now the Carolinas and Virginia areas, an elaborate system of gift exchange had developed as a means of bonding tribal groups together, maintaining the power of local elites, and, as Mallios believes possible, of redistributing wealth (p.12). With this in mind, any presentation of food or goods or ceremonial welcoming on the part of one Indian would have demanded an equivalent reciprocation on the part of another. Mallios makes clear that this could be a stifling system that frequently placed burdens of debt on the part of recipients that they would try to avoid by pre-emptively giving their own gifts, thus releasing them from an obligation and placing that recipient in a position of obligation to them. In this socio-economic system, gifts were valued at more than their physical worth; they also symbolised the strength of spiritual bonds. A failure to operate within the bounds and conventions of this system was not just socially unacceptable; it was equivalent to spiritual death.

 DOI: 10.1163/157407808X382836

Contrast this to the European system of commodity exchange based on the open marketplace, and we can already see how misunderstanding would result in more than just confusion. When the Spanish missionaries failed to reciprocate gifts with those they were intending to convert (believing that their offer of spiritual salvation gave them the upper hand), and then traded with rival tribes for food, Don Luis felt himself fully justified in exacting retribution by his own offer of a false gift—the building of a church—and then by murdering the Jesuits. When the English settlers at Roanoke and Jamestown failed to adequately reciprocate local tribes, individual Indians felt themselves justified to take what they should have been given—in these cases, a silver cup and a hatchet.

What must have been equally baffling to the Indians was that there were individuals amongst the colonists who did seem to understand the conventions of the gift exchange system, which made violations by other colonists harder to accept. The mercurial John Smith at Jamestown proved highly adept at reading the cultural standards of the natives, and successfully exploited the system by giving and withholding gifts whenever doing so would benefit the colony. The Jamestown merchant Christopher Newport was held as a paragon for the appropriateness of his behaviour, and was used by Chief Powhatan as a standard that made Smith's deliberate violations harder to bear (p.111). Relations between the settlers and the natives tended to break down when elite intermediaries such as Smith and Newport were recalled to Europe and were no longer able to manage the system. Following these departures, the less capable colonists were guilty of flooding the local market with European goods, thus debasing their value and further undermining the gift exchange system. Further offence would be caused when colonists failed to understand the link between gift giving and status, and traded without regard for social position.

Mallios' deceptively slender study covers a broad range of material admirably and concisely, and it acts as an effective synthesis of existing work on the nature of the gift-giving economy, as well as of the pioneering socio-anthropological work of Marcel Mauss and Claude Levi-Strauss. A lengthy preamble on the nature of the written sources, which are inevitably of European origin and carry an "aura of whiteness" (p.5) comes at times to resemble a *mea culpa*, but Mallios is clear that an analysis of these conflicting exchange systems can revitalise "otherwise stifled investigations of these historical records" (p.37). By drawing together the Spanish and English examples, he demonstrates that what links the different European experiences in the New World is far more important than what separates them. He is also quite clear that conflict over the nature of these different exchange systems is one of the causes of conflict between European settlers and native Indians, but it is not the *sole* cause. In studying what could be portrayed as monolithic cultural or economic forces, he is also careful to emphasise individual agency, stating that the identity of differing tribes and their own struggles for dominance are as important in explaining the breakdown in relations between the two groups. It is also impossible to imagine the Jamestown settlement without the presence of John Smith and his own personal talents as a leader and mediator. This approach could be in danger of making Mallios' conclusions too diffuse, but he makes an effective case for his study acting as a catalyst for further research, and he does this without raising more questions than he is able to answer.

The gift exchange system is an appropriate metaphor for the gulf of difference between the European settlers and the indigenous Indians. Paraphrasing Mauss, Mallios concludes that the gift exchange system binds individuals and groups in a social contract, one that should guarantee peace, but that it also has a negative counterpart. The violation of this system may be done in complete ignorance, but when two such contrasting groups are concerned, the outcome is always going to be violent. The "gift" is "simultaneously the offer of alliance and the mandate of reciprocity" (p.123), as this sharp and effective study demonstrates.

INDEX

 DOI: 10.1163/157407809X413083